Short Hair Detention

Short Hair Detention

Memoir of a Thirteen-Year-Old Girl Surviving the Cambodian Genocide

CHANNY CHHI LAUX

ARCHWAY
PUBLISHING

This book is a work of non-fiction. Unless otherwise noted, the author and the publisher make no explicit guarantees as to the accuracy of the information contained in this book and in some cases, names of people and places have been altered to protect their privacy.

Archway Publishing books may be ordered through booksellers or by contacting:

Archway Publishing
1663 Liberty Drive
Bloomington, IN 47403
www.archwaypublishing.com
1 (888) 242-5904

Because of the dynamic nature of the Internet, any web addresses or links contained in this book may have changed since publication and may no longer be valid. The views expressed in this work are solely those of the author and do not necessarily reflect the views of the publisher, and the publisher hereby disclaims any responsibility for them.

The cover photo of me was taken in Phnom Penh, February 1975. I was visiting Phnom Penh as a reward from my parents for passing the seventh-grade entry exam.

ISBN: 978-1-4808-5293-8 (sc)
ISBN: 978-1-4808-5294-5 (hc)
ISBN: 978-1-4808-5295-2 (e)

Library of Congress Control Number: 2017915338

Printed in the United States of America.

Archway Publishing rev. date: 10/20/2017

Dedication

To my mother, Chheng Ly: I have written this story in memory of your everlasting love and strength. To my daughter, Natasha Laux, and my son, Richard Laux: I hope this story gives you strength to never give up on your dreams and to always have faith.

Contents

Preface

I was a happy thirteen-year-old girl when the Khmer Rouge took over Cambodia and killed at least two million people over a period of four years. During this time, I was forced to work in labor camps, some of which were far away from civilization and my family. Living through this difficult time, I endured never-ending challenges of starvation, harsh working conditions, and sickness.

This story recounts the intimate details of my journey through those devastating years (1975–79). It progresses from the first six months of starvation to the agonizing moments when the Khmer Rouge separated me from my parents and how I learned to survive year-round unforgiving conditions and constant threats to my life. Throughout the journey, I experienced constant reminders to keep faith in God and to not lose hope that my family would somehow be able to survive.

My feelings and emotions were constantly challenged by the freedom that was lost and the hope that things would get better. Throughout the story, promises were made, and we sacrificed many things for each other. I made special friendships along the way, and there were undeniable moments of giggling that I had with my starving teenage girlfriends, even under the direst circumstances. Those friendships, along with numerous kind-hearted people on the journey, helped me to keep sane with small strands of hope to cling to.

My story also reveals the animal instinct within me that took over my conscience, the self-inflicted emotional pain that weakened me, and the love that I had for my mother (Em) that saved me. It was this love that helped me to look past my own misery and to strive for survival, for I could not bear to imagine Em's suffering if she had lost me.

While enduring horrendous crimes committed by the Khmer Rouge, I thought many times that if I were lucky enough to survive, I would share the experience with my future children. This book is the result of that promise.

After reading *The Diary of a Young Girl* by Anne Frank, I began collecting notes for my story. In the summer of 1992, while I was in the hospital bed nursing and admiring my firstborn (Natasha), I began chapter 1. Soon afterward, I organized the chapters and spent the following years recounting the horrific and tender memories as if they happened yesterday.

After shedding many tears while reliving painful memories, I have come to greatly appreciate the catharsis I experienced from writing the story. It took me twenty-five years and many more life-changing events: the birth of my son Richard, Natasha turning thirteen years old (my age when the Khmer Rouge took over), my mother passing away in 2010, and finally my current unemployment to complete this book.

My original goal of sharing my experience evolved naturally from a tale of nightmares to a true love story between me and my mother. Through this book, my mother's love will never be forgotten.

Acknowledgments

I wish to thank my friends who read and commented on the manuscript: Catherine McIntyre, Curtis Roelle, Jane Gray and Nancy Flowers.

I would like to thank my nephew Joseph Smead, who bravely accepted the task of editing the very first draft of the manuscript, and Jimmy Kong for his creativity and skills in preparing the cover photograph.

Thank you to my brothers Mark Chhi and Ken Chhi, and my sister Chenda Chhi for bravely reliving and sharing private and sensitive memories in support of this story, as well as their thoughtful feedback on the manuscript. For my brother Ken Chhi for his creativity in drawing the French Village hut, and for his unwavering support and encouragement.

I especially wish to express my utmost appreciation to my husband, Kent Laux, for his tireless effort in reviewing this story from cover to cover multiple times. I am genuinely grateful for his patience, his constant encouragement, and for unselfishly supporting me in completing this writing.

Last but not least, I would like to thank each and everyone who helped spread the word of my book through social media. I am blessed to have your support! I would also like to acknowledge the following supporters who gave me their trust in completing the book and sharing to the world by backing me though crowd funding: Mark Mercer, Steph Parker, Jason Uechi, Syla Ly, JoAnne Jennings, Nancy Gausman, Jess Turner, Michael Owen, Curtis and Cheryl Roelle, Richard Laux, Wayne and Verla Roelle, Mark and Sherry Hammer, Michael C. Kovalich, Neal Herman, Lynda Larsen, Jackie Laux, Oliver Crespo, Michael Burns, Sue and Paul Whitted, Mellany Travers, Fran and Al Keif, Christian Tse, Michelle Maasz Brouwer, Kristen Kraupie, Kirk Laux, Vivan Brown, Natasha Laux, Jason and Katie Slabach, Surmeet Gill, Chenda Chhi, Ken and Kandi Chhi, Andy Chhi, Rachel Chhi, Alan Chhi, Mark and Cathy Chhi, Reenie Thummel, Joseph Smead, Ron Fifer, Haing Hoc and Sovany Lam, Dorr H. Clark, Jan Smith, Linda Zhu, Taé Tran, Sandy Joe, Bret and Lisa Gengenbach, Dale and Arlene Gengenbach, Jun Deng, Kristen Kraupie, Charlie Gorwood, Ray Martin, Jane Kendall, Douglas Petry, Janelle Shook, Janell Adams, Soosan Rejai, Millie Howe, Chantell Kuhlmann, Thavary Krouch, Susan J. Mills, Stefani Chikos Murrell, Pat Collins, Joanne Roa,

Catherine Doyle-Segura, Beverly Lu, Kandy Fabreo-Montelongo, Paul Owens, Jas Duggal, Sharyl Iwata, Cristina Carter, Kevin B. Murphy, Neha Pathak, Albert Lui, Marcia Gates, Bill Tynes, Sam and Vera Tous, Christopher Chiu, Maybelline Alejandro, Brenda and Jesse Liu, Steven Conston, Ryan and Jolyne Chhi, Rita Chhi, Jessica Chhi, Damian Neighbors, Jonathan S. C Tan, Carolyn Buan Talosig, and many more supporters who choose to be anonymous.

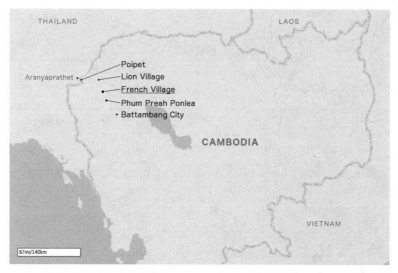

Overview Map—My family moved from Battambang City to Poipet for a quick exit to Thailand should the Khmer Rouge take over Cambodia. After the Khmer Rouge seized control of the country, we were detained in French Village and the surrounding area. *(Adapted from National Geographic MapMaker Interactive by K. W. Laux, 2017.)*

I have created the character table below to assist readers in keeping track of the people listed because they are mentioned in different parts of the story. Many others are in the story, but they are not included in this table since they are not referenced in multiple parts of the story.

Name	Relationship
Aunt Nay Hak	Pa's younger sister, Cousin Ou's mother
Aunt Sareth	Mother's half-sister, Pros's mother
Bong Nick	Friend. We met in Seur girls' camp and stayed together in Chamnaom sick-house.
Chenda	Sister
Ee	Oldest brother
Hong	Second oldest brother
Jair Lai	The Meeting Creek neighbor who Em loved like a daughter. She had a sick son: PL
Kheang	Younger brother
Linda	Second cousin who lived with us many years before the Black Uniforms took over, Mair and Ouv's daughter

Name	Relationship
Mair	Mother's first cousin, Linda's mother
Ngy	Cousin, Uncle Tre's daughter
Om Leung	Neighbor in Meeting Creek Village
Ou	Cousin, Aunt Nay Hak's son
Ouv	Linda's father
Pros	Cousin, Aunt Sareth's son
Tahry	Best friend. We met in a girls' labor camp.
The Savan	The neighbor in French Village
Uncle Khemm	One of Pa's younger brothers. Pa provided financial support so Uncle Khemm could continue his study in Paris before the Black Uniforms took over.
Uncle Song	Pa's oldest brother
Uncle Tre	Pa's second oldest brother, Cousin Ngy's father

The Chhi (徐) **Family**—The photographs of Pa, Em, Chenda, and me were taken a few months before the Black Uniforms began their reign on April 17, 1975. Ee and Hong's photographs were taken in July 1976 at Aranyaprathet refugee camp in Thailand, three months after they had escaped the Black Uniforms. Kheang's photograph is not available.

Chapter 1

Before April 17, 1975

It was the end of the 1974 school year. Cousin Ngy and I spent a lot of time together, but we were not playing. We were studying and testing each other on everything we had learned since first grade to get ready for the seventh-grade entry exam. The pressure to pass the test was tremendous. My biggest fear was that if I failed the test, I would have to stay in the sixth grade for another year, and the fifth-grade students would catch up with me, and I would be labeled as the stupid one. Em[1] constantly reminded me that if I passed the test, she would take me to visit my cousins in Phnom Penh, the capital city of Cambodia, in an airplane. However,

---

[1] *Em* is what we call our mother. In my parent's Chinese dialect (潮州 Chaozhou), *Em* means "older aunty," but for superstitious reasons, it was believed that if we called our mother Em, we would have more chance to survive infant mortality.

if I failed the test, I would have to help her around the house and cook for my sister and three brothers while they would be going to school. Helping Em around the house didn't sound too bad, but I didn't want to cook for my sister and brothers.

The trip from my home town of Battambang to Phnom Penh in an airplane sounded exciting. I had never flown in an airplane before. None of my friends had ever flown in an airplane. I imagined the cost of flying at the time would be out of reach for most people in Cambodia. Sometimes while I was studying, I would daydream that I was seeing birds through the aircraft window and that they were flying around the airplane so they could study this big strange bird that sang a terrible song. The very idea made me smile and stopped me from daydreaming.

A day or two before the exam, Em made a special effort to visit one of the teachers. He was going to be the monitor in my exam room. Em brought me with her for the visit, along with a basket of fruit, two whole cooked chickens, and other goodies as if we were going to pray to our ancestors. At the time, this kind of trip was considered to be courteous and humble.

The teacher lived in our neighborhood. However, we had never visited his house. Looking from the street, I could see only the red roof that stood behind the tropical

fruit trees and the lower shrubs. The white column bal-
ustrade fence in front of the trees indicated the house
had belonged to a French family when Cambodia had
been a French colony. It was very pretty. The bottom
was a solid block of some kind of clay painted white. It
was about one foot thick and stood up about one foot
off the ground. On top of this block stood another two
feet of carved white columns with small slits between
them. The slits were narrow enough that it would be
impossible to try to force a leg through them. The top of
the fence was a carved slab that was there to support the
columns. The slab's functionality was overshadowed by
its beauty. The front gate was a pair of carved panels
that swung open from the middle with the help of small
roller wheels on the bottom. A sign that read Beware of
a Mean Dog, hung on top of one of the panels.

As Em and I approached the gate, two German
shepherds greeted us with their loud, vicious barks.
They showed us their big, white, long, healthy teeth.
My heart was dancing faster than the barking tune.
With my hands full of gifts, I could not grab Em's hand,
but I did use my invisible hands, and Em knew I was
scared. The dogs had their two front legs up against
the gate. Looking at them, I was glad the gate's lock
was working.

The dogs turned into friendly, fluffy little things

when a maid came to the gate and let us in. I was relieved, not only from the dogs' transformation, but to get on the other side of the fence as soon as I did. This way I had less chance to be seen at the examiner's front door with gifts. The walkway to the house was laid with red bricks covered with damp moss and shaded by the fruit trees. I tasted the sweet, cool air that had been fermented by different kinds of ripe fruit that still hung on the trees. I was thinking that they must not have any children in this house. Otherwise the fruit would not have had a chance to be at its best. While I was thinking, I began to feel the brightness of the sun and its powerful heat. I turned my eyes away from the fruit and the trees, and there I saw the cutest little brick house. It was like in a fairy tale. It was worth the trip and passing through the gate.

I was scared and embarrassed to meet the teacher. I knew him from school, but he didn't know me. He had a reputation of being the meanest teacher in my school. I had heard a story that he once spanked one of his students so hard that she wet her skirt. When he appeared, I was shocked to learn that Em already knew him. They talked like casual friends. She introduced me to him and told him that I would be taking the test in the next few days and that I had been studying a lot. She asked him to keep an eye on me.

On our way home, Em told me that this trip didn't guarantee that I would pass my test. I would still have to do my best. The trip we just made was expected of parents of children taking the test. I learned that all my cousins had to endure the same trip, and so did most of my friends whose parents could afford to do so. All of a sudden I didn't feel shame, only sorrow for my friends whose parents could not afford the trip.

The night before the test was very hot and humid, and I woke up in the middle of the night soaking wet. At first I thought it was sweat, but then I realized that I had a bloody nose. Em tried to stop the bleeding by making me tilt my head backward while she splashed cold water on my forehead. I felt the blood flowing from my nose to my throat. It was an awful feeling, so I pulled my head forward to change the direction of the flow. I preferred it to drip out of my nose rather than swallow it into my tummy. *I am not going to swallow such a disgusting thing*, I thought. My head rocked back and forth between Em's hand pushing my head backward, and my neck muscles fighting to lean forward so the blood would drip on the ground instead of flowing back into my throat. When the blood eventually stopped, I felt cold from the wet clothes that were catching the splashes of water Em put on my forehead. The maid helped Em to clean up the mess. I remember feeling special when Em and the maid pampered me and took me back to bed. I also felt relief from the pressure of passing the test the next day now that I had a good excuse in case I didn't do well.

The morning came sooner than I wanted it to. It was a special morning. The breakfast was ready, and Em was at the table waiting for me. Usually, Em would be standing and serving us even when we had enough help from the maid. She was gentle and smiled to me and said: "You have tried your best to get ready for the test. Now don't worry and just do it." My oldest brother Ee gave me a pep talk: "If I can do it, you can do it too." At that moment, I realized that this was what I needed the most, a pep talk from Ee, for I knew Ee was not as smart in school as Hong (my second older brother) nor Chenda (my older sister), and he still passed the exam. Also, I considered myself as good as Ee.

Em watched over me like a hawk to make sure I was in optimal condition for taking the test.

"Don't eat too fast. Don't eat too much. Go brush your teeth. Go to the bathroom."

It was her way of kissing and hugging me, and I loved it. That morning, I didn't have to clean up the breakfast table.

As ready as I could be, I walked to school to take the test. The whole town seemed so quiet for it knew today was the exam day for sixth graders to advance to seventh grade. I felt so important marching with the other sixth graders to school like we were in a parade. All the grandmas and grandpas, mothers and fathers, aunts and uncles, and brothers and sisters were lined up to cheer for us. With their smiles and cheers they encouraged us all the way from the first step out of the house to the school ground. I never thought it would be this way.

My heart was beating so fast while my head was trying to go over the problems that I was not sure about during my practice. The consequences of passing or failing the test did not matter to me anymore. My weakest point was spelling. I was good at history, geography, and biology because I liked those subjects. But I was not so good with math, and I was terrible at spelling.

The exam was given in a different school than the one I had gone to, with an assigned room and seats. I was told that the exam rooms were usually above ground level, so that there would be less distraction by activity outside.

I didn't know anyone in the examination room, which didn't help. When the examiner that Em and I had visited a couple of days before appeared, I felt relief, and I was hoping he still remembered me. The time had started, the test was given, and I worked as fast as

I could. I was intensely focused on the test, so much so that I forgot about the possibility of getting a hint from the teacher. All I could think about was completing this important test. My head was down, and my neck was stiff from holding my face about six inches above the exam paper. My upper arms squeezed my body for comfort. My fingers moved constantly. Even when they were not writing anything, they pounded the exam paper as part of my intense focus.

To say I was extremely nervous would not be sufficient to describe the situation. It was awful. At one point during the exam, I found myself so shocked that my mind went blank and every muscle of my body went through spasms. Just then a ball of crunched-up paper struck the side of my head. It must have been thrown through the window from the ground floor. My body stiffened and straightened up from the shock such that my head was above everybody else in the room, and naturally all eyes fell on me. My head felt numb from rays shooting out of all the eyeballs in the room from every direction. The paper ball hit the floor, rolled about three or four rows away, and stopped at the examiner's foot. He picked it up, and without opening it, he rushed to a window and searched intensely for the culprit. He must have found one because he rolled the paper ball tighter, aimed, and swung his arm to throw the ball back to its owner. Furious, he clenched his jaw and slammed all the windows shut.

I wondered what I should say. That paper was not intended for me. Neither my brother nor any of my older cousins would have tried to help me cheat. Cheating was never acceptable in our family. It was one of those unspoken rules. The paper could have been for anyone in the room who was taking the exam.

To my relief, the examiner didn't try to find out who it was for. All he said was, "Continue with your work. You will not be bothered again."

I thought, *Wow, what a nice guy!* I had heard of these paper balls in the exam room before. They contained answers to all the questions in the exam. Somehow the exam was disclosed prematurely to the public every year before test day. So older male (never female) relatives would get their hands on it, solve the problems, and pass them through windows, hoping their relatives would get them without being caught by the examiner. Sometimes young men threw paper balls that contained no writing into the room as a joke.

The examiner marched slowly from desk to desk. Every time he got to my desk, he stood and looked over my work.

How in the world is he going to give a hint without being obvious? I thought. How am I supposed to ask for help without saying a word and have him answer without speaking? I found myself unable to think straight every time he was near my desk. In my head, I repeated the words "Go away, go away." One time when he stopped and looked over my work, he pointed with his index finger to one of the math problems that I had already finished.

Ahh, this is how you help me! I took it to mean that I was wrong on the problem. I was so tickled by the sign language. At last Em's gifts were not wasted.

The test took all day with an hour lunch break. By the time I arrived home, I didn't care how I did on the test. I felt so tired yet relieved.

A week later the test results were posted. Ee took me on his motorcycle to find out my result. I was much more scared than when I took the test. It felt like I had run out of air to breathe, and my body was light as a dead leaf falling from a tree swaying with a soft wind. Once we got to the school grounds, I saw a lot of people were already there. By the small bulletin board, young men fought to get a peek at the result for themselves or for their sisters. Some were jumping and yelling with excitement, and in the process of doing so, they hit and banged other men next to them. I watched these men and hoped I did not disappoint my brother.

Some came out from the crowd slowly and quietly,

trying to keep their heads up and take the bad news as well as a person could. There was no expression on their faces. I peeked at them and followed them with only my eyes. When they were out of the corner of my sight, I thought, *I hope I don't disappoint my brother.* I watched my brother fight the crowd to get a peek at my score. My eyes were fixed on the back of his head, and then his head sunk into the crowd to take a closer look at the score. I was wondering why he was taking so long. I bit my fingernail and waited for his head to emerge and hoped I wouldn't disappoint him.

My eyes grew tired from squinting, and when I looked back up, I saw Ee was already outside of the crowd and walking toward me. There was no expression on his face. He was walking slowly as if he had no energy to talk about anything. He didn't smile. At that moment I knew I had disappointed him. My whole body was shaking, especially my lower lip. I couldn't see Ee anymore, and my eyes filled with tears, tears that came out faster than I could blink them out. There was no sense in trying to look at Ee, so I put my head down. Now the tears dripped straight to the ground, making no tracks on my face.

What was I going to tell my parents? Everybody would know I did not pass my test: my neighbors, cousins, aunts and uncles—the whole town would know.

More than shame and embarrassment, a feeling of abject sadness quickly consumed me when I thought of Pa. What would Pa think of me? If only Pa could be proud of me, I would be living in a perfect world.

"Why are you crying?" Ee said, tapping my head. Is he telling me that I passed? Ee added, "So what if you fail? We all know that you tried your best." Oh no, I couldn't take it anymore. I broke down and cried out loud like a baby.

"But you passed!" Ee exclaimed.

I hate you! I hate you! How could you do this to me? I was thinking. I couldn't get a word out. My emotions were so strong with happiness and exasperation. All I could do was laugh and cry at the same time, and I kept hitting his upper arm muscles with excitement. I was relieved. Who cared about flying to Phnom Penh? I was as happy as I could be.

A few weeks later, I flew to Phnom Penh with Em. The flight was not as fun and relaxing as I had thought it would be. It was a rough ride all the way, from the time it took off until it landed. I felt so sick that I never wanted to fly again.

We visited my aunts, uncles, and cousins in Phnom Penh, but most of all I got to see my father and tell him the good news about school. Pa had an import and export business in Phnom Penh. He spent most of the time there and sometimes in other countries on business trips. He frequently traveled to South Vietnam and Thailand. Occasionally, he went to Hong Kong and Singapore. I remember being so proud of my father for the simple fact that he went to other countries. It always amazed me that he spoke five languages: Khmer, Chinese, Vietnamese, Thai, Loa, and he was learning French and English as well.

Pa was rarely home. When he came home from his business trips, he would spend a day or two at home then go back to Phnom Penh for a month or two. Sometimes he would spend the whole month with us. Every time he came home, he brought gifts for everybody from different countries, and he always brought treats for us and all the other kids in the neighborhood. One time he brought soggy sandwiches and told us the French people eat them like we eat rice. I thought they were one of the best treats besides the chocolate Dove egg candies that Pa brought from Saigon. He told us the American soldiers love them.

I was so proud of him. He was a man who left a memorable impression wherever he went. Nearly everyone who had known him had some fun and inspiring stories to tell about their times together with him. His generosity, friendly personality, and loyalty to friends and family, not to mention his good looks, made him very popular in the neighborhood. I felt proud watching him walking tall to his coffee gathering in his dress pants and white shirt each morning that he was home with us.

When he was not home, we would write a lot of letters to him because we didn't have a telephone. Most of the letters repeated the messages of the previous ones, telling him words of love and at least two to three repeating sentences that said "I miss you." He chose not to move us to Phnom Penh because there were many bombings there. In our hometown, we never saw signs of war.[2]

Living in Battambang, my family never had to experience the impact of the war. People believed that the Khmer Rouge would not bother Battambang because it was the most productive agricultural state in Cambodia. Destroying Battambang would mean destroying their reliable food supply.

To compensate for Pa's absence, Em made many trips to visit him, but just this one time she took me along. While she was away, my Grandma Chiv Heang and one of my aunts would help with the house and take care of us kids.

---

[2] The Cambodian civil war started in 1970 between the established government backed by the United States and the Khmer Rouge backed by communist China.

I was very excited to start my 1975 school year. After all, I had passed the seventh-grade entry exam, and I was going to a new school with students from seventh to twelfth grades. The fact that I was going to share a classroom with boys was exciting, for I had spent my first to sixth grades in an all-girls school. All I saw were girls, and we all wore the same uniform. I was also eager and looking forward to high school romance, which I heard so much about already from older girls in the neighborhood.

Em bought me some new outfits and a new bike for the new school year. The first day of school started with a cool morning breeze. I had my school bag ready the night before. The new school was in the same block as our house. I wore a blue skirt with a white shirt since blue and white were the uniform colors. Just steps after entering the school, a man told me to go to the office.

"But why?" I demanded to know.

"Just go and wait for me there," he commanded, without looking at me straight in the eyes. He was busy looking at everyone who passed through the door.

Not sure where the office was, and wanting to be with my friends, I asked again: "Why? I will be late for my class."

"I will give you a pass. I am the principal here." He looked irritated at me.

What had I done wrong? I had no idea. Whatever it was, it was never good when someone was called out by the principal. I quickly got out of his way and walked toward the office. When I got there, I saw that I was not the only one waiting for the principal. There were about ten other girls, and none of them knew what they were waiting for. The school bell rang. Students from each class gathered in rows and columns in the school court-yard, all facing the flagpole. The short people stood in the front rows and the tall people stood in the back rows. They formed perfect rectangles. They sang the national anthem and saluted the flag. Then they turned away from the flag and walked in rows to the class.

I missed my first flag salute in school and missed the chitchat with new friends before class. It was not the good first day I imagined it would be. The principal walked in the room and told us to stand in line.

"None of you is dressed like a lady," he said with a loud and angry voice. He went on to lecture us how a lady should dress. In my case, and like most other girls there, we should not have worn skirts cut above our knees. Other skirts were not the right blue color for the school. He kept talking for at least fifteen minutes, then he let us go with a slip. I walked out of the office feeling very small and angry. I felt as if he was watching me and saw every shape of my body. It was a terrible day.

In home economics class, all the students were girls. The very sight of all girls and not a single boy in the whole class made me feel at ease. The teacher made us all stand up. She walked around the room with her whipping stick and signaled about five or six of us to stand in front of the class. I was one of these girls. I was excited to be picked among the girls. Little did I know how quickly she would remind me of how my day had been. She marched up and down in front of us selected girls and told the rest of the girls in the class how and why we, the selected few, were a disgrace to the all the girls in the school because of the way we dressed. At this point I was more mad than embarrassed by the unnecessary humiliation.

I thought, Didn't the principal talk to you? Didn't you talk to the principal? Or maybe you did talk, and that is why you did this to us again, to make sure that we would never ever repeat the same mistake. Oh, it was a terrible day.

When Em asked me how my new school was, I broke down and cried. I felt that I never wanted to go back to school again. I could not find the words to speak, and my tears gently flowed over my cheeks. I felt my throat stiffen as though it was packed with glue. Em didn't comfort me. She was tough with her words. Perhaps she thought that if she was soft and comforting,

I would stay out of school. She showed disbelief and disgust with my emotion. I stood and waited until she finished preaching, then I went upstairs and threw my-self on the big bed that I shared with Chenda and my younger brother Kheang. I wasn't thinking about any-thing, just crying, just emptying the tears out of me. I was happy to be in my bed with my pillow.

Chapter 2

April 17, 1975

News reports said the Khmer Rouge were getting closer and closer to taking control of the whole country. Pa came home from Phnom Penh to be with us. Every night before bed, Em would make us rehearse what to do if we were awakened by gunfire or explosions.

The time came when nearly every night we could hear bombs exploding in the distance. Then it happened: All of us were awakened by the rumbling sound of bombs and some gunfire near our house. Unfortunately, we had the opportunity to put Em's rehearsal schedule to use. Each one of us knew just what to do. We all went into the small bathroom beneath the big stairway and hoped the thick concrete of the stairway would give us extra shelter. The bathroom was too small to hold all of us, so the men stayed nearby, but outside the bathroom. In the morning, we learned that the airport had been bombed and destroyed.

People in town were restless. Some were happy that the war was close to the end. Some were afraid of change. Everyone that we knew was afraid of the Communists. Many families were refugees from other provinces, and they were happy, thinking they would soon be able to go back to their hometown and start to rebuild what they had lost. My family belonged to the people who were afraid of the changes. My grandfather Yong Hao Chhi, who escaped from Communist China, used to tell his children the story of starvation, confiscation, and suppression that his family had had to endure living in Communist China. The story was told to us over and over, so naturally we were afraid of what might happen. The Communists might march into town and take everything away from us, and we would starve and not be permitted to speak words of love for family or friends but only for the government.

There were fifteen people living in our house at the time: our parents, the five of us kids, the maid, and two of my aunts with their families. Aunt Sareth was Em's half-sister. She was vacationing from Phnom Penh with her six-year-old son, Cousin Pros. My other aunt, Aunt Moy, was Em's cousin, and her family of five were refugees from Pursat province. Aunt Moy's oldest daughter,

Linda, was like a sister to me. She had been with us ever since I learned how to jump rope. Linda was sent to live with us so she could continue her education in Battambang. Later on, when her hometown got raided by the Khmer Rouge, Linda's parents and two younger sisters also came to live with us. We called Aunt Moy "Mair"[3] and her husband "Ouv,"[4] the way Linda called them.

Every meal in the house was served twice: first for kids and then again for the adults. One day at the dinner table, the conversation became serious as Pa began talking about having all of us move to a different town.

Pa stated, "The war is getting closer and closer to us. We should leave and go to our house in Poipet." He was trying to justify his suggestion by adding, "There are going to be a lot of changes. I heard that if the Red are winning, a communist country is certain. If it is anything like what my father told me about Communist China, we can't stay here."

For a long moment, there was silence. Em broke the silence. "When do you think we should leave?"

"The sooner the better. It does not look good," Pa said.

---

[3] *Mair* means "mother" in the Cambodian language (Khmer).
[4] *Ouv* means "father" in Khmer.

"A lot of my friends are gone already," Ee added.

Pa took a deep breath and responded: "Yes. I think it's best to pack tonight and get going tomorrow."

"Have you talked to your brother in Poipet yet?" Em asked.

"He won't mind. Besides, the house there belongs to us. I will let him know we are coming," Pa replied.

"You guys go ahead. I will stay here and look after your place. One of these days I'll go back to his father," said Aunt Sareth, looking at her boy.

Ee showed no expression one way or the other and said, "I'll stay with Aunty, Pa."

Pa looked at Mair and asked, "What about you?"

"I lost my home a long time ago," Mair answered.

"You are welcome to go with us. I am pretty sure my brother won't mind you coming along."

"Thank you," Mair said with relief and added, "You know I will never get used to war, bombings, and dying. Some people say they are used to it, but not me. Every time I see it, it gets into me more and more. I'm going to run as far as I can and take my family, too. I don't care about the kind of government it might be. I am just too damn scared of the bombing and killing." Mair stopped herself, feeling that she had already spoken too much.

Ouv declared, "I'm going to stay as long as I can. You

go ahead and take the kids with you. I'll be right behind you if things get worse."

Mair didn't protest her husband's decision. To Pa she added, "How long do you think we will have to stay in Poipet?"

"I don't know; we'll just have to wait and see. We may come back here, or we may go on to live in Thailand. I prefer not to leave the country, especially not to go to Thailand, if possible. Many Thai people that I have dealt with in business are cruel and are not so honest and trustworthy." To Ouv he said, "Despite what we have been told for generations, the Vietnamese are honest business people."

That night we packed our bags for the trip to Poipet, a border town to Thailand. For a moment, I was happy and excited. The idea of going to live in a different town was exciting, not to mention a different country. I was also happy that my parents decided to do something for the family so that we could get away from the bombings.

Reality began to hit when Em said that I could not take my pet dog Blacky with me, and that I wouldn't have the chance to say goodbye to my cousins living in the next block. I started to feel very sad, knowing that I would be a refugee escaping from bombs to live in a different town. I never thought that it could happen to me.

Heartbroken, I asked Em, "What about our schools, Em?"

She answered with a calm voice, "We just have to wait until the country becomes peaceful again." I started to cry, and I felt the tears come all the way from my stomach. Em knew very well that my crying was not just for the school. It was for everything.

In the morning, we were ready to go. Pa agreed that Ee (then eighteen years old) would stay with Aunt Sareth and her son to look after the house. At the time, it was impossible to have proper police authority in town. If left unguarded, the house would surely be looted the next day. Pa must have also felt that Ee was old enough, smart enough, strong enough, and quick enough to escape the country if he had to, especially when he wouldn't have to herd all of us through the border like Pa would. Or perhaps Pa felt justified to have Ee stay with Ouv, who used to be a farmer. Ouv was the strongest, biggest, and tallest Cambodian man I ever knew. With his dark skin, strong distinctive face, and head full of healthy curls, Ouv looked more Australian aborigine than Cambodian. He was so gentle with us kids, and we all loved to play with him. Ouv was a Buddhist monk before he married and became a farmer.

Off we went—ten of us in a station wagon taxi with our belongings on National Highway 5 to Poipet.

In Poipet, we shared the house with Uncle Tre, Pa's second older brother, who had rented from Pa for many years. My Cousin Ngy, who studied with me for the seventh-grade entry exam, was one of his daughters. He also had eight other children. The oldest was eighteen years old, and the youngest was not even in preschool yet. With the addition of our family from Battambang, we were twenty-two people all together living in that house. It must have been tough for the grown-ups, but for us kids, it was a blast to be with each other.

Things seemed so slow. We had been waiting at least a couple of months for some news of the war. We didn't do much. We had not gone to school since we left our home in Battambang, and my father's business seemed to stop. Every morning he would go to a noodle house in town to meet with his friends, probably to talk about the changes that might come. My father always told his friends that even if Cambodia became a communist country it would not be as bad as what happened in China because Cambodia is a self-sufficient country. "I can't imagine Cambodians starving for food," he would say. He would also say that it is very hard to live in a new country, but at the same time I had a feeling that he was not fully confident in his thinking. At least in Poipet we could easily cross the border into Thailand should things take a turn for the worse.

My father had a business partner in Thailand who lived not too far away from the border in a town called Aranyaprathet. We crossed over into Thailand often during our stay in Poipet, most of the time just for fun— shopping, dining, and visiting family friends. One time when we visited, Em took along most of her personal belongings and left them with my father's business partner. Pa assured us that he was a good and honest man. It was also known that he was much more prosperous than any other person we knew in Thailand, so to leave our savings with him would be safer than with anyone else.

Em was sitting in his house and started to open handkerchiefs to reveal the precious jewelry she had collected over the years. Among Em's jewelry were two gold Omega watches that my father bought for my two brothers, her diamond ring and earrings, gold and diamond bracelets, necklaces, a diamond pendant with at least ten half-carat diamonds packed together, and the most precious thing—my Apsara gold bracelet.

Em kept some of her other jewelry that was less valuable with her. At the time, jewelry was not just for fashion. It also served as a means to manage a family's savings. Banks were for business, whereas personal savings were converted to jewelry. Em divided her remaining jewelry into little bags that she sewed into the crotches of our underwear. She told us it was just in case we had to flee and were separated from each other, each one of us would have something to survive on. Along with the precious underpants, each of us had a small bag next to our bed. In case of an emergency, we would only have to grab the bag and go. In my small bag, I packed some clothes along with brand-new underwear that Em's friend had knitted for me. I also packed my brand-new bell-bottom pants that Em bought during one of our trips to Aranyaprathet. The pants were too big for me, but Em bought them anyway so I would not feel left out when Chenda and Linda got theirs.

Every night she made us wear the treasure undies when we went to bed. Chenda and I were having fun laughing at the way they felt every time we put them on. It was hard at first, but after a while we got used to it. First thing in the morning, we would shed our treasure undies and hand them back to Em.

I thought that Em was being too paranoid about the whole thing. Jewelry in underwear? Give me a break! I didn't think that it was possible for me to be separated from her. All I had to do was follow her with my feet and keep my eyes on her. I was thinking that I was big enough to keep close to her. But then I remembered some of the refugee kids in Battambang who were homeless and without any parents or relatives. I began to realize what Em meant when she said that we might be separated. Thinking about the possibilities made me cry softly to sleep.

One morning Pa was with Em, enjoying the family in the living room. It seemed so peaceful at the time. Then a man on a moped stopped in front of the house. He came in and greeted my parents. They had a small talk, but the next thing that came out of his mouth was: "I'm going to Battambang. I thought you'd like to come with me," as he was looking at my father.

Without any hesitation, Pa agreed to go with him. Perhaps Pa was bored staying in Poipet with nothing much to do for a couple of months. Em pleaded for Pa to stay. She was afraid that he wouldn't be able to come back, and if we needed to cross the border to Thailand, he should be with us. My father didn't listen but went anyway with that guy on the moped, all the way from Poipet to Battambang.

A couple of days later, we learned that the road from Poipet to Battambang was controlled by the Khmer Rouge, and they stopped all traffic to and from both cities. Em was restless; she blamed herself for not being more demanding that Pa stay with us. I thought repeatedly, *It was that moped; it was that man.* Most of our friends had already gone to stay in Thailand. Em couldn't decide what to do. She was waiting for Pa and watching her friends leave one by one for Thailand. She wanted to leave, but she didn't want to go without him. After all, she was a housewife, and she had no record of Pa's business. How would she survive in a new land? Perhaps if it was just her four children and herself, she would have gone to stay with friends in Thailand, but the maid and Mair's family of four were also with us. She decided to stay and wait for her husband. With eyes that seemed to migrate to her forehead, she waited and watched every man that passed by the house. I wished I could do something for Em.

After we heard the news about the road to Battambang, the days went by painfully slowly, with no signs or any news from Pa or Ee. They were nowhere to be found. Em waited and waited. That was what her heart was telling her to do, so that was what she was doing: waiting without sleeping and waiting without eating. Perhaps in her heart it was too late to decide otherwise, so she waited and wished she had gone to Thailand like her friends.

One day a new sound came rumbling and roaring from the small road in front of the house. All twenty-two of us went rushing from every room in the house to get closer to what was making the sound. In front of the house, I saw trucks and little men dressed in all-black clothes passing by the house. People were chasing the trucks and yelling: "Hooray! ... Hooray!" Some were dancing in the street and singing, but mostly yelling: "No more war on Khmer land!" and "Peace to the Khmer people!" Many expressions of emotion were heard all over.

One woman held her toddler on her hip with one arm, the baby's legs wrapped around her side, while her other arm waved in the air frantically to convey her emotions. I found myself hearing nothing and seeing nothing but her. She was looking frantically between the passing trucks and the arriving ones. Moving in the direction of the passing trucks, she was crying and laughing at the same time. Catching her breath, she put her toddler down, wiped her tears, lowered herself to her baby, and said: "You will meet your Grandma!" With tears in her eyes and her lips stretching and twitching, she added with a whimper, "We are going back to our hometown, my child."

I had to turn away to hide my tears. Was it to give the mother and the child some privacy, or was it because I didn't have much to share? Or it was because I didn't deserve the same emotions the woman seemed to possess? Or was it because I didn't want my cousins to see me cry? Whatever it was, I knew I was caught in a stream of emotional fires, which I will treasure and never forget. God had shown me that the love between a mother and child is so strong that it will touch other people around them.

While I was still gathering my feelings about the mother-and-child scene, I noticed some in our group of twenty-two people were cheering and hooraying affectionately, but our maid displayed the most feeling. Her emotions were so strong that she could not stand still. She jumped up and down and screamed until her eyes met Em's.

Busted! I was thinking in my head. *You are too big to jump like a kid. Your tits are flopping!* A year ago, she was only thirteen years old when her parents sent her to Em for an amount of money that they would get every year. She had become like a sibling to me, a nice one. When we fought, I would always come out feeling better. She could be grumpy and grouchy, but she would not yell at me like Chenda would. She was the same age as Chenda and only a year older than me, the youngest maid we ever had.

Most of our maids were young women between the ages of sixteen and twenty. Em never had a maid who already had a family. Em thought that they become more stubborn as they got older, and when they have a family of their own, their husbands come with whiskey breath to ask for more money for the labors that their wives endure.

Unlike most other bosses in Cambodia at that time, Em would never raise a hand or stick against any of our maids. The last maid we had did not want to go back to her family when her father came to reclaim her. We were all very sad. Every kid in the house was crying, and our maid cried the hardest. The whole neighborhood watched as her father walked her out of our house because she was moaning so loudly. I miss her so much. Sometimes I wonder where she is and what is she doing. I know for certain that if she is alive, she is thinking of me as I am thinking of her. Her name was Yert. We called her Bong[5] Yert. To say her name still makes me feel warm.

Em gave the maid a disapproving look. "Don't be a fool! You haven't seen their true colors yet."

I took a second look at the men in the trucks. They had to be some sort of army, for each one of them carried a gun over his shoulder. I was thinking quietly, *Are they Khmer Rouge soldiers? If they are, what happened to their uniforms?* The plain black uniforms looked like pajamas, making them look smaller than they were and not as strong as they should be for an army that had just won a war. Where were their helmets? Each

---

[5] *Bong* is a Khmer word used to refer to someone with respect as in an older sister or brother.

of them wrapped the bright red and white checkered *krama*[6] on his neck. They looked weird, like a bunch of fancy farmers.

Something else was even worse: These men did not reciprocate the emotions that people showered them with—none whatsoever. They were sitting as still as statues packed in the trucks.

Inside the house was a strange new atmosphere. It made me halt and hide any emotions that I was feeling. It was almost silent. I don't remember Em saying anything much, but I do remember feeling scared of the uncertainty. My seventeen-year-old brother Hong rushed into the house with his face completely pale and gasping for air. With a dried-up voice, he managed to splutter out what was on his mind: "Most of them are very young, Em. Twelve, thirteen, at most fifteen years old. With guns. They are smaller than their guns. They're guarding the border. Nobody can get out now. One of them cocked the gun at a man who was asking their ages." None of us had ever seen a gun pointed at a person before. Little did we know that this was only the first step on our way down to hell.

---

[6] *Krama* is a Khmer word referring to a two-color cotton scarf made with a small rectangle or checkered pattern. It is used for many purposes, including head wraps, hammocks for children, pouches, and wrapped as short sarongs for men.

That night we slept with our special underwear. I was wishing that there was something that I could do to help Em feel better. I wasn't thinking about the soldiers or Hong's story about the border, and I didn't miss or worry about Pa and Ee. I didn't wish to be anywhere else but next to Em, and I wished I knew a way to help her feel better. That night Em was the only and last thing in my mind.

Chapter 3

April 18, 1975

Early dawn the very next day, I woke up to the sound of intense gunfire. My heart was out of bed before my body. The gunfire continued, and it was coming from all directions. I felt my heart pounding its way out of my body, very hard and very fast. For a moment I sat up on the bed and thought, *What's going on? What's going on?* Another round of gunfire shook me out of my thoughts.

For a moment I thought that I was dreaming, but then I heard Em cry, "Hurry, hurry my children." It was not a nightmare. It was worse. It was real. Before I could get out of bed, there was more gunfire, this time very close. Em was still crying to get us all together. "Hurry, hurry my children. Go downstairs."

I got out of the bed, and without thinking I found myself hidden behind the door, looking through the crack, over the balcony, and down the street where the last gunfire had come from. There I saw two men dressed in simple black uniforms with bright red-and-white checkered krama. They had long shotguns in their hands; they looked like twins. With their guns pointing into the sky, they hustled in a general direction, but every step they made they shifted left and right, turned around and walked backward and forward as though they were possessed by a devil.

"Out! Out! Everybody out! Right now, before I kill somebody!" one of the men yelled from the bottom of his lungs, so loudly and so viciously it sounded almost as if he was speaking a language I had never heard before. He was the smaller of the two, but it seemed that the devil got the best of him, much more than it did his partner. I stood still in my corner as if wanting to make sure the gunfire was from these two devil-possessed souls. For a split second, it appeared that the smaller man with the shotgun was looking straight at the door and into the crack. He chilled my face through my left eyeball with his devilish look. I turned my head away and stiffened myself like a log, gently sucking that last breath and holding it inside me as if it could protect me. Again I heard gunfire, each shot firing one after another so fast, faster than any index finger could move. My adrenaline took over my curiosity, and I found myself shaking uncontrollably, like a wet rat. I wished that I never looked at them. I felt my blood thinning, rushing from my feet to my heart—the heart that it was familiar with, but was acting strangely that morning. I grabbed my emergency bag from near my pillow and ran downstairs in one breath.

Downstairs, my uncle and his family were already gone. There wasn't any time to say goodbye to my cousins, no time to think about it or reflect, and no time to cry. It was time to leave. But where would we go? Nobody knew. We would have been in Thailand already if it wasn't for that moped and that man who stopped by to take my father away. Now that Pa was not with us, we had ten people in our group: Em and Mair, two boys, and six girls. The two boys were my older brother Hong, and my younger brother Kheang, who was nine years old at the time. The youngest girl in the group was Linda's five-year-old sister. We needed a strong man to help us carry food and whatever else we needed, but we had to do the best we could with what we had. Everybody was depending on Em to know what to do and how to survive. Mair and her family had been living with us for the last two years. Having no money to survive on her own, she decided to stay with us. The maid's family was in a different part of the country, so she came with us as well.

The street in front of the house was packed with people, cars, oxcarts, horse carts, motorcycles, bicycles, tricycles, and whatever other mode of transportation they could get hold of. The black-uniformed people in front of the house seemed nicer than the two monsters in the back street. They walked from house to house with a bullhorn in their hands, telling people not to take more than two or three days of food, and saying there was no need to take many belongings because after two or three days of reorganization, everybody would be back in their houses.

No gunfire came from these men. As they spoke, they referred to all the people as brothers, sisters, fathers, and mothers. The way they talked sounded strange to my ears. I thought quietly, *I don't trust you. I have heard of people like you before through my grandfather's stories. You are not to be trusted. You don't distinguish between your mother and any other mothers in the whole country. You treat them all the same, and with less love than for your government. I will never be like you.* At the same time, these men were gentle in voice, and they made me think that perhaps they were in the same boat as us: They didn't have a choice.

The black-uniformed people must have thought we were good followers for we didn't bring anything much with us at all. But we didn't have any means of transportation. Every one of us had to use what God gave us—our two feet. There wasn't time to think about what was best to bring. The only time we had was to get out of the house as soon as we could. So off we went, out of the house and away from the border. We each had a bag, and there were a few extra bags that Hong, Mair, Linda, and the maid took turns carrying. We took with us some clothes, blankets, dried food and rice, some plates, spoons, and cooking pots.

Em could not help much in carrying anything other than herself. Her breathing became increasingly difficult as the heat from the sun intensified. Her asthma medication was not strong enough for a day like this. But her stomach did not seem to bother her as it normally would. She was not drooling like in the months before. Perhaps her stomach problem was replaced by four other stomach problems, if not nine others. They were different stomachs with different kinds of problems, and they all seemed worse than what she had.

Every once in a while, Em warned us: "Stay close together, children." I was determined not to let Em worry about me. Sometimes I carried extra bags using my hands, my arms, my shoulders, or my head. Whenever I could, I used my young and innocent look to get some sympathy from men who had oxcarts. Without asking, I would hang some of my bags on the side frame of the oxcart, and would put the rest of the bags on top of the ones that I hung. I felt ashamed to impose my burden on these men, but I knew that if I asked, they would say no, and I remembered my father often told us something like, "When you are down, and you need to survive, put on a thick face. Don't be too shy." In other words, "Swallow your pride, and get ready to lose your face." Well, I was down and I needed to survive, so I did put on a thick face, even though it was not easy to do.

Most of the drivers were kind men. Some of them told me to put only half of my load on the cart and carry the other half myself. And some said: "Be sure you don't sit on it. It is too loaded already; you might break it." There was one driver I remember the most; I can still see his face today. When he realized that his cart had been invaded, he turned to me and raised his hand with a switch. He was going to whip me; I really thought he would. Quicker than he could unleash his switch on me, I took my bags off his cart. I felt my blood getting hot and rushing to my face. I felt as if he was already striking me. He moved on, swearing at me. I could not hear everything he said, but I was confident with my imagination. Perhaps a kid had broken his cart once already. Whatever it was, I learned one thing from this to add to my father's advice: "Don't forget to check his face before you put on your thick face."

A thought came to mind that if we had stayed at our home in Battambang, we would be in a better situation than we were now. In our move to Poipet, we had left behind a brand-new car (a 404 Peugeot), a moped, and four bicycles.

We set out marching down National Highway 5 for at least three hours. There was no more yelling, screaming, and crying to locate a family member. If a mother could not find her child, it was of no use to howl any more, but just to cry quietly and hope. I was grateful that Em was not one of those mothers who stopped along the highway, wondering if they should speed up or slow down to reunite with their lost little ones. It was an agonizing moment to witness a mother in that situation and not be able to offer help. All I could do was look at them, then walk away and pray. The highway seemed so sadly silent. The people with cars had long gone, those with oxcarts were less often to be seen, and those of us with two legs were too exhausted to talk, so we just walked gently and quietly, one foot in front of the other. The sun was unforgiving, and there weren't many trees along the highway. Had the highway been designed for walking, it would have had more trees. Every shaded spot we walked by so far was overflowing, occupied by exhausted faces.

My shirt was soaking wet from my own perspiration,

more than I ever thought I was capable of. Oh, dear God, what have I done in my previous lifetime to receive this punishment and witness these hardships? Can't you do something? However, the sweat began to show me its main function, and I started to feel cool. Oh, dear God, forgive me for doubting you. I got a second wind to boost myself ahead of everybody in my group. For a while I would speed up ahead of everybody and then wait for them to catch up with me. When they caught up, I would go again, using my hands, arms, shoulders, and head, and once in a while using a kind man's oxcart to carry my load. It was a game that kept me going for a little bit longer.

At one point, I saw a woman carry her belongings in two baskets suspended on each end of a bamboo carrying bar that she placed on one side of her shoulder. Her load was so heavy that she could not walk straight. She took each short, crooked step quickly to keep the momentum going. I heard her strong, short, and quick breaths as she passed by me.

What is she carrying? Gold? I gazed at her load and noticed something in one of the baskets was moving. I looked again and saw it was a baby—*two* babies. Twin toddlers. Identical! How cute! For an instant, they brought a smile to my face at this strange time. Not a sound came out from either one of them. They had smooth, brown baby skin, but not a single hair peeked out of their heads. They wore no clothes, no hats, not a shred of fabric to protect them, just their brown baby hands holding onto the rim of the baskets, and their bald heads, sitting like two-year-old baby Buddhas in each basket suspended from each end of the bamboo carrying bar.

They must have been hot but were probably enjoying the gentle motion of the ride from their protective mother. They were smiling when they saw me, trying to tell me that they loved this new experience. Enjoy it while you can, but this is not normal. As their mother was huffing and puffing along, I prayed for her: May God be with you, care for you and your children. For the love that you show to your children you deserve nothing but good things. The mother reminded me of what I saw earlier in the day: mattresses on top of cars, furniture in the trunks. Were these people too frightened to think straight or too selfish to help others like this mother?

I saw a big tree in the distance and could already feel the cool shade, but then the thought came to me that it was probably packed. Without looking back for my family, I started stepping toward the tree. To my disappointment, my suspicion became a reality. There was no way that my family could fit anywhere under this cool tree. I lost hope for a break. I was unable to control the heaviness of my heart, my jaw stiffened, my lower lip shook, and I felt a tingle on the tip of my nose and water in my eyes. I blinked the tears out of my eyes and turned away from the exhausted crowd. I wasn't crying because of the shade. I was crying because I couldn't help it, and it felt good.

I was sitting in the sun by the edge of the shade with eyes that never left the highway, watching for my group, when I saw that one of the families in the shade was leaving. I felt proud of myself for getting a shady spot for the group, but too tired to mention it when Em arrived. Mair unpacked and got some precooked rice and some dried fish out for each of us. None of us seemed to be hungry, but Em and Mair insisted that we must eat.

Every now and then, we saw people that we knew passing us by. They all asked about my father. "How unfortunate," they all said when they learned about the moped and the man.

"Where are we going?" they asked each other.

"Away from the border. And stay on the highway: that is where they want us to go," one friend told Em.

"Get your kids and keep moving as soon as you can. You don't want them to rush you with guns," one man advised Em.

No longer than thirty minutes after the break we were on the road again. Cars that had run out of gas were abandoned along the highway. There were also other belongings that must have been too heavy to carry that had been scattered along the road.

Afternoon came with cool air that was refreshing. I felt as though I had a burst of energy that was just too vigorous to contain. Kheang and I were racing each other on the empty highway. All of the tiredness that I felt earlier in the day seemed to have vanished completely.

It was getting dark, and we still didn't know where to stay for the night. "If we cannot find a place to stay, we may have to sleep in the field along the highway," Em told us.

That would have been okay with me. Quietly and to myself, I was determined to support Em no matter what she decided. God must have a heart, or Em must have passed his test, for not long after Em decided we would spend the night along the highway, we heard a family pacing behind us, one of the families that we knew well from Poipet. The lady of the family told Em that she had an aunt who lived in the next town that would be so kind as to take us all in for the night. The next town? I had never thought that I could walk from town to town. I had never even heard in my life that people could walk from town to town. That day I did it with my own two feet.

It seemed to take forever to get to the house. I was exhausted. My legs felt so heavy and my neck was sore from carrying the bag on my head for the first time in my life, not to mention the distance that I had hauled it. The highway must have been situated at the edge of town because I saw only a few houses along the way. The people who were in these houses looked at us with puzzled faces. Kids watched us as if we were some kind of parade of homeless people. Even though I was tired, I was feeling ashamed, as if it was my fault that I was in this situation.

A dirt road led us from the highway to the house. Closer to the house, to the right of the dirty road, was a big vegetable garden. Living in Battambang city, I had never seen a garden that big before. The wood house was about eight feet off the ground. The woman of the house stood at the top of the stairs by the entrance. "Come on up. Come on up," she invited us, before we even asked for help. "There is nothing to be afraid of. There is room for the night. Come and rest."

"God bless you, God bless you, God be with you," Em whimpered to the woman.

We each took our turn slowly crawling up the stairs to the house. The woman showed us where we could stay for the night. We lost track of our good friend who had brought us to the house, which was packed with people the woman had rescued for the night. She told us that she had made a lot of winter melon soup and cooked some rice and that we were welcome to serve ourselves. We went down the stairs to wash and came back up to have dinner. It was dark as we sat in a circle on the floor and had dinner by a kerosene lamp. I felt like I was eating in the dark. The kerosene was nothing like the fluorescent light that I had been used to. Nevertheless, I was very grateful to the woman of the house.

When I took my first spoon of the soup, I almost threw up. The saltiness, stinky aroma, and strong flavor of the broth overwhelmed the simple sweet squash soup that I was expecting.

"Squash soup with *prahok*,[7] Em?" I was confirming my shock quietly with Em.

"Rural Cambodians use prahok like we use soy sauce. Eat it, my child, so you can have strength for tomorrow. The woman has been very kind to us," Em whispered back to me.

After dinner Em lay down, and I reached over to

---

[7] *Prahok* is salted and fermented fish paste that is used in Cambodian cuisine for umami, savory flavor.

massage her legs. She insisted that I get some sleep. "I'm not too tired. Let me massage you a bit more," I said. A few minutes later I tried to get some sleep, but I found myself tossing and turning. When I slept on my back the bones in my spine hurt. Sideways, it was my shoulder, elbow, and knees. Sleeping on a hardwood floor was nothing like sleeping on a soft mattress. *How can anybody sleep without a mattress?* was the last question I remember asking myself when I fell asleep, only to be woken up in the middle of the night by my calf muscles twisting uncontrollably, trying to get to the top of my shin bones. I was in excruciating pain, but most of all I was scared because I didn't understand what was going on with my legs. Would I have them back and be able to walk the next day? I didn't want Em to worry. I must have made a shrieking noise when I woke up Em.

"What's wrong? What's wrong, my child?"

"My legs. My calf muscle is twisted."

"It's all right. It will go away. It's called the alligator twist."

"Alligator twist?"

"Caused by walking too far. Try to massage it with your hands."

I bit my lips, trying not to moan. I was shaking with pain. My heart throbbed from the pressure that I didn't let go through my mouth. I sat up and reached over to bring the baby alligators back where they belonged, and in less than three minutes the pain subsided and I was fast asleep, but I woke up again and again with the same painful experience. That night I woke up many times from the alligator twists, for the day before I had walked the longest walk in my life.

Chapter 4

THE LION VILLAGE

Planting Season of 1975

I woke up the next morning to Em's hustling voice. "Up, up, up. Hurry, hurry my children."

I was up with my bag in my hand and ready to follow her instructions. People were scrambling around the door, trying to get down the stairs. Babies were crying, and adults were directing their families. One of the men who came from Poipet with us stood by the staircase and reached up to help mothers with babies to get down and out of the house as soon as possible. He cried out, "Out, out, they're chasing us out again." His strength and kind gesture to the families around him was comforting. I found myself wishing for my father—for his strength and security. Much earlier than the previous morning, we were out of the house and onto the same National Highway 5. We didn't get a chance to thank the woman or her niece who brought us to the house.

My body felt sore from the day before and from the alligator twists. The sun wasn't out yet, but I was already tired. I kept telling myself that I would not let Em worry about me. So I kept moving my legs one at a time.

The highway was crowded again with refugees. It was not as crowded as yesterday morning, but there were more Black Uniforms. They were directing us, making sure we didn't get off the highway. They seemed vicious and devilish in a way I couldn't really describe, perhaps because I would not dare to look into their faces. Still, I could feel the chill and darkness of their spirits when I walked past them.

On this second day, we took more breaks. I sensed that my luck was slipping away when I noticed there weren't any oxcarts to be seen for at least two hours. I was no longer the leader of the group. I didn't care if Kheang took the lead. I was too tired to play any game with him. Walking together with the group, I saw Kheang was still in his pajamas from two nights ago and was not carrying any bag. He just managed to carry himself, but looked determined not to be a burden on the group. *Kheang, what a good boy you are!* Quietly in my head, I was proud of him. Through this whole ordeal, not a single complaint ever came out of his mouth, and he was just nine years old.

We walked quietly, without even the smallest conversation—just walking. In my case, I didn't even think of anything. I was too tired to think straight anyway.

Something about fifty yards ahead of us caught our attention. People were crowded to look in the ditch alongside the highway. I picked up my speed to try to satisfy my curiosity, only to get stopped by Em and Mair. I looked at Em's face, the face that always gave me comfort, and it told me everything will be all right. I latched on and held it tight to my heart while my legs managed to pick up even more speed to get away from whatever it was that Em was so horrified to even let us get a glimpse of.

"Dear God, why let him die like an animal?" pleaded a woman as she walked past me.

By now the sun was up, but it was still early morning. As I walked I was daydreaming that Pa was on the same moped, with Ee on the back seat, coming toward us from the opposite direction. How nice that would be. We would be together, and they could help me carry the load that made my scalp numb and my neck sore.

I was glad whenever we saw people that we knew. I was glad for the familiar faces in this strange time, but most of all I was glad because every time Em saw our friends, I would get a break from walking while she talked with them and asked many questions. Her friends would ask questions back, but none of them had much to comfort each other with.

We still did not know what our destination would be, but we sensed that wherever it would be, it was no longer under our control. I took comfort in knowing that if we kept marching forward on this highway, we would be back in our hometown, Battambang, even though it would take us many long days.

A familiar voice full of mixed emotions called for Em from behind: "Is that you? Chheng?" We all stopped and turned around. It was Aunt Lonn and her family. Aunt Lonn was one of our old friends of many years. She was traveling in a group of eight, including her five sons, a daughter about six years old, and her elderly mother. Before Em could respond, Aunt Lonn said: "You are the last one that I expected to see on this road. For sure I thought you would have gone to Thailand. Where is your husband?"

Em could not get a word out. Her face turned red, and her eyes filled with tears. Mair stepped in and told Aunt Lonn about Pa. The three ladies were silent and turned their faces away from each other, dabbing and wiping their tears with their fingertips. Aunt Lonn's husband had passed away not too long ago. Just when I thought things could not be worse, Aunt Lonn turned back to Em with a gentle voice, slowly and almost too quiet to be heard, and added: "I heard that they evacuated Battambang too."

"Dear God, what am I going to do?" said Em, bursting into tears.

"Stick with me," Aunt Lonn responded with a hint of anger in her voice. "Do you remember the medicine man in Lion Village (*Changha*)? He made the holy waistband[8] for our husbands."

"Yes, Lok Krew[9] Preuk. I thought he was with the Khmer Rouge," Em replied with a puzzled look on her face.

"He was with the Khmer Rouge, but he is still a good man. He is going to try to help people that he knows to go to his village. The people in his village respect him, even the Khmer Rouge."

There was a quiet moment, and the hesitation was clear in Em's face.

"Come with me. We will look out for each other." Aunt Lonn pleaded to help.

---

[8] It was customary for a Khmer man to wear a blessed braided string or gold chain around his waist. For they believe that the blessing on the chain provides protection from bad karma.

[9] *Lok Krew* is a Khmer term that refers to a teacher or a master.

In my head, I was also pleading: Say yes, Em. At least with Aunt Lonn we have a destination.

"Yes, you are right, we must look out for each other," Em said firmly and slowly.

Thus, our group had grown from ten people to seventeen people. As we marched, I wondered what this medicine man looked like. I had heard of him and his wondrous magic before. Once I was told that this man had the ability to "shrink the road," and once Pa had traveled with him on one of these shrunken roads, and it was proven to be true that he made better time than a car on the highway. It was said that on this same trip they were confronted by a tiger. The tiger looked right into Pa's eyes, preparing to leap. Then the medicine man said his magic words, and the tiger eased its focus and walked away. On that day, the medicine man became Pa's master.

We were told that the medicine man was waiting for us somewhere ahead on the same highway, so we picked up our speed to ensure we would not miss him. Along the way Em would tell all the people that she knew: "If you ever see my husband, please tell him that I will be with his master at Lion Village."

In the distance, on the right side of the road, I saw a line of people turning away from the highway. The change in course made all the parents restless. Would we get to the master before we have to turn? I wasn't sure. The question must have been on everyone else's mind, too, as we all seemed to move faster and faster, heads up and looking for an old man that might be standing by the road and waiting for his people. I already saw Black Uniforms standing across the highway with guns in ready position. But where was the master—the master who promised to rescue us? Master always keeps his word.

As we moved closer to the turn, we saw a small group of people turning in the opposite direction from the main crowd. "Do we have a choice? Which turn is best?" Someone in our group was directing us to turn the opposite of the main crowd: "Over here. Over here."

My eyes were on Em, following every move she made. Em had told us many times before all of this happened: "Watch for me, and follow me. Do anything you can to stay with me. I can't always watch for everyone. In a split second, if you lose sight of me, we may never see each other again." So I watched her and followed her, and whenever possible I looked into her eyes, but this time her profile was all I could get ahold of. Em was never out of my sight. Not looking at every one of us, Em kept chanting, "Stay together. Stay together. Come closer. Come closer."

We were all huddling behind Em when a Black

Uniform swung his rifle around, herding us as if we were cattle to turn right and shouted, "Go!"

Someone in the group exclaimed, *"Lok Krew!"* Things were still for a moment. Then the Black Uniform repeated his command again, only this time louder than before. The last person in the group that turned left was about thirty yards into the field when he turned around and ran back to the highway. He raised his arm and waved it to get the attention of the Black Uniform. Sure enough, the Black Uniform seemed to freeze at the sight of this man, who marched resolutely toward him. I thought that he must be the master.

"These are my people," said the marching man.

"My apologies, master," said the Black Uniform, who had turned soft and kind. He turned to us and, still swinging the rifle, hurriedly commanded: "Go, go! Hurry up!" We ran as fast as we could, away from the main crowd toward the small group being led by the master.

"You are so lucky. He wasn't going to wait any longer," a woman in the other group told us.

I had thought the war was over. This was worse than when the war was active. Was this a new war? Who was fighting whom? These thoughts and many other unanswered questions occupied my mind.

The master was catching up with us. He was a

small, quiet man in his sixties, but he was walking faster and stronger than any of us. Aunt Lonn and Em were talking to him while they walked, but I couldn't hear a word of what he was saying. To me he was larger than life, and I felt safe having him in our group.

We took a lunch break under a shade tree along the trail to Lion Village. Mair started to unpack our belongings to get some food for us. This time, however, the precooked rice was already finished. She found three big pieces of hard clay that she formed into a triangle and made a fire with twigs in the middle. It looked to me like Mair had done this many times before. For the moment, I was happy and excited to really be doing what I only read about in books: surviving with the bare minimum, cooking in an open field without a coal or gas stove. I felt like I was on a school field trip. I felt proud that I contributed to our survival by collecting twigs for the fire. The hot rice tasted so sweet, and the few slices of preserved pork that Em made in case of emergency were a big treat. The thought came to mind: *I can deal with this. This is not too bad. I can contribute to our survival, and I can help Em.*

We were still on the road to Lion Village as the sun was setting very low on the horizon. I was tired and sore, but we could not stop. We had to stay together, marching to a village that we had never even heard of. I could tell that we were getting closer because the trees around the village were getting bigger. I heard countless insects and animals crying near my feet and all around me, but I could not tell what they were. I never heard any of those cries before. Now I was hearing all of them all at once telling each other: "Beware! Strangers!"

I found myself getting closer to the group, leaving very little space to the next person. At the edge of the village, I saw lights from kerosene lamps scattered between shadows of trees, and I could smell a strong and stale and unfamiliar smell that lingered in my nose and stuck in my throat. We walked through an opening in the line of tree fence that led us to the master's house.

The master had a small house that was raised above the ground on wooden stilts that were no thicker than his leg. The stairs to his wood floor were only wide enough to let one person through at a time. Each step was smaller than my foot, so to balance myself I held on to the small rail as tightly as I could. At the top of the stairs, I had to bend my head down to avoid knocking my forehead. When I got to the main floor, I found it was packed with people, most of whom we knew, but not as closely as Aunt Lonn. I greeted the master's wife and was told to go back downstairs, where we were to spend the rest of the night.

Downstairs? Where? How could we stay downstairs? Oh—what is that smell? Somebody help me, get me out of here! I'd rather sleep in the field than in this place. I hate this village already. I was desperate, but there was nothing I could do to change it.

Rice and salted pork was what I had for dinner that night. I could not believe that I could swallow anything with that strong smell in the air, but I did. I had seen many things that day that I had never seen before, smelled things that I had never smelled before, heard cries that I have never thought were possible. All of my senses were busy registering new things, but my heart was with me, embracing me, telling me everything would be okay.

There was an oversize bamboo bench underneath the house where we slept together, packed, body to body. That night I closed my eyes, praying, pleading, and asking, "Why, what have I done?"

The next morning, I woke up in a different world. Why did I have to wake up? I didn't want to face the new reality. Lying on the bamboo slats, I tried to be as still as I could, for moving was like torture. My whole body—not just my legs—was sore beyond words, and every muscle felt as though it was infected. I wanted to cry, but why? We were all in this together.

The awful smell was still there. "What is that smell? Em?" I asked.

Mair was already up and rescued Em from my question. In a plain voice, she said, "Cow shit."

"Gross!"

"Stop it. You're only making things worse for your mother."

"What is that hill?"

"Cow shit!"

I shrunk with Mair's last response. The cow dung was piled up into a hill almost as high as the wood floor of the master's house. It was about five feet away from where we were sitting, eating, and sleeping. Why in the world would cow dung be piled in a hill? Why so close to a home? Why did I have to be here? My feeling was beyond feeling. I had never heard or read of such a living condition. I finally had to get up, and just like every morning, I had to respond to nature's call. Where was the bathroom? I did not want to find out, but I had to.

"Linda, why don't you take your sister and wake Kheang to go too?" Em asked.

Kheang pushed himself to get up on his own two feet. He was moaning and groaning, and it took him a while to straighten up. Linda took us past the tree fence and toward the edge of the village, into a small area with shrubs and bushes scattered around. "It stinks! Can we go somewhere else?" I pleaded with Linda.

"No, this is it."

"I can't."

"You have to. There isn't anywhere else."

Kheang didn't hesitate. He went right ahead and didn't want to stick around. "Hurry up so we can get out of this stinky place," he said.

I walked to one of the bushes and was so worried that somebody might see me as I adjusted myself that I stepped into someone else's deposit. I tried to get up, but it was too late, so I was between getting up and sitting down when I had to let go. I shut my eyes, tightened my lips, and held onto my breath, but I could not shut out the experience that was so awful. I stopped myself short of completion and ran away with wet underwear. Disgusted with everything, I tried to walk it off, scraping and cleaning my shit-covered thong flip-flops with the dusty dirt along the trail.

How can there be a house without a bathroom? Why does it have to be this way? I hate this village.

Back under the master's house, I was restless because I didn't finish my job behind that bush. I was determined not to go there again. No matter what, I would not go back there. Even if my intestines burst and I died, I would not go back there.

Lying down on the bamboo slats seemed to help control the urge. While I was lying there, I saw the master's daughter come down the stairs. She was about

Chenda's age, wearing a sarong so well that she didn't need elastic to hold it up around her waist. At the bottom of the stairs, she turned around, gave us a quick smile, and walked toward us.

"Does anybody want to go with me to see people dancing at the pagoda?" she asked.

Every head turned toward Em. Now that the master's daughter mentioned it, I could hear the music. For sure I knew what Em was thinking: "You don't go to watch people dance unless you want to be asked, and dancing in public is out of question." So the answer would be no.

Instead, Em looked at us and said: "Go ahead and go, and look out for each other." I was shocked and sat up, only to realize that I really had to go to the bush again. So I pleaded with Linda to take me, but not without dancing, twisting my body, and many facial expressions.

Linda warned me: "Next time I will not take you back if you don't finish your job the first time."

I heard the music get louder and louder as we meandered between small huts along a dirt path. It was a new experience, and I found it interesting and amazing that families could live in such small huts. It would be a fun adventure to live in a small hut. *I might even enjoy it*, I thought with a bit of guilt.

The huts along the Pagoda had set up little stands that sold snacks for a small price. I stopped by and bought a snack and was curious about the taste, for I never had seen snacks that looked so unattractive. I gave it one small bite and was not impressed. After the second bite, I wanted to find out what was in this snack. It was nothing that I could identify. It was a grayish white color that had no aroma. It was dry, crumbled with each bite, and had a hint of sweetness to the taste. I had not seen or tasted any snack like this before.

"What do you call this?" I asked.

"Cake, can't you tell?" the woman snapped at me.

I didn't dare to ask what kind of cake it was. Somehow it seemed so hilarious, and once out of the woman's sight, Kheang and I kept repeating: "Cake, can't you tell?" and laughed our heads off.

At the pagoda, I saw many young women and men dancing and singing to the live drumbeat rhythms of traditional Cambodian new year music. There was no electricity to amplify the sound nor any other instruments but the pure sound of a single drum controlled by a pair of bare hands. The music was simple but very engaging. The young men and women wore ordinary cotton clothes. Although their clothes seemed new for the celebration, there weren't any bright-colored silks that were customary during new year celebrations at a pagoda.

Watching the dancers and trying to contain my excitement, I sensed eyes were on me like I was some kind of alien. They were kids' eyes. A group of kids were hobbling around us and looking straight at me—at my shirt, my skirt, and my face. These kids ranged from as old as Kheang to as young as a toddler that just had learned how to walk. I found myself fascinated by them as well, for most of them didn't have any clothes on, and they were all so grayish black. I realized then how different from us the village people were.

I noticed that none of the newcomers were in the dance circle. Standing outside the circle, we watched the village people dance and looked at each other, thinking that we didn't belong here. They were celebrating while we were suffering. We were so different in the way we dressed, the way we talked and walked, and even the way we looked at each other.

On the way back to the master's house, I wondered: Maybe these kids had never even seen a car or truck before. Unless they got a chance to travel outside of the village, there was no way they would know what a car looks like or sounds like because there weren't any roads in this village except the small trails between huts.

I couldn't wait to tell Em about my experience in the village. Kheang and I took turns telling her the "Cake, can't you tell?" story and even had the cake with us to make the story more exciting, but Em refused to taste the cake when she took a look at it.

I told her about the huts. "There are no houses, Em, only huts. And there aren't any shops at all, only a wooden pagoda where people bring things to sell in its yard." Em listened without any comment, and I added one last thing that I thought was really scary about the village. "The people are so different."

"Just be grateful that they let us in," Em said, jumping at me.

It had been at least three days since we last had a bath. The sweat and the dirt that we collected along the highway was dry and crusty on our bodies. A bath was very necessary at this time, but not without a price. We had to walk to the end of the village and fetch the water from a well with a bucket tied to the end of a rope. Linda lowered it, then brought it back, only to see that half of the water was gone on its way up.

It was impossible for us to cleanse ourselves in public, so we chose to carry the water back to our place. With semi-privacy, I managed to soak a piece of cloth into the water and wiped myself clean, leaving some fresh water for Linda and Chenda to do their cleansing at night, for they were young ladies, not just girls like I was.

The process was beyond my imagination, and I hated the village. How could people want to live there, with no river and no pump, only a well that was so deep that it was pitch-black at the bottom?

Just a week ago, we were living in a different world. Now, as bad as it got, we knew that it would be worse, and there was no plan to prevent it. We had rice and pre-served pork twice a day every day since arriving at Lion Village. Yet every day before my meal, I found myself hungry for the same rice and pork. Fruit, snacks, and candies between meals were things of the past. There wasn't much for me to do except sit under the master's house, fearing for the future and wishing for a second chance with the past. Every dusk, the sun turned deep orange, and the birds seemed to sing the saddest songs. The air filled with smoke from burning dry cow shit to keep the mosquitos away.

My body was recovering pretty quickly from the walk, but my neck was still sore. I noticed four or five lumps the size of my little finger clustered behind my left ear and around the base of my skull. There was nothing I could do about them except hope that they would go away.

A few days after we arrived in Lion Village, the first

rain of the season came. The rain fumigated the whole village with a spice of dried cow shit and human excrement. Our dirt floor turned into steamy, musty, moist earth. I didn't want to get down from the bamboo slat floor; I wanted only to cover myself with a blanket and cry my head off. I tried to think of one good thing about this village ... but there was nothing. I was doomed. I saw kids out laughing and showering in the warm rain, but still I could not relate to their excitement when I saw their toes covered with mud. Em learned from the natives to put buckets, pots, and pans out in the open to collect the rainwater.

Late that afternoon the village people were all excited. "No more dry food," they were saying. We were not sure what they meant until the master's son, who was about the same age as Hong, asked, "Would you like to go hunting frogs tonight?" He reassured us, "The first rainfall of the season brings the best catch."

Hong went out in the dark of night, hoping to get some frogs for us. The master's son coached Hong: "Better leave your shoes here. They will not stay on your feet in the muddy field." So Hong was in bare feet with a flashlight and a funny-looking bamboo basket hanging over his shoulder. I wished he would not go; I didn't want to see him that way.

The croak of frogs echoed through the whole village

non-stop and so loud it was more like the roar of a lion, a roar that warned us of the worst to come. I sat and waited for my brother to come back. I did not want any frogs. I did not want to acknowledge that he was accepting this new way of living. A couple of hours later, Hong was back with an empty basket. Thin, cold, shaking, and tired under the moonlit sky, he summoned an explanation. "I saw lots of them Em, but couldn't catch any." Quietly I chuckled at the way Hong described his experience, but then I saw Em gently put her hand on his head, pat it softly, and gently say, "It's okay, my child."

That night I begged God to stop showing or teaching me this kind of living. I begged him to take me back to where we once were and promised to never again take life for granted. *Dear God, I know you can't talk to me like a regular person, but please show me a sign; tell me in my dreams what will my future hold for me.*

As soon as I woke up in the morning, I could not wait to tell Em about my vivid dream. In my dream I saw Pa and Ee racing to pass the gate that was coming down slowly to separate them from their loved ones. They just barely passed the gate when they turned around and pleaded with the Black Uniforms to bring Aunt Sareth and her son with them. I saw these images like a movie that I couldn't control, and I let it go through its point of no return. I watched Aunt Sareth's desperate hands reaching out to Pa and Ee as they walked away from her and toward us with their faces down. The dream all happened right by the tree fence, in front of the master's house.

"Maybe your dream will come true; maybe Pa will find us," said Em.

In my dream, I sat on the bamboo slat floor and could see through the gap in the tree fence that Pa and Ee were coming through. Not that Pa or Ee could change things, but I would have loved to see them again and get their sympathy for what we had gone through. If Pa could be with us, he would have a plan for our future, to get us out of the village, or at least to move out of the master's place since we were becoming an obvious irritation to the master's wife and daughter. That day I sat and watched the gap along the tree line, wishing my dream would come true.

Around four o'clock in the afternoon, Pa came pushing a bike with a small load, and Ee was walking right behind him through the gap in the tree fence. My dream came true! Kheang ran to Pa, and everybody was screaming. Em's face looked awful as she tried to control her emotions. With tears in her eyes, she sobbed and spoke words that could not be understood to release the jolt to her heart. She ran and held her hands together up in the air as a gesture of thanks to God, landed them on Pa's arm, and rested her head on his shoulder, and everything turned completely silent.

It was a sad, bitter experience to witness. Pa had changed so much in such a short period of time. His face was darkened from the sun, yet pale from exhaustion, and tightened up to reflect his emotion. It was the first time I saw him cry. We cried with him and followed him up the stairs then knelt down and bowed to his master. He could not bring himself back up to face the master. His hands that should have been flat on the floor turned instead to cover his face, and because he could not suppress the feeling any longer, his body shook, and he let out sounds that sent an aching shock wave to my heart. I had never heard any grown man cry, let alone my own father. I felt tears swell up in my eyes in shock, but more in fear.

The master's warm voice calmed us all and gave us hope again. He said, "I begged you not to lose hope. Just remember: What goes around comes around. You have been a good man, and God has eyes; he will be with you."

We could not wait to tell Ee about our unbelievable journey and ask the many questions we had for him: Where were Aunt Sareth, our little Cousin Pros, and

Ouv? Did you walk all this distance to find us? How did you know we were here? What happened to Blacky?

Ee and Pa left our home the same time we left Poipet. Ee told me that Blacky, our spaniel puppy was left by the house to tend to herself. Part of me got mad at Ee and Pa for not even trying to take Blacky with them. The other part realized that if they had taken Blacky, they eventually would have had to carry her for she was such a tiny dog. I was grateful that I did not have to witness her abandonment.

The plan was that Ee and Pa would try to find us, and Ouv was to stay with Aunt Sareth and her son in a village call Phum Preah Ponlea, which was one of the villages where the Black Uniforms moved people from Battambang to. Once Pa and Ee found us, we would again be reunited with Aunt Sareth and Ouv. Once I heard this plan, I thought of my dream. In the dream, Aunt Sareth was not able to come across the gate. I started to feel goose bumps all over me. I asked God for a sign, and I received one. I remember being scared to receive the sign.

Ee and Pa had continued their journey on the same National Highway 5 that we were on, but they were going the opposite direction, aiming toward Poipet. They traveled for about a week on this highway, trying to get any information they could about us. Sure enough,

Em's message got to Pa. A friend told him: "Your wife and children are with your master in Lion Village." So they continued, first on a moped, and when they could not find anyone who would take money for gas, they exchanged the moped for a bike. They slept when it was dark and continued even before the sun came up to try to beat the heat. They slept in the open field most of the time, but once they were able to find an empty shack. They had the best rest that night. They even found pillows to rest on, so they slept until the sun was too bright on their faces. When Ee rolled over to get up, he was startled by the sight of blood spattered everywhere in the shack and on his bedding, including the pillow that he was so thankful for. From the look of it, a body must have been not too far away, but they were eager to get out of the place rather than look for the body. If they found it, they could do nothing but walk away. They hurried to get out of the hut, and when they did, they murmured and asked for forgiveness from the spirit of the dead for they felt that they had intruded on its resting place.

Oh, how things changed. Only a week earlier, if you were to initiate a trade of your moped for a bike, you would be looked at sideways as if you had lost your mind. Now everything was turned upside down. A bicycle was worth more than a motorcycle, and an oxcart worth more than a car. Fortunately, money was still worth something, and Em still had some.

The next day, a rumor was spreading that the new government would not allow traveling between villages. What about Aunt Sareth? Oh, my dream was so true that I was afraid to repeat it to anybody else. For some reason, I felt as though it was my fault for dreaming such a bad thing that came true. Not a word came out of my mouth that day.

Pa was restless about the news. He told Em that we could not survive in Lion Village. He wanted to move us to a village along a river that he had come across when he looking for us. "Who would want to do any business in a village like this? If we move closer to the river, we will be more in touch with the moving world. Besides, a river will always provide fish."

The master acknowledged Pa's plan and encouraged him to move as soon as possible. With his encouragement, we could tell that the master was losing his influence on the Black Uniforms.

Em bought a pair of oxen and a cart that afternoon. We were privately packing our bags but didn't load them on the wagon so that people would not suspect our plan.

As the first rooster crowed, and before anyone walked about, we were up and ready to leave the Lion

Village. We all went upstairs and bowed in front of the master as he gave us his blessing. He was such a kind man.

Aunt Lonn watched us break our promise to stay and look out after each other. We didn't offer for her to come along, and she didn't ask, nor did she beg us to stay. I felt the lump in her throat as she watched us depart. At the packed cart, a man was ready to drive the oxen out of the village on the same dirt road that we had been on about two weeks ago when we were forced out of Poipet. The first few steps were slow and heavy until we got past the tree fence. The man on the oxcart told us to move as fast as we could so we would not be seen. He had once worked for Pa, and as a kind favor, he was willing to lead us out of the village.

After a couple of hours of brisk walking and taking turns riding on the oxcart, we were in the middle of an open field with the frog village just a small cluster of trees at our backs. As we walked, Mair showed us what water spinach looked like so we could help her pick some for lunch. In the dry season, water spinach looked nothing like the kind we usually bought from a market. The stem was small, and the edible part was too short. It looked more like a weed than like the water spinach that we were used to.

Kheang and I had fun picking water spinach in the

field along the trail. I heard a sound that was unfamiliar, cooing gently and peacefully. I asked Mair what it was. She pointed out a pair of doves in the field. Living in the city, I had never seen a dove before. I was so happy to see the gentle birds with smooth feathers that seemed to glide when they flew away. Watching the two doves fly in the middle of the openness, I took a moment to enjoy the tingling warm feeling that I suddenly had. It was a feeling of love, sadness, and fragility—for what and why, I was not quite certain.

The man led us to a shack by the road for a lunch break. There was a little pond near the shack, and Mair was fetching clear water for cooking when I noticed something was moving as she sunk the pot into the pond.

"What's that?" I asked without even thinking.

"Leech."

"Oh, so cute!"

"Wait until it sucks your blood."

"Ugh."

For the first time in about a week, we finally had something green with our meal, the water spinach that we picked. I never thought that I could be so happy to have some vegetables to eat, but they were very satisfying.

Right after lunch, the man told us that we would

have to continue our journey by ourselves because he had go back before he was noticed. He pointed his finger toward where we should be headed to get to the river. We could tell where the river was. The foliage was thicker and more green against the horizon. None of us except Mair and the maid had ever been near an ox before this past week, so Mair volunteered to be the new driver. The oxen did not like their new driver. It took a while to persuade them to move forward.

As we continued walking, my neck problem started to get worse to the point that I felt feverish. I decided to tell Em.

Her first comment was: "How so unlucky? Why now?" I felt betrayed by Em's comment, I thought for sure that she would be feeling sorry for me.

Pa saw what was going on and added the painful question, "What is wrong with her now?"

I kept telling myself that they were just tired and didn't mean to sound so bad, but I was still hurt. I wished that I had never told Em about my fever because Em's response struck a nerve as I was marked by the family as an unlucky child. Everybody in the family knew that as soon as I was conceived, Pa was sentenced to about a year in jail due to trumped up charges that were totally unfounded. During that time, Em—four months pregnant—was left alone to care for three children by herself. All her pregnancies except mine were lucky. The best pregnancy that brought ultimate luck was Kheang. He brought the family the best fortune and happiness until a week ago. So knowing that I had brought bad luck to my parents, I tried very hard every time to be strong and not cause any trouble. The rest of the trip I pushed myself to walk with a fever and throbbing neck, insisting that I felt all right when others offered to let me stay on the wagon longer. My emotions were wilted and saturated with pain by the two people I loved the most in the world.

French Village Hut—During the first six months living under the Black Uniforms, my family lived together in this hut before being separated. *(Ken Chhi, 2017)*

Chapter 5

THE FRENCH VILLAGE

Planting Season of 1975

Once we reached a village, Pa confirmed my fear. "Things will never be the same from now on. We will have to be strong to survive this one," he said.

This village was much livelier than Lion Village. Homes were lined up along the Mongkol Borey river with all different kinds of shrubs, bushes, and trees. The river looked so alive. The village people didn't look too different from us. There were some who had skin as light as ours. Houses were much bigger and stronger than those in Lion Village. There was one brick building in the village that was bigger than any of the other houses. We learned later the building was a church that French missionaries had built at the time of colonization, hence the name: French Village (*Phum Barang*).

Pa planned for us to spend the night in French Village with Uncle Tre's sister-in-law's family (the Savans), and continue our trip the next morning to Seur, where Uncle Tre had moved to. It would take another day of walking along the river to get to Seur. However, as soon as we arrived at Mrs. Savan's house, we were informed that no one was allowed to leave the village. "Don't bother finding relatives; they mean nothing to you. Your government will take care of you. Stop your journey wherever you are and make yourself useful," the Black Uniforms would say.

We were fortunate that the Savan family let us stay with them until we had a place for ourselves. They also sold us a small lot downstream and across the river, next to their farmhouse, which was at the end of the village. They let us work together with them to plant some cucumbers and squash in exchange for a share of what they produced. We were very grateful for their generosity, but we realized we needed to be on our own soon. On the small lot that Mr. Savan sold us, we had to somehow build a place for ourselves. We didn't know anyone else in the village except the Savans, and we had nearly exhausted our welcome with them. None of us knew how to put together a bird house, let alone a hut. We didn't even own a hammer back home. Mair convinced Pa to sneak around the Black Uniforms and go get Ouv to help with this unfamiliar lifestyle, for Ouv would know how to do farming and fishing and how to build a hut. Ouv was in Phum Preah Ponlea with Aunt Sareth and her son during this time.

A couple of days later, Ee, Pa, and Ouv arrived back at the Savan family's house. Aunt Sareth didn't come with them. She decided to stay with Pa's sister (Aunt Nay Hak) and her family of four strong sons and her husband. Perhaps she understood that it would be too risky to sneak around the Black Uniforms with her little boy. Or perhaps she knew that neither she nor her son could endure such a long walk. The next day, without any break, the three men began to build the hut.

Every day, all able bodies left the house to help build the hut and take care of the garden. Kheang, my two little cousins, Em, and I stayed at the house. Kheang and the two cousins were too young to work, Em was cooking, and I could not work because my neck was getting worse. Every day I had a slight temperature, and my neck throbbed with pain. I could not look straight in front of me. To compensate for the pain, my neck was fixed at about forty-five degrees to the left. I moved only my eyes to look around because moving my neck was too excruciating. So I spent most of my time lying down to ease the pain and waiting for people to come home. When they did come back, I felt guilty for not being able to help them. They looked so different with their muddy clothes and tired expressions.

As days went by, my neck didn't get any better. One day I could not eat or sleep, and the pressure behind my left ear was unbearable. I could not do anything but lie on the wood floor with a pillow pressed against my throbbing neck. I could not stop myself from moaning and groaning with pain that brought tears to my eyes. I was certain that whatever it was, it was eating its way through my skull and my neck bones. Without any modern medication, Pa had asked a medicine man to treat me. I had never been treated by a medicine man before. I had heard that one of the medicine man's treatments was to literally burn his patient wherever the pain was. I was so scared. Hoping to change Pa's idea about the medicine man, I tried to cry my way out.

The medicine man came with a bag of tricks in his hand. He took a look at my neck and reached over to feel it. When he began speaking words of comfort, I noticed the black teeth that he had from many years of chewing areca nuts, betel leaves, and tobacco—and no brushing. I could also smell alcohol on his breath, and he didn't look like he was sure what to do. I started to cry and fought to stay away from the man when Em and Pa lifted my head off the floor. I felt as if my parents were pushing me toward the devil. In my head, I was pleading: *Please don't let him touch me. Please leave me alone. Don't treat me. Let me be.* My crying must have been so annoying that when Pa raised his voice to silence me, he said: "Stop, you bad luck child!" Not a sound came out of me, only tears that I could not stop. Why did he have to say that? The emotional pain was worse than the throbbing on my neck. I felt so empty and so little, and I couldn't hear anything else after that, only my own heartbeat. It didn't matter what the medicine man was going to do to me. I didn't care.

Before I knew it, the man said, "There, that should take care of it." I felt the slimy saliva with pieces of betel nuts on my neck, as they lowered my head back on the floor. I could not stop the silent tears, and I was wondering whether Pa would care if I died.

The medicine man's magic did not seem to help. I felt as though there was a big worm living inside my neck, and it was torturing me with its persistent twitches. In the middle of the night, when everybody was sound asleep, I found comfort by breathing with the rhythm of the twitching worm and repeating under each breath: "Stop ... stop ... stop." My mouth was so dry, but my eyes kept shedding tears, and my breath was not long enough to summon any prayer other than one pleading word: "Stop ... stop ... stop ..."

With the next twitch came a wet and warm sensation around my neck. The twitches were gone, there was no more throbbing, and instantly no more pain.

But I was in a panic. Surely there had to be some worms coming out of me. I called out to Mair for help. She hustled to try to get something to catch the oozing of the thick, warm liquid. The fluid kept coming out; one shirt after the other was soaked. I was so happy that a smile leaked out of my lips. It was a good thing we were in the dark and Mair did not see it. I was sitting up and holding the last shirt up against my neck when Mair could not take it anymore. Because of the thickness of the liquid, it was sticking on her hands, and its smell was too much for her stomach. She started to convulse and vomited her dinner. I felt sorry for Mair, but I could not stop being happy that I was no longer in pain. I felt the weird hollowness of the puffy reservoir. I changed my soaked shirt, tossed away the dirty pillow, and fell asleep immediately.

The next morning, I felt like a new person: happy and hungry. My neck was still sore, but it was nothing compared to the throbbing and the pain that had been happening for the last few days. I was well enough to go down to the river and wash all the shirts that were soaked from the previous night's episode. To my surprise, there was hardly any trace of blood, just dried gunk. I spent most of my day taking care of myself. I went around the riverbank and picked a particular kind of weed seed pods to cure my infection. When I put the pods in water, the seed pockets would pop and let out tiny little seeds that expanded and clung together at the bottom of the bowl. I collected the clump of seeds, squeezed the water out of them, and shaped them into a patty to cover the infection. As they dried, the seeds contracted and sucked the yucky goo from the infection. I knew that the seeds were doing their job because I felt the suction with a gentle throbbing as they dried up. And when I couldn't stand it any longer, I would take them out and saw the stained milky stuff on the seed patty that smelled like rotten meat. The seeds took out the things that should never be in one's body. I was amazed at the effectiveness of this new medication, and was proud to be able to take care of myself. I realized that I gave no credit to the medicine man, and that was just fine with me. If I had to, I would probably go to him again, but somehow, I wasn't sure that his magic did the trick.

After many days of no markets and no buying or selling, people began to realize that money was worthless. Our stay with the Savans was not so friendly anymore. All the money that they got from us so far was worth no more than a piece of paper. On top of that, Mr. and Mrs. Savan had asked to have Linda marry one of their sons, but they were refused. A day after they were told that they could not have Linda, they asked for Chenda instead. I had heard of people in the rural area marrying their children young, but Chenda! She was only fourteen years old. I was not surprised when Em and Pa told Mr. and Mrs. Savan no. So the next best thing that Em could do for them was to share one of the cows that we bought from Lion Village. Em had the cow slaughtered, which pleased Mr. Savan for a couple more days.

I was glad to know that soon we would have our own place. Even if no one cared to, I was going to make sure we would have a decent place to use as a bathroom. To me, the worst part of staying with the Savan family had been the times that I needed to relieve myself. Mr. Savan had dug a deep and large rectangular hole as a bathroom. He had laid two slats of wood with a gap between them across the length of the hole, and between two posts, one on each end of the hole, he had tied a bamboo pole for a rail.

The hole was so deep that when I finished my job I could not hear the landing. If I ever fell in, I was sure that I would be buried in excrement, with maggots crawling into to my mouth and all over me, and there would be no way to escape without a ladder. I learned not to look down. Frenzied maggots were all I could imagine. Some of the maggots found their way to the top of the hole, but I preferred to step on them with bare feet rather than wearing shoes and taking a chance on falling in off the dirty, slippery wood slabs.

With all these fears running through my brain, I would suppress my need as long as I could, and when I couldn't do it anymore, I focused only on the rail and the dirty slats, and I held my breath until I was done and out. One good thing about the hole was that it was surrounded by banana bushes that provided some privacy. If someone was there before me, I could see their head before their body. Still, every visit was awful, and I was sure there was no way that I could get used to this.

The hut was not quite done when Pa decided that it was time to move from the Savan house. Getting to our new home required crossing the river with a water level that had been rising with the onset of monsoon season. I was scared to step into the canoe since I'd never ridden in a canoe before. Once we got to the other side of the river, we had to climb up a steep set of stairs to get to the riverbank in front of Mr. Savan's farmhouse. To the left of the farmhouse stood our hut, with a freshly built thatched roof and thatched walls. On skinny legs, the hut provided shelter above the uneven soil, ready and waiting for us, so sad and quiet.

I walked slowly toward the hut, eyeing and studying her like a kind stranger. As I stood under her roof, next to an open area, I felt the bamboo floor barely brushing the tip of my fingers. I moved my fingers as if to pet her, and she sent a warm wave to my heart and brought tears to my eyes.

She had a compartment with four walls and an opening that was big enough for us girls to duck into and out of. Right outside this compartment was the common area for Em to prepare and serve food. On the other side of the common area was the boys' sleeping area. Unlike the girls' compartment, the boys' sleeping area had only two walls to provide some shelter from rain and privacy from the Savans and the trail in front of the hut along the river. A step down from this common area and the boys' sleeping area was a raised dirt floor where Em did her cooking. For someone sitting in the common area, the hut offered the view of a large and beautiful tamarind tree at the edge of the riverbank, and on the other side of the river was a thick wall of tall bamboo bushes.

Looking away from the river beyond our hut, I saw a row of bamboo bushes that were not as thick as the one across the river. Beyond the bamboo bushes was a rice field. On the left of our hut was a walkway through the opening in the bamboo wall into the rice field. On the other side of the walkway, I could see the garden where our family had helped Mr. Savan plant cucumbers and squash. Our new hut was the smallest place we stayed since we left our home in Battambang, but she was also the best place, one that I could call home again.

It took me a while to get used to the small hut. Many times, when I woke up in the morning, my head would bump against the roof. It didn't hurt, but it was a wakeup call telling me that I lived in a different world, a world that I wished I didn't exist in.

Now that I had my own home, I had to do something about the bathroom, something that would be more decent, somewhere near a bush where I could dig and cover every time I used it. But there was no such bush. I would have to plant the bush that I was thinking about. Closer to the bamboo fence would give some privacy, but I couldn't sink a shovel into the earth because the bamboo roots were more like twisted wires than natural roots. So I still had to share the same spot with Mr. Savan's family. There was a tree branch that hung over the riverbank, and when squatting on it, we would be hidden by the leaves from other branches. For better or for worse, at least that spot would be washed with every monsoon rain.

At a village meeting in the old French church, we were told that everything in the village belonged to the government: the land, the houses, and the animals. There was no yours or mine, only the government's. Whatever we needed, the government would provide.

Everybody was to work the same hours and get the same rations. There was no need for a lazy monk, no need for a cheating businessman, and most of all no need for money. The doctrine stated: "Money is the source of corruption."

A leader was picked out of every ten families, based on what they were doing for a living prior to the new regime. We told them that Pa was a truck driver, which sounded much better than an import-export business-man. We were able to lie to them because we were so new to the village that there wasn't a risk of someone discovering our secret. The only person that we might be worried about was our maid. However, we were confident that she would not reveal the truth about us because we were good to her. Our maid had more work than us, but she ate the same food at the same table with us. I referred to her as sister instead of just a plain name, or worse, by her title like other families would. We had no reason to fear her. On top of that, Em told people that she was a niece. To the new regime, if you had not been sweating every day, you were a crook. So if you had had a maid living with you, then you would auto-matically be considered a crook. One of the peasants in the village was selected as our group leader.

The only government representative that we had to deal with was this group leader. His job was to make sure every able body was put to work. He was also to provide the rations the government provided to each of the families. Our leader let his young wife and his mother-in-law run the group. They didn't like us, to say the least, and we did everything we could to not cross them. We were told to go to work, except for Kheang, who was too young, and Em, who was to cook for us and watch over my two little cousins.

The first day reporting to work for the government was more of a torture to Em than to any of us. She converted our clothes to be suitable for field work. It was the very first time I wore pants. As we were leaving the hut, Em and Kheang stood and watched us as if we were going to jail. I could feel the pain in her eyes.

We met at the leader's place. It took a while to get started on this first day. Getting to the field required wading through knee-high soupy mud mixed with cow dung. The village people were in and out of the muck without any hesitation. If they could do it, I could, too. So I stepped in, ignoring the smell, the feel, and the look, but I could not ignore the slippery hard clay earth beneath it all. I slowly felt my way through the muck with my bare feet, but this was too slow for our maid, so she galloped through the muck and splattered it all over my clothes. She was so disgusted with us. She knew that she was better than us in these outdoor skills. She felt the need to be recognized, so she left us in the muck and went to walk beside the leader's wife. I noticed that there were two other families who were stuck in the muck like us. We looked at each other and moved our lips slightly, to try and smile a greeting.

Mair told us the trick about walking in the muck. "Don't put your weight in one place too long. Just make small and quick steps. Then you won't feel slippery or get stuck." I believed her, but I did not want to take the chance of falling in the stinky mud. It was easier said than done.

By the time we were out of the muck, most people were way ahead of us. To try to make up lost time, we walked as fast as we could. When we caught up with them, we ran into another obstacle. This time it was a patch of weeds growing low on the ground that had sharp, short thorns with hooks on them. Again, I saw that most of the people calmly walked on them as if they didn't exist. How did they do that? As I froze in my first two steps, I put my arms out to balance my stand. People were laughing at me. *Oh come on, little girl you can do it. It won't kill you*, I told myself. So off I went, panting in a rhythm with each sharp, prickly step, so as to get my mind off the genuine pain in my tender feet.

In the field we pulled, cleaned, and prepared young rice plants for replanting in a larger field. Mair showed us how to pull the young rice plants so that we would not snip the roots.

Our maid yelled at us with a disgusted look on her face: "This is how you do it! Give it to me!" Too tired to talk back and too hot to work, whenever I had a handful of rice plant, I took the opportunity to stand up and straighten my back.

"Why are you just standing there?" the leader wife warned me. With mud up to my ankle and water halfway to my calves, I could not sit down and I could not stand up. I spent most of the day bent down and arching my back toward the hot sun. I felt the heat on my back, but after a while all I could feel was numbness and stiffness as though I was locked in bent position.

When I got up the next morning, I felt a burning sensation on my lower back. I reached back and with my fingertips felt a patch of blisters, all different shapes and sizes and packed next to each other on the exposed skin that must have snuck out between my waistband and the hem of my shirt the day before. If I'd only known the sun can cause painful blisters on one's body, I would have been more careful. My poor skin. The pain was not as bad as it was shocking to feel those big, soft, warm blisters. When I showed them to Em, I was sure that Em would tell me to stay home. Instead, Em's sad face pleaded to me to keep going. "Don't stay home, my child. Don't give them another reason to look at us sideways."

Every day I woke up and walked to the field, worked until lunchtime, then came home to Em. Then out again until dark, then home to Em. But every day I came home, there was less and less to eat. The once-a-week ration of rice and salt lessened each time it was given. So every meal Em fed us with a new cooking style so that our stomachs would be filled, but it was mostly with water and water spinach; it looked more like pig food than anything else, but it was filling. After a couple of times urinating, my stomach was empty again, so I would purposely hold my urine for as long as I could. It would also keep my mind away from thinking about food all the time. Instead, all I could think about was going to pee.

I found myself consuming rice broth more than I thought I could. My stomach seemed to expand. I drank at least a half gallon of rice soup every meal. Not everybody in the village was as desperate as we were. The village people always had some food stashed away for the monsoon season, so they had enough for their families. Some even had more to exchange with the newcomers like us for gold and fancy jewelry. In the case of Mr. Savan, there was enough for his family, and on top of that he had the patch of cucumbers and squash that provided a good supplement to his dietary needs. Every day we watched Mrs. Savan pick the squash that we helped plant and weed, and fetch water from the bottom of the river. Not a single cucumber or squash was offered to us, and on top of that, her little children would warn us not to go near the patch. How funny— people change so much. The garden that we helped plant was now producing, but all we could do was look at its fruit while we were so hungry.

"It is so unfair," I told Em.

"It is their land, and they have their family to worry about."

Not satisfied with Em's reasoning, I felt I could rightly help myself to some of those cucumbers. As I eyed them, I marked and estimated my steps from the hut. The night came, but the moon was too bright to snoop around, so I decided to wait for a cloudy day or a dark moon. One good dark night, I went into the patch and grabbed four or five cucumbers and ran back to the hut. My heart was pounding. It was the first time I ever stole anything from anyone. I gave the cucumbers to Em and didn't care what she would have to say. She took them from me and said, "Make sure you never take more than four or five." That night we had cucumbers for dessert.

Even with Em's creative low-ingredient porridge,

our ration from the leaders didn't last through the week. So Em made a plan to sneak out of French Village and go to an orchard village called Banana Village (*Chamkar Chayk*) that was a couple of hours of walking from the river. At the time, it was better for a woman to sneak around than a man. If a woman got caught, she would get a slap on the wrist and be let go, but if a man got caught, the consequences could be life-threatening. So Em decided she would take Chenda to go with her. Banana Village was located east of the river and almost halfway to National Highway 5. It was far enough from the river to provide the dry land necessary to support orchards. Just hearing the name of the village alone, I wished Em took me instead of Chenda. In the past, the people in Banana Village would bring their produce to French Village during the monsoon season, but now, since there wasn't any market for them, they were sitting on piles of produce. To better control its citizens, the new government preferred not to distribute excess produce to other villages where food was scarce.

I watched Em collect remaining jewelry from our special undies. Pa took off his twenty-four-karat protective waistband that had his Lion Village master's blessing. Cupping it in his two hands and raising them above his head, he closed his eyes and begged for forgiveness. To him, he had betrayed his master; he had parted himself from his master. As he put his hands back down, he slowly opened his eyes, but they were empty, too empty to look at. Em tried her best to bring some life back into Pa's eyes. She said, "Lok Krew's blessing will still be with us, for we have never in our lives done a bad deed to anyone."

The next day, we all headed out to the field except Chenda. She was supposed to be "sick," ready to sneak out with Em soon after people went to the field.

While working in the field, I kept thinking about Em and Chenda. I prayed that they would find the village, for they had never been there. We had only overheard from others who went there for food exchange. I felt sad and warm within my emptied stomach, imagining the mother and daughter walking desolately in the middle of the flooded fields in the rain to avoid being seen by the Black Uniforms. I was so proud of Em, how she became so strong and determined to keep her family alive. I wished I could hug her and tell her how much I appreciated and loved her. I hoped she knew how I felt, for we were raised not to express our feelings openly.

At the end of the day, it was dark and raining, and we were sitting in the common area of our hut, waiting for Em and Chenda to come home. They were supposed to be back home before we got back from the field, but now it was past that time. As I waited, many thoughts and unanswerable questions rushed through my mind. *Did they get lost? Did they get caught? Or maybe they just have too many things to carry so they cannot walk as fast. They have to be cold and shaking in this rain. What if either Em or Chenda can't take it anymore and have fallen down with their last breath?* Imagining that last scene made me crawl to my bedding and quietly let my tears out. I felt so cold and alone in the darkest night of my life. *Dear God, please let me be with my sister and Em again. Bring them back to me.*

A soft and gentle voice called across the river: "Pa, Pa."

Oh, Chenda, Chenda, I love you. A sad and happy song sang in my head as I tried to get out of my bedding. As I crawled back to the common area, I could not stop the happy tears that were dancing on my cheeks and my jittery lips. I was so happy. Looking across the river from the common area, even in the dark, I saw two figures standing and waiting for us to bring the canoe over.

They were cold and shaking but could not wait to show us what they had brought for us: bananas, sweet yams, beans, rice, salt, and tobacco. "Tobacco? Why?" I asked with disbelief, but I quickly changed my mind when I saw Pa reach over with a little laugh in his sigh, and he smiled and blinked the tears off his eyes. Ee reached over and put out his hand for some of the tobacco. It was shocking to all of us to learn that Ee had started smoking prior to the Black Uniforms era.

My hunger spiked when I saw all the food. Even though we already had dinner, Em decided to cook rice mixed with mung beans for us. It tasted so good and felt so good to have rice and beans heaped on a spoon instead of running off it with river water broth. Em kept reminding us not to eat too much. She was afraid that we might get sick from overeating.

Pa told us: "In China, I was told that some people died from overeating when they came out of starvation and had enough to eat for the first time in a long time. They ate so much that they could not breathe, then they passed out. I never thought that Cambodia could be in the same situation as that of China. China is a poor country with too many people. When the Communists took over, its government could not feed its people even if they wanted to. Cambodia is a self-sufficient country. Who would ever think its own government would be starving its people? Never in the history of Cambodia did the people ever starve for food."

Em signaled to Pa to cut it out. By now, Black Uniforms would roam around at night and take you away from your family at any chance they got.

Pa finished off his food with a sniff of the tobacco that Em got him. If only we had a piece of paper to roll the tobacco. For the time being, he had to wait for the next day until Em could flatten a particular kind of leaf (*sangkair*) between two warm bricks so that it would be wilted enough to roll and dry enough to burn.

It was the first time in a long time that there was conversation after the meal.

"They have everything," Chenda told us about the people in Banana Village. "And they are very generous. One woman served us a meal and gave us boiled sweet yam for the road. We didn't get lost or anything like that. We just lost track of time."

"Gold for salt." Pa was in his own world, not hearing anything Chenda was saying. "Gold for tobacco. Now all I need is a cup of coffee. Then I can die in peace."

Quietly I thought, *How long will the new food last? What do we do next? Did Em use all of her gold and jewelry?* I found myself wishing that Em would not share everything with Mair and Ouv's family, and especially not the maid.

That night we all went to bed with a full stomach. I wished for a way to get the food inside me to last longer than one day, for I knew tomorrow would be back to hunger. But at least that night we all slept with a full stomach. To our disappointment, the satisfaction of going to sleep with a full stomach didn't last very long. I woke up at least three times from diarrhea, and every time I was up, somebody else in the hut was up too. What a waste of precious rice and beans! They were too good for our starving stomachs to handle.

As time passed by, every day seemed to last longer. Every morning I blamed God for not taking my life while I was sleeping. Why did I have to wake up to this world? The rations were becoming smaller by the week, and the rules were getting tougher and tougher. We were told by the Black Uniforms, "If you are lazy, you don't deserve to live. In that case, you are better dead than you are alive, for dead you will provide fertilizer for the field. We are here to cleanse the whole country. We are ready to do whatever necessary to achieve our goal, even if it means eliminating the whole village. We are ready to do it." There was no doubt in my mind that they meant what they said. Another phrase that always stuck in my mind was: "For that kind of person, we should not waste the bullets. Just use a bat with a quick whack right in the middle of the forehead." I didn't want to find out if that was just a threat or the truth.

These Black Uniforms gave us rules, kept food away from us, and made us work from dawn to dusk, but they themselves were in a different world. They were fat and never showed up in the field. They spent most of their time patrolling the huts and the houses to find out who didn't go to work and why. Every new moon and at night they would trot around the huts and listen to our conversations. Obviously, you would never talk bad about the new regime, but you would also get in trouble if you were to talk or wish for the food and life that you used to have. How bitter they were! I wonder what their lives were like before the new regime took over. Why take such personal revenge on a whole village, or perhaps on the whole country? I didn't have a way to find out.

The food that Em had traded for did not last very long. It was clear to the maid that she was better off attaching herself to someone other than us. So she left to stay with the leader. She had been very unpleasant since the beginning, but she got worse as time went by. She was demanding and yelling at us as she showed us how to work the rice field. She even yelled at Pa. I put my thick face on anytime she told me to do something. I did what she said without any anger or fear. I just wanted to stay low. But whenever she yelled at Pa, anger scorched my face. I feared that Pa would not be able to control his temper, in which case for sure I would lose him to the Black Uniforms. One morning we had to get in a canoe to go to the field. As Pa's weak legs struggled to get into the canoe, the maid hurried him with her hash words: "Why don't you hurry up?" I felt the little blood that I had left boiling in my stomach, but at the same time I was hoping Pa would just do as she said. Pa's body jolted at the tone of her voice and sent a tilt to the canoe.

"Watch what you're doing!" she added.

"Don't lose it, Pa. Don't lose it, please," I whispered to myself.

Pa was amazingly calm. He sat in the canoe. The nine or ten people that were in the canoe, including the leader, were completely silent. They knew that a man can take only so much. Pa broke the silence with a calm voice. "I want to ask you a question."

"Please, Pa, don't," I pleaded quietly to myself.

"Why do you treat me so badly?"

"What do you mean?" she responded with a furrowed brow.

"The way you talk to me. The tone of your voice," Pa said, confronting her.

There was no response. My heart was changing from fear to curiosity. *Yes, why?*

Pa broke the silence again and with his dried mouth he asked: "Have I ever done anything bad to you? Did I treat you the way you treat me?"

"That's enough!" was her response.

I felt so good. *Yeah, think about it, you devil!* I was so proud of Pa. It was just a perfect amount of spice served up for her to taste. I was happy about this even though the silence continued all the way to the field. On top of that, I felt that now the leader knew for sure that we were good to the maid regardless of what she may had said behind our back. That was the last time the maid ever spoke to us.

Many times I thought of Bong Yert, our previous maid. I missed Bong Yert and knew she would not have treated us like this maid did. Em thought that Bong Yert's father was a Khmer Rouge member and that he knew things would change rapidly, and that was why he came and took his baby back not too long ago. If Em was correct, Bong Yert might be wearing the black uniform now. If so, she must have looked for us in our house on that first day. Or perhaps she was still looking for us in the villages near Battambang. Had we stayed in our house, maybe she would have found us on that first day. I was certain that Bong Yert would look for us, for she was like a sister to me, and she loved us.

Our ration was reduced to one cup of rice per person per week. Salt was given in a teaspoon per family, but was not always available every week. Mr. Savan's cucumber patch was drowned by the monsoon floods and was no longer producing for us to snitch from. We had to do our best to survive, so Ouv taught Pa, Ee, and Hong many techniques for catching fish in the rice paddy and in the river. Every night before they went to bed, they all went out to set traps for small fish along the riverbank and lay lines of hooks in the rice field. The next day before sunrise, rain or no rain, they dragged their paper-thin bodies out to collect the traps so that they could be back in time to report to work. They usually caught three or four good-sized fish and some smaller ones, but some mornings they came back with empty hands and long faces. We girls also pitched in. Em made Chenda and me new jackets from Pa's old khaki pants. She added patch pockets that came up to our chests with the toughest fabric she could find. The pockets were a bright green that could be seen two fields away. Needless to say, we didn't care how we looked. We were happy to have such strong multipurpose jackets. From the field, we filled our pockets with dead crabs, snails, small fish, frogs, and even toads, and some wild green vegetation. I had never in my life heard of anyone eating toads, but after removing their skin, they resembled skinny frogs. I was told toad eggs are poisonous, so when I cleaned them, I emptied the eggs even though they looked so tempting.

No matter how much we tried, our stomachs were empty most of the time. We tried eating things that only pigs would eat. If pigs could live on it, we could live on it. Besides, there weren't any pigs left to consume these things. So we tried rice dust that had been purchased as pig feed before the Black Uniforms era.

First Em added some water to the rice dust and cooked it on a low heat in banana leaves. It was filling, but it was hard to swallow because it had a lingering odor and flavor of machinery oil. Next Em roasted the rice dust instead of baking. The smell of machinery oil was lessened by roasting, and we consumed it dry. Every night we passed around a bowl of rice dust. The only problem was that the rice dust stayed dry a long time in our mouths so that when we ate it, we had to keep our lips shut together for a while. Kheang and I would get in trouble, because as soon as we put the dust in our mouth we always felt the urge to giggle. The harder we tried to close our lips, the stronger the urge to laugh, and when we could not hold our lips together any longer, the dust would fly out from our faces. So we were allowed only a tiny bit at a time. Each time I put a scoop in my mouth, I couldn't stop saying, "Oink, Oink," quietly in my head.

For the next few days, until it was all consumed, the rice dust was a hot subject in the field. People made a joke of it and gently insulted our new government.

"If I knew rice dust tasted so good, I could have saved a lot of money in the past."

"I just witnessed the most amazing thing. I went to a bush and saw human footprints, but the dung was a pig's."

One day I had a high fever, so I could not go to the field. I was in and out of consciousness. While unconscious, I had the best time. I could taste all the food I used to have. I was having fun; I was laughing, playing, and was happy as I could be. Then I had to come out of it. My dry mouth and bad breath woke me up to the reality and summoned me to throw up, but there was nothing in my stomach to come out. I felt my abdomen rolling and tightening, but only liquid came out from my stomach. I felt heat escaping my eyes and my mouth, and my head pounded in pain with each beat of my heart. There was no medication, but there was Em. She sat next to me with gooey, crushed neem leaves in a bowl of water that she used to coat my forehead. I found comfort in the treatment and in my own silent chanting under every breath: "I'm hot. I'm hot. I'm hot."

The treatment must have helped because when I woke up again, I was not as hot. My head still hurt but was not throbbing. I lay still and contemplated my body's needs. I was hungry. How strange that I was hungry even when I was sick. Never in the past did I want to eat when I had a fever. Staying sick in the hut, I was hungrier than when I was working in the field. I daydreamed of noodles, rice, meat, and a taste of salt. Right before I went to my first year of school, Pa and Em took us to visit Angkor Wat. We also went swimming in a large body of water where I unknowingly took a gulp of the salty water. I wished we could at least live near this body of water. We would have all the salt we needed. I thought of the times that Em used to get mad at us for not finishing our plates. How I wished to have that problem again! I wished for a chance to live in the past just one more time. If I was given the option of eating as much as I wanted of anything and then being executed, I would take it.

Em was working by the fire when I decided to beg her for a favor. "Em, could you make me a little bowl of rice? A small bowl, three or four spoonfuls of rice, but real steamed rice, not watered down."

"No, I can't. You know I would, but I can't. Hearing you ask me is tearing my heart apart."

My hot tears rolled along my cheeks as soon as Em said the word *no*. I felt guilty for asking her, but at the same time mad, thinking I was on my deathbed—she still said no.

By the time everybody came back from the field, I was thinking that I would not stay home the next day even if the fever persists. At least in the field I was working, listening to the conversations, and laughing at jokes that made the time pass by more quickly. By now there were not many distinctions between the villagers and the newcomers. We could do all the things that the villagers could and work as fast as they could. Or perhaps they were slowing down. As I was thinking of my plan for the next day, I realized how bad it must have been for Kheang and my two little cousins who had to stay home with not much to do but wait for mealtime every day.

That day was worse than any other day because I could not sit still and wait for the meal. Still having a bit of a fever, I jumped in to help around the fire while Mair was cooking. Mair told me to get out of her way, but still I was moving around her and doing something else, not completely out of her way. "I said get out of my way!" Mair yelled as she raised her hand to knock the knife out of my hands.

In shock, I quickly stood up and stepped back from the fire area. Simultaneously, in the corner of my right eye, Pa's hand swung from behind and landed on the side of my head. I felt the fall in slow motion, then blackness followed. A few seconds later I found myself lying on the muddy floor, crying in self-pity. The adults were all talking at once, but they were not in my world. My world was quiet and painful. As I covered my tingling face, I felt my hot cheek with my shaking hands. I ran my tongue against my teeth, and they were all still there. The wetness on my face was just mud and not blood. I was okay, but I would never be the same again—for Pa had gone too far.

Em wanted to know what had happened. I told her without any emotion. My feeling seemed to freeze in a neutral zone. She tried to say that the hit was not toward me, it was his anger toward Mair. For Mair to yell and hit one of his kids in front of him was most disrespectful—a thing that would never have happened in the past, when he was continuously supporting Mair financially and helping to raise Linda ever since she was a young girl. I did not doubt what Em said was true, but it didn't make me feel any better. I wondered—if Chenda was the one that had gotten in trouble with Mair, would Pa have hit her as hard? I was sure that would not have been the case. In the past, every time Chenda and I had a fight, Pa would grab me and spank me, but not Chenda. Many times Em would say, "What about Chenda?"

A couple of days later, Mair and Ouv left us to share a wood house (not a hut) with a village family. They took Linda with them. The first thing that came to my mind was that Em would have fewer people to cook for. It was better that they left, but why take Linda? She was my sister more than she was their daughter. She was old enough to make her own decision, but she did nothing about it. *How can you leave us?* I supposed that just like the maid, my parents could no longer provide for them better than others could.

After the first meal with just our family together, Ee busted out his opinion about Ouv.

"Let him go; we can survive without him. I can never forgive him after that time we slaughtered the cow." He paused and then added: "Did you know that the cow was pregnant?"

Everybody froze.

"Yes, she was," he added angrily.

"Ouv and everybody else did not want to do the job. They were looking at me like I should do it. I was wondering why they wanted me to do it. I knew nothing about cows, let alone how to slaughter one. Someone in the group said: 'You do it because you are the owner.' I looked at Ouv. He didn't say anything. So I delivered the first ax blow. Not too long afterward, I learned that the cow was pregnant. I knew then that all those farmers including Ouv knew it, and that was why they didn't want to do the job. But they didn't tell us. They knew that we wouldn't slaughter a pregnant cow."

Silence followed Ee's story. Then a question that I often thought but never asked came into my mind again: What happened to all the beef? It seemed to me that we should have preserved some, but none was left after a couple of days. Again, I never asked.

Now that we had so little, people were leaving us. They were with us until there was no more to suck on.

Soon after Ouv left, the fish didn't seem to bite as much, and Em kept running out of wood to burn. After work one day, while the boys were out trying to catch fish, Pa, Chenda, and I went to the village cemetery. In the peak of the monsoon season, the cemetery was the only place near the village that was not covered with water, so it was an easy place to fetch firewood. Not knowing what to expect and with my imagination going wild, I felt light-headed as we got near the cemetery hill. Pa told us along the way to be sure that before we did anything, we should ask for forgiveness from the spirits that we were going to intrude upon.

Cambodians believe that the human spirit lingers long after death, especially following unnatural deaths. To disrespect their resting place, such as by walking on top of graves or disturbing the soil around graves, unsettles the spirits, provoking them to haunt you and cause many bad things in your life.

As I stepped onto the hill, I felt the hairs on my neck standing and my heartbeat increasing, thrusting up against my throat. There were no marks anywhere in the cemetery, but the new graves were obvious with fresh, loose dirt on them. I tried to stay away from the loose dirt and close to Chenda and Pa. Wood in small branches was everywhere. Pa stopped at one thick bush, asked for forgiveness, and began chopping the branches. All three of us used our best calm voices to repeatedly ask for forgiveness while chopping.

"Please forgive us if we are in your way or stepping on you. We have no way of telling. If we had a choice, we would not be here. It is a matter of surviving."

Our asking for forgiveness sometimes turned into pleading for help. "Please help us if you can. As you can see, we are desperate."

I found myself feeling less and less scared the more I spoke to the graves. After a while, the chanting ceased to come out loud, but continued only in my head.

We were making good progress when my ax slipped from a small branch and landed on my lower left shin-bone. When I first looked down, I saw more of the white bone than the blood. A few seconds later, the blood started to flow continuously. On the way back to the hut, I hesitated with every left step. I didn't have a choice but to sink my foot into the mud and feel it scraping the cut. When we got to our hut, I was happy to show Em the wood that would last her for a while. I was surprised that my cut was no longer bleeding. After I washed it, all I could see was the white bone and not a drop of blood. I thought that stepping in the mud must have helped stop the blood from flowing.

The graveyard became our private wood yard. We didn't have to compete with anybody for the wood.

People in the village called us "stupid Chinese." One day the leader's mother-in-law stopped me and asked: "Aren't you scared to go to the graveyard?"

I ignored her.

"You are a stupid Chinese girl! Someday you're going to lose your soul in that graveyard. Then you'll stay there permanently." She was disgusted with me.

To most villagers, especially the group leaders, we were Chinese, based solely on our light skin color. They didn't think that we valued Cambodian culture as much as they did. On top of this, to the Black Uniforms, we were ghosts from the past. They despised us because we were mostly business owners and thereby automatically the cause of inequality that led to suffering and unfair practice to the labor workers. How ironic that the Black Uniforms hated us for being Chinese, for they were backed by Communist China. To me, I was happy that Em always made us feel special. She would tell us: "You are lucky to have Chinese blood because half-Chinese and half-Cambodian kids are the smartest kids." So every time I experienced discrimination, I quietly thought. *But I am smarter than you.*

The leader had called us for the ration. There was no salt again and only one cup of rice per person per week. When it was our turn to receive the rice, the leader's wife, with heavy eyelids and dry face, looked at us like we didn't deserve any rice. With each scoop she twitched her wrist and let some of the precious rice fall back into the basket before it got to Em's handkerchief. Did Mair say bad things about us to make the woman despise us? I wasn't sure, but I noticed that Mair seemed to get a heaping cup and a steady hand for every scoop with a friendly gesture from the woman. Her relationship with the leader's wife was good, and we had nothing to say to each other when we crossed paths. When she looked at me, I turned away. I didn't want to listen to her or say anything to her.

On those days, all I could think about was finding or doing something to satisfy my hunger. I was not dreaming of any particular food, but I was on a constant search for any moving creatures. In the field, I often took a long bathroom break and walked across the field, scanning for crabs and snails. By then it was no longer possible to catch small fish because the water was covering most of the fields, and those fish were no longer confined to small areas. Many times the crabs were too small to keep in my pockets, and they would be crushed to nothing by the time I got back to Em. In the earlier days, I would just let them go, but these days I was happy to find them. Too small to take to Em, they were perfect to eat on the spot without any guilt. The first time I opened my mouth to bite on this tiny creature, I had to close my eyes. The first one tasted so bad I had to spit the whole thing out. For the next one, I removed the tiny eyes and the cap and tried it again. My eyes relaxed with pleasure, and the flavor was satisfying. Even though I was starving, I had to hide my crab-eating habit, for it was so unnatural and undignified the way I ate them. For sure, if a village girl ever caught me eating one, she would be repulsed by me and would spread the word about my new snacking behavior. Not that I wanted to impress them. I just didn't want to give them another reason to talk about me.

Bael fruit was plentiful. When it's ripe, you can boil and scrape off the flesh inside the hard shell of the fruit to eat, but the seed compartment of the fruit will make you sick. One day I came home with pockets full of bael fruit. They were still small and nowhere close to ripe, but I didn't want to wait. Some people looked at me as if I was crazy. Some yelled at me and told me that I was being wasteful. At home, Em boiled them for us. The texture of the flesh was like that of the boiled sweet yam. They were not sweet like they should be when ripe, but they were good. I could not resist the temptation to sneak around to take a bite of the seed compartment. It was gooey and sticky and didn't taste good, but it was filling. So one bite after another, I continued until I was halfway through. I felt nausea and was drooling constantly all day. I told myself, "Never again. Never again. Not this fruit ever again."

I was so hungry every minute that all I could think about was food. I would eat or try anything that moved, but I didn't eat to survive like most people think of it. To survive meant there would be hope after it was all over. There was no hope within me, but my stomach did not understand that.

Fish were harder to catch, and all the green vegetation was either not growing fast enough or drowned. Without much to add to the rice soup, Em kept adding water until the soup looked more like hot water than anything else. Even then there was not enough for everyone, so Em decided to stop adding more water into the rice soup and instead gave us rations for every meal. Rations for the rice soup and rations for salt, salt that Em got from exchanging small sections of Pa's blessed twenty-four-karat waistband. Every meal, we sat in the circle and watched Em silently and closely as she dipped the ladle into the rice soup. She was good. She was always fair to every one of us. Quickly and silently we ate, with nothing to talk about, nothing to say. When Pa finished his portion, Em would give him some of her portion and say, "You are a man. You need more than us." Pa would never refuse. In my own mind I was asking, *How could you take it from her?* But I would not dare to let the thought come out.

One day Ee spoke out exactly what I was thinking: "How could you take it from her?" Instantly I felt guilty to even think what I was thinking of Pa because the words that came out from Ee were so harsh and humiliating and without any grain of respect remaining. Before Pa could respond, Em pleaded, "Dear God, please not like this. Please stop." The two men looked at each other with the same amount of guilt on their face, but their focus was on Em. As a result of Ee's comment, Em decided to give Ee some of her portion as well. Again she said to the rest of us: "They are men; they need more. The hunger affects them stronger than it affects us."

After the meal, Pa would turn to his bedding corner and say his usual prayer: "Motherfucker." Kheang would never complain. He would go to his corner, the opposite corner from Pa, and just sit there, out of the way. Ee's face was more pale from anger than hunger.

Chenda and I helped Em rinse the plates, which didn't take much time at all. Still hungry after each meal, together we sat, but without a word to each other. Not even a word of encouragement, but quietly in our minds we were free—free to think of anything we could think of, dream any dream we could imagine. Many times I found myself thinking of Blacky. *Would we turn her into food?* I was glad that Blacky was not with us.

I found myself asking questions and answering them myself.

What ever happened to all the food that was supposed to be in the market? Somewhere in the country the food was waiting for us. Where were all the strong men? Where were the heroes? Why did no one stand up for their rights? Oh, yes: They left their families and went to the meeting that was called by the Black Uniforms and never came back, those poor old regime soldiers. What about the rest of the men that didn't go the meeting? Their guns were taken and they are starving and their spirits have left them. Why don't we just walk westward toward Thailand? So what if we get caught? it would be better than living like this.

A couple of times before bed I overheard Pa talk about taking all of us westward toward Thailand, but Em thought that it would be suicidal and rejected his idea. I doubted that we could make it to Thailand, but I wanted to try so badly. Many times I wished that I could turn myself into a bird and fly out of there.

One day after the meal, a frail-looking woman from Lake Kair stopped by our place. She was pleading to exchange her gold for food. As she was talking, Em realized that the woman was an old friend from Poipet. How much the woman had changed! In less than six months she was unrecognizable. Only her voice was still the same; the rest had gone. She told us we had changed too, and we didn't doubt her. We didn't have anything to offer her, but she was happy to see us.

"Aren't you afraid to get caught? Nowadays they will consider you an enemy spy, you know," Em could not wait to ask the woman.

"No, I welcome death. I just don't have the will to do it myself. Every morning I blame God for keeping me breathing. I am not afraid of dying." She added with a softer tone, "I have nothing left. My baby died in my arms because I could not produce milk for her. My husband took his last breath while making rice soup. His body ended up in the fire pit, partially cremated."

Tears coated her red eyes, but not enough to form a drop.

She continued: "The last time we were called to collect our ration was three weeks ago. Many families were wiped out within the last week. You are lucky your family is still with you."

The woman listed all of our friends who had not survived. "Many, many more; I could not say it all," she added. Then she looked at us in a puzzled way and asked, "How did you get here from Poipet?"

Em told her about Pa's master who helped pull us to his village instead of to the place that the woman got pushed into.

Knowing that we could have been in a worse situation somehow gave me the energy to try harder to survive, even though I questioned its purpose.

Even though it was raining nearly every day, I pushed myself to wake up, get out of the hut, and go to work. Wet, cold, hungry, and sometimes sick, I still went to the field. Staying in the hut would worry Em and draw the attention of the Black Uniforms. On my way to the field, I often thought of the old times when I had wished to go to Mair's house to see how she planted rice and what rice plants looked like. Now that I was in it, I wished to never set foot in a rice field ever again.

In the field, there was no incentive to work hard. If you were a fast worker, you could not go home any earlier than the rest of the group. So no one seemed to try hard, just showing up in the field was half of the work already.

There were only two jobs for the whole village: care for water buffaloes and cows or work in the rice fields. Hong was told to care for the animals. The rest of us were to work in the rice field. Since almost everyone in the village had to work in the rice field, the fields were done with planting before the planting season was over. To keep us busy, the Black Uniforms told us to transplant mature rice plants in unprepared fields. This practice would not have happened in the past because doing so would not be considered a good return on investment. We were to work on fields near lakes that had never been used for planting rice. Even the villagers were disgusted with these farming methods.

Once we were told to work on a field that was basically part of a lake. The field was known to be infested with leeches. Normally a good field would be covered with water that came up just below the knees when working in it, but in this particular field, the water came up past the knees to halfway up my thighs. As the water gets deeper, leeches can get to more places on your body. I was told that leeches could get into girls' private places and live and reproduce there. The idea of leeches reproducing inside my body gave me the creeps.

I stayed close to Mr. Savan's nephew, Bong Seurn, who was always kind to me. I learned to trust him, for he shared the same ideas as my family. He had a child, and his wife stayed home and cared for the child. The fact that he had a young family of his own made me less shy to be with him. He was my dedicated leech remover. So I almost always worked next to him, especially on the infested field. As soon as I got off the canoe and put my foot into the water, I could see leeches wiggling from a distance in the clear water to come and greet me. When I pulled my foot back up to the canoe, a few of them would already be clinging to the side of the canoe.

"I can't get in there," I pleaded.

"Come on, I'll help you," Bong Seurn encouraged me. "Just make sure you tie up the bottom of your pant legs really good. You should be okay."

I followed Bong Seurn's suggestion and tightened up the strings around my ankles to the point of cutting off proper circulation, but I didn't care. I just wanted to make sure that leeches would never find their way into me. In the field, Bong Seurn always reminded me not to make sudden movements. Being calm and relaxed was the best way to not attract them. I took it that he meant to let the slimy creatures go to the other girls that were screaming, yelling, and splashing. I tried moving slowly and gently in the water, but my heart and my eyes were not those of a calm person. I felt a nip on my inner thigh, and I froze and forced myself to feel the spot. Sure enough, the soft, slimy creature was near my underpants. As I jumped and screamed I thought, "How did it get through the tight string around my ankles?"

Bong Seurn grabbed ahold of me and asked where the creature was. "In my pants," I whimpered, spreading my legs and pointing to where it was. I must have looked like I was pointing to my crotch, so I corrected myself quietly in a high pitch that came out of nowhere: "On my inner thigh." This time I pointed with much better accuracy.

"Stay still," he told me as he felt and grabbed the creature from the outside of my pants. "I got it," he said.

I knew that the only way to really get it out of my pants was to have Bong Seurn reach into my pants through the waistline. With a short, sharp jitter, I whimpered in confusion and turned my face away as I reached over to open my elastic waistline for Bong Seurn. As soon as he yanked the sucker out of me, I stumbled backward uncontrollably watching the feisty sucker trying to puncture Bong Seurn's wrist. He spat on it, and the salt in his saliva curled it up, making it twitch back and forth in his palm. It was a big one that filled up Bong Seurn's palm. He continued spitting on it, then he cupped his hands together to shake and roll the creature in his saliva. Bong Seurn stretched out his arms and legs and swung the slimy sucker as far as he could. The water splashed where it landed.

I took a deep breath, still shaken by the incident. I was reluctant to move or do anything else, but I didn't have a choice. Bong Seurn talked to me and eased me into planting again. And again, as I bent my body down to try to plant the rice in the deep-water field, another sucker hooked itself with one end on my cheek near my ear and the other end right between my shoulder blades. The right side of my face froze. I reached out and tapped the water with my left hand as I cried for Bong Seurn. Again he helped me.

The field was too deep to be able to find a spot nearby to go to the bathroom. As far as the eye could see, there was no sign of any dirt above the water. Without thinking twice about it, I just bent my knees a little bit and let it go in the water. I imagined everybody was doing the same thing. It seemed that as soon as I started to do that, the suckers appeared less and less. Something within urine seemed to send them away. The next day, both of my inner thighs were itchy and burning with red rashes.

There wasn't much planting done on that day. It was more torture than labor. Continuous screams of agony—leech phobia—were heard all over the field from the village people and the newcomers alike. Without the Black Uniforms patrolling us, the leader decided that we would quit early.

On the way back to the village, we rowed past an area filled with water spinach. So people were out of the canoe and trying to collect as much as they could. (Wild vegetables growing nearby the river and village had already been consumed.) Pa and I went to one area and started to pick the greens. Exhausted, wet, and cold, we realized that we could not pick fast enough before the canoe took off. So Pa went deeper into the lake to pull the water spinach, new and old growths alike. He wrapped them like a rope around his elbow and his hand and brought them to me at a shallow part of the lake, then went back for more. In the shallow water, I was to watch for the canoe so that we would not be left behind. As I was standing and watching the canoe while waiting for Pa to come back, I noticed that I had been a blood pool to many leeches that were so little that I didn't notice their bites. They were all over every part of my bare calves and in the water, all around me. I jumped up and down in one place with all the strength that I had left—hands flopping in the air, water spinach in the water—and I screamed: "Pa, Pa, too many leeches!"

"Shut up! Put up with it!"

I wished that I had never been born. *God, why you are so cruel?* I stood there shaking more from the experience than from the cold wind. Staring into space, not waiting for Pa or watching for the canoe, I let the little suckers have a feast on me. Pa came back with his white shirt no longer white, dress pants that did not belong in the field, and water spinach strapped over his left shoulder and crossed over to his right hip. He picked up the water spinach that I had dropped. Without a word, we walked together to the canoe. I carried nothing, and he carried everything.

In the canoe, people gave us a hard time for carrying so much of what they called "inedible parts." They wanted us to throw away some of the old growth. "It's too heavy for the canoe," they said.

Pa didn't respond, but he scared them with his expression. People always leave a crazy man alone.

Sitting in the canoe, I picked off some of the tiny suckers left on my legs and threw them back into the water. It seemed that I was not scared of them anymore, at least not the small ones. My legs were coated with lines of blood from each bite flowing to the bottom of the canoe.

In the hut, we had the water spinach to fill us up for a couple more days. Some of the stems were no doubt strong enough to be twined into rope, but Em managed to chop them into a good size for our meals.

Every time we were able to fill our stomachs, we seemed to have more to say to each other after the meal. Hong mentioned that if things ever changed, we should never forget this time. "Even if we could have everything like before, we should make this kind of meal once a week as a reminder that we should not take life for granted."

"Do you think it will ever change?" I asked.

"Do you remember the song that goes something like this?" Hong replied with a smile while he was trying to remember the lyrics."

Even though the horizon is far away,
you can see all the birds are happy,
singing and flying across the sky.

It is so wrong that people are always fighting.
They curse each other from this lifetime to the
next lifetime, holding on to anger.

If you do good, a good heart will find you.
If you do bad, you can count on a black heart
to reach you one of these days.

If you still have life, you will always have luck.
You must not lose hope.

There's always a clear sky after a big storm.
Don't be afraid to smile
and hope for your day to come.
("The Hope Song")[10]

Hong added: "When you look at them, you see black
and evil, but you must not give up."
I had heard that song before and thought it was

---

[10] After listening to many Khmer oldies for months I was unable to
find this song. So I decided to sing it from my heart as I remember it.
http://shorthairdetention.com/resources/hope-song.html

boring. I didn't understand what it was trying to convey. But when I heard Hong say the lyrics and Chenda join in with the last verse, I realized that I still had a heart, and a tear dropped. I asked Chenda to repeat the last verse a couple more times so that I would remember and make that song mine.

Our work kept taking us farther and farther from the village, closer and closer to the Thai border. There was a rumor that some of the people from the nearby villages had escaped, banded together to become a resistance group, and lived in the jungle between the Cambodia-Thailand border. Several times while working in the far-away fields, we heard booming explosions in the distance. They gave us hope. I was very happy every time I heard an explosion. I felt that I had a chance to live again, that someone out there in the world cared about us. I thought that this regime that was so unnatural could not last very long. I just hoped it would be over faster. I wondered how and when had I become happy to hear an explosion. It seemed odd to think a bomb could give me a chance to live.

I heard Bong Seurn and Pa talking about some kind of international organization that existed with the sole purpose of protecting all countries and people around the world because things like what was happening to us were not acceptable. Whatever that organization was, it was my hope that it did indeed exist. Surely the world would not tolerate watching as a whole country turned into concentration camps.

One day I was certain I could not go on anymore. I was awake but could not get up, or did not want to get up. Em kept pushing me, "Get up, my child. Get up and try harder."

I'm sorry to let you down, but I can't go any more. I told her quietly in my mind, too tired to say it out loud.

"Try harder for us, my child."

I was so sure that it was my last day. I wanted it to be my last day. My only wish in the world was to hear Em agree with me and say, "Stay with me my child. You can't go to the field like this."

I said to myself, "Let me go. Let me be. Let me give up. I do not want to try harder any more. If I don't eat today, perhaps I won't wake up tomorrow. Suffering will be over."

Em didn't give up; she kept pleading with me. I got up with frustration, unsure if it was directed toward Em or the whole situation, but I felt the big lump stuck in my throat. I was thinking: *Why try harder? For what? One more day, one more week like this? Em, you are going to feel really bad if my last breath will be in the field.*

God did not make things easy for me. I did come back from the field and still wanted to eat and felt guilty for being frustrated at Em. *What if she is the first to go?* It was too painful to imagine. In fact, she had lost more than half of her weight, but somehow she was the strongest among us. In the beginning, we were worried about her, for we had no way to refill her modern medications. I thought for sure she would not last very long, but the opposite was happening. Her asthma stopped bothering her, she stopped drooling from her upset stomach, and her weight problem was no longer an issue. As I sat and thought about how Em had been the strongest one in the family, I could not help but scan the hut to see who the weakest one was. Hong wasn't back from the field yet, but he was not the weakest one. Besides, he had an easier job than us. Watching animals, he was not so much under the gun. He was able to snoop around more than any one of us. The animals didn't know how to snitch.

Pa. My Pa was the weakest one. He was very thin. I watched him lying flat on the bamboo floor, his stomach touching his backbones. His whole body was like a skeleton covered with a gray, thin, wrinkled blanket. I wished there was something that I could do for him. He wasn't sleeping, but his eyes were barely open. He wasn't relaxing, but he had no choice. The gravity was too strong for him to fight. I watched life slipping away from my father. For a moment, I couldn't tell if he was still breathing. Before I could get a closer look, Pa moved a bit and mumbled, "Motherfuckers." Instantly I smiled with pleasure, knowing that he was still with me and that they deserved his wrath.

When our meal was ready, we could not start because Hong was still somewhere in the field. Anxiously, we waited and wondered what was taking him so long. I thought, *Why do we have to wait?* The answer was obvious. We waited because we could not stand watching him eat after us, and he would not like it either. Em and Pa were getting more and more restless. Em, Pa, and Ee went past the bamboo fence into the field and started calling for Hong. Ee and Pa went farther into the field, but Em stayed close to the bamboo fence and marched back and forth as she called for Hong in as calm a way as she could. Chenda, Kheang, and I sat and watched Em from the hut, wishing Hong would answer back to her calls. There was no answer, and no one else came out to help her look for her son. When Pa and Ee returned without Hong, Em started to lose control of herself.

"My boy. My dear boy. Where is my boy?" Asking without expecting any answer, she was whimpering and crying, but there were no tears, not even enough to coat her eyes. What happened to the tears? Why were they not coming out? Had she used them all up? Her face was full of pain, and her eyes shifted in all directions but none in particular. Her head moved around, trying hard to turn away from the world. Her arms bent up and down as if she was thrashing for air; she had no soul left. She could not summon herself to call for Hong any more. I wanted to hug her, but somehow I just sat there stiffly, like everybody else. I saw Pa comfort her and bring her back to the hut. She was still whimpering, and all she could do was chant, "My boy. My boy. My boy."

I found myself imagining what had happened to Hong. Was he so tired that he fell and gave up? Did the water buffalo hurt him? *Dear God, please don't take him back this way. Dear God, please don't take Em's baby from her.*

It was getting pretty dark. If Hong was still alive, he had probably decided to rest somewhere in the field until the next day. We all gave up on him, except Em. We sat like a bunch of skinny, despondent monkeys on a branch, watching Em going back to the field and calling for Hong. She didn't give up. She was determined to march and call for him as long as she could. The last call she made, a response came.

"Yes! Em."

"He is back! He is back!" She ran back to the hut and back to the field. I sensed her glee and saw her broad smile and happiness beyond words. Her tears came out like a reservoir from a broken dam. Hong walked through the bamboo fence. He was shaking from his drenched clothes and wearing an old krama hanging over his neck that stretched out into two big pouches that were full of something.

"Sorry, Em. I lost track of time when I was picking these wild bean flowers (*phak snoaw*)." He was apologizing, but his face was proud as he showed us the contents of the pouches.

The pouches were stuffed full of the wild bean flowers. They looked so pretty and tasted even better. God had given us a bite of food for one more day, but what would he bring tomorrow?

Despite starving and despising the work in the field, I still found pleasure in looking at the green rice plants gently moving in the soft wind as we passed by in the canoe on the way to and from the fields. If I could have enough to eat, I would probably enjoy being here. As the rain continued to pour day and night, the river overflowed its banks, and water was everywhere. It was a good thing that the big tamarind tree was by the riverbank to mark where the river started and where the path along the river used to be. Our dirt floor was covered with water except for the spot where Em had her fire.

Every morning Em would tell us to shake our work clothes before we put them on. Every morning I ignored her—until one morning, as I pushed my right arm into the sleeve, I got a terrible stinging sensation provided by a big, ugly scorpion. It was painful—very, very painful. Ever since that morning, I made it a habit to shake off any possible flood refugees before putting my clothes on.

At night, when we needed to empty our tanks, we just got up, squatted at the corner of our bedding, and let it go through the slats of the bamboo floor. One night we could hear a lot of splashing under the house, and for sure we thought they must be fish jumping. In the morning, when we looked down through the bamboo slat floor, we saw many fish. The excitement rumbled through the hut. If we only had a fish hook and a nylon string we could catch some. There had to be a way to catch some of those fish. Pretty soon we saw people hustling through the knee-deep water in front of our hut with big fish and smiles. One man told Pa there were schools of fish passing by the village and that they would be gone in a couple of days.

The village people, including the leaders, found it hard to go to the field. They sent a few members of their family to please the Black Uniforms, and the rest were trying to catch those fish while they still could. We did the same. The riverbank was lined with people using all different kinds of tools and tricks to catch fish. I was told to stay home and try to catch some fish somehow. Perhaps I could help people who had the means to catch the fish and hope they would give me some. So that was exactly what I did. I stood behind a woman and helped her empty the fish from the net into a bucket. When she was tired, she let me borrow the net. She hesitated, thinking I might tear the net or break the handle, but she didn't have the heart to say no. I caught fish. I felt like I could live again. Every dip of the net into the river I brought back at least five or six good-sized fish that were straining and struggling to escape the net. I saw the fish swimming all around me. I was in heaven. I brought every bucket full of fish to Em and Kheang at home, then went out again, even in the rain. I was cold and shaking, but I didn't want to stop. I could not stop. It was the rain that kept the owner of the net in her hut. I caught many buckets of fish that day. This must have been the reason Pa brought us out of the Lion Village to the river. We were alive, we could have hope again, just like the song said:

If you still have life, you will always have luck.
You must not lose hope.

There's always a clear sky after a big storm.
Don't be afraid to smile
and hope for your day to come.

For a while we boiled fish with no spices, no salt, and no rice. We ate nothing but boiled fish and they were so sweet. We went to bed with stomachs full of boiled fish. The only thing that was bad about it was that we had to put up with the diarrhea, but it was not painful or life threatening. The fish provided us enough oil to light our hut at night. With full stomachs and fish oil lamps, we had more to say to each other at night. Em, with her silly hope, told me to wash the persisting infections and rashes on my legs very well so that I would not have marks when I could wear a miniskirt again.

"Miniskirt again?" I repeated, chuckling in disbelief.

"You never know," she responded firmly but gently while she ran her fingers on the rings of rashes by my left ankle.

Yes, I do, I thought. *I know I will survive.* The fish will last us for a while until something else takes their place. There will always be something else. God is very unpredictable. I will survive, but not by resisting the Black Uniforms nor by help from some international organization, but from doing the best I can. The last thing I'm worried about is marks on my legs. I love you Em, but I can't think like you.

Pa often expressed concern about his two younger brothers, Uncle Khemm and Uncle Hoc. He had provided financial support so they could continue their education in Paris. "I wonder what is happening to them. Without money from us, will they be able to finish their education?"

He was also concerned about his sister, Aunty Khim, and her family. He had bought their house so that they could leave Phnom Penh to go to France just before the Black Uniforms took over. At the same time, he praised the luck that they possessed—unlike him and his own immediate family. I listened to him and looked at him, but my heart was with *him* not with my aunt and uncles. How sweet it was that he always opened his arms for people.

If Pa had been educated like his brothers or sister, would we be in France too? But Pa had never spent a day in a classroom. We were told that when he was a young boy, Grandma and Grandpa were poor, and he was best at selling Grandma's cookies, so he was kept away from school to help her. He had learned to read and write from a good-hearted teacher who allowed him to stand outside the classroom by the window while class was in progress, and this way Grandma and Grandpa didn't have to pay the school.

Later on in life, he learned to read and write in Chinese because his business required him to. He picked up French when he was in detention with a Frenchman for about a year. Pa picked up some English in later years, when his business brought him to Saigon. He spoke seven different languages and made friends with everybody, ranging from army generals to ex-convicts. Everybody who knew him loved him, even the guard in the detention camp. He had a heart and a way with everybody—everybody but the Black Uniforms.

We had now survived the first six months of misery living under Black Uniforms brutality.

Chapter 6

SEPARATION

Harvest Season of 1976

T he schools of fish did not last long. Without enough dry places to smoke them or salt to preserve them, we were back to the same old faces. No smiling, no jokes, nothing to laugh about, to talk about, or to fight for. We were getting better at handling our starving stomachs. We would just be real quiet and listen to them growl.

The monsoon season had gone through its peak, and the floodwater was on its way back to the river. Some rays from the sun beamed through the cloudy skies. The season was changing, but we were thinking of nothing but food—anything at all that might be chewable or edible.

"Ee, when I die, make sure you bury me with my head toward the east," Pa said to break the silence, but then it continued. No response, no shock, no emotion, just dead silence. Pa believed that with a proper burial his children would be blessed. I would replay that request many times in my head, and will for the rest of my life. Even thinking about his last breath, he still wanted to take care of us.

I wasn't thinking about dying or surviving. I wished only to fall asleep. That was the only way to escape the torture.

Then small flashes of light and splashing sounds came from the muddy path next to the hut, grabbing our attention. Hong jumped onto the muddy floor and rushed to the flashes and splashes that were still happening.

Ee joined in, "Be careful, be careful, Hong."

"Hurry up, hurry up!" whispered Em.

Under the full moon, I saw Hong kneeling down on all fours, chasing and wrestling a fish along the path in the mud. I could tell the fish was healthy since its scales easily reflected the moonlight. All of us waited anxiously and quietly to avoid being noticed by the Savan family.

Hong brought back one more drop of life from God. He had in his hands the biggest fish our family ever caught. For the first time since we left our previous life, I said my thanks to God. It was truly a miracle. My heart was pounding, and tears came with feelings of joy for the gift from God and fear of his power. How could I say he does not care?

"God has eyes. God has heart. Dear Lord, you hear my prayer." Em spoke for us all, but she was interrupted by her own shaky voice. The rest of the words stuck in her chest and throat. Only the involuntary sound of her heavy sigh escaped. Her display of emotion sent an electric shock to my heart. At last I felt my heart beating again.

The next morning, all the young men and women were to go to the village meeting. There was a sense of restlessness in the air. Former peasants and masters alike feared the uncertainty of the situation. The previous village meeting called for all former military members to attend. None returned to their families.

Em and Pa let Chenda go to the meeting. They believed the Black Uniforms would be more likely to spare a girl's life than a young man's. Ee and Hong were supposed to be too sick to go to the meeting. Linda came to the hut, and both Chenda and Linda were sisters again. They walked to the meeting with many other young women and a few young men. The village was quiet. Not even a baby was crying. Em sat in front of the fire and picked at the coals with a stick, struggling to keep her tears silent.

After an hour or so, Chenda came back alone. She choked up when she saw us. She went to Em and started crying without a word, dropping her face toward the ground and covering it with her two pale, skinny hands. Em gently caressed the back of her shoulders. The two bodies jolted with tears that came from nowhere. There was still not a word, but it was clear something must give.

Mr. Savan came by and said, "Please stop crying. It won't do us any good. They will take my two boys, too."

Chenda had been instructed to come home for her belongings and regroup at the village meeting place for a journey without a destination. For Chenda, Em packed about one cup of rice, some sticks for a fire, and the one or two sets of clothes that she still had.

Chenda stood at Pa's feet and summoned the words, "I'm leaving, Pa." He was covered from head to toe in a blanket. There was no response—not even a twitch for an acknowledgement. Pa chose not say goodbye. Chenda cried; we all cried. It was the first time I realized I was going to miss my sister. *Will I see her again? I want to see her again. How can they do this to us? Why are they doing this to us?*

Em gently pulled Chenda from Pa and said, "It is too painful for him to see you go, and you must understand that."

Chenda had no soul left with which to prop up her bony body. She swayed like an ironwood branch in the wind as she pulled away from Pa and knelt down on the muddy floor to get a blessing from Em. Holding a bowl of water in her left hand, Em dipped in her right hand and took it out to shake the water over Chenda's head.

She said with tears and lumps in her throat, "I am

not a priest and I am not a monk, but I am the mother of this child, and I ask you to help me bless this child who is so precious to me." She ended her blessing abruptly. Only an agonizing sound came out of her as she quietly moaned for help. Chenda rose and comforted Em as we all watched and felt their pain along with our own pain. The mother and daughter walked away from the hut toward the riverbank while someone rushed up and down to hurry all the young women and men. Em let go of Chenda's hands, stood still, and watched her baby girl walk away from her. Chenda continuously wiped her tears. Each step she took was slow and painful for her, but I kept looking. I watched her walk away from my life, my only sister ... I watched ... *Will I see you again?*

Em cried and refused to stop until Pa comforted her. In his own way, he came out of his cocoon and said gently, "Please stop crying. If you continue like this, you are killing me. I beg you." Ee and Hong were probably feeling the same as me: guilty. I was sure that if I had gone, then Pa would not feel as much pain, for I was not his favorite kid. But I was too scared to go away from the most secure place on earth, next to Em. I was too scared to take Chenda's place, and I didn't even offer.

Not long after Chenda left, they took Ee and Hong as well. I don't remember how it happened or what Em and Pa were doing, nor do I remember how they felt when Ee and Hong were gone, only that one day I woke up and it was just Kheang and me with Em and Pa.

It was so quiet, or perhaps it was just me. I talked to no one in the field and just worked hard. I wasn't working hard for the Black Uniforms, but somehow working hard made me feel at ease and at peace with everybody around me. Mair would try to help me finish my work load, but I never even tried to acknowledge her generosity. I was not mad, not holding a grudge. I was just happy to be quiet. Occasionally I would talk softly to Em, and I would also respond to Kheang in matters of trivial sibling rivalry.

I stopped talking to Pa completely, but it wasn't intentional. I was afraid of him. He was in a constant state of anger whenever he talked to me. I would obey him and do things for him without any question, and I was happy that way.

"Are you mute?" Pa snapped at me one time. The words slashed me like a razor blade. *Why does he have to be so mean? He hates me*, was all I could hear in my head. Once I helped Pa to make a basket from a fresh bamboo stalk. I sat next to him, intent on what I was doing, when he swore and yelled: "Why do you have to make that face?"

I dropped the carving knife, went into the hut, and

let my emotion flow down my cheeks. Quietly I repeated in my head: *I hate you, too.*

Later that day, Em came to me and asked why I was so quiet these days.

"I don't know, Em."

"Are you holding a grudge toward your father for losing his temper on the day he slapped you?"

"No, I am not holding a grudge."

"Why aren't you talking to your father?"

With tears in my eyes, I replied to Em: "Do you think Pa ever loved me?"

"What kind of question is that?"

"He hates me."

"All parents love their children in different ways, but all the same love."

I had made my point to Em and didn't want to hear how good Pa was any more, so I shut the world out and went inside myself to listen to my own heartbeat. Perhaps my excuse was that I was a starving teenager. Now that I am a mother, I wish I had kept my pain to myself so that Em would not be sad for me.

The monsoon season completely passed, and the cool wind came. It blew softly but constantly. Our bodies, which were previously coated with milky water every day, were dried up. Our stretched and cracked skin revealed some of the blood that barely kept us alive. My lips were cracking, so Em collected and cooked crab butter[11] for me to put on my lips. It worked much better than any lip balm that I had used in the past.

Most of our clothes from the monsoon season were torn. The shredded items were used to salvage the others. There were patches over patches and stitches over stitches, but some patches were too thick and heavy when they got wet, and the original fabric gave in around them. Em took out her precious silk *somput*,[12] which she had carried all the way from Poipet, and proceeded to reshape it with scissors that she borrowed from Mrs. Savan. Em stood up and held the bright-colored somput against her body. From the look of it, the waist of the silk somput could fit two of Em now.

Pa looked at Em and added, "There is no doctor or any diet pills better than the communist pills." He chuckled and continued, "If only I had known." Em looked at herself and shook her head and smiled.

As she lay the silk somput down and began cutting, I thought, *Good thing Em was a big lady before all of this*

---

[11] Crab butter is made by removing the tiny yellow fat from the shell and cooking it over low heat to extract the clarified liquid fat from cooked solid.

[12] A *somput* is a formal sarong, prefolded, fitted and sewn to retain its shape, usually made from silk and worn by Khmer women on special occasions.

happened, but any other fabric would have been better than silk. Em made me two new bright pairs of pants with drawstrings (elastic bands were a thing of the past). She looked at me as I tried them on, and had me squat, bend, and take long strides. It seemed to feel good, but when I checked her face for confirmation, I saw something else behind those eyes. They weren't checking to see how the pants fit. They were mellow with sorrow. There must have been tears behind them, but none to be seen. She took a deep breath, sighed, quickly looked away, and ordered me to put them in the mud. Just then I realized for better or for worse we were erasing another piece of evidence that we were financially better off than most before everything turned upside down. Most people in the French Village probably did not own silk clothing of any kind.

I thought the process of dyeing fabric was fascinating. I was eager to get started with this science project and forget the fact that it was Em's silk somput. I went over to the field and shaved off a kind of tree (*trawkow*) bark and brought it back to the hut to boil and reduced the simmering water to one third the original amount. I took the bark out and let the black water cool down. While the water was cooling, I went to the field behind the hut and scooped up a bucket of black clay mud and brought it next to the hut. Now I had all of the ingredients, and I couldn't wait to get started. With a stick in the black water, a bucket of mud next to it, and the bright pants on my arm, I started to feel guilty and not sure if I could do it. I felt as if I was going to drown the silk. *Quicker is better,* I told myself. The moment I dropped the silk into the black water, I felt my heart gently bump against my rib cage. Watching the bright color sinking slowly into the black water, I wished I didn't have to do it. In my head, I saw Em in the silk skirt smiling and happy with family and friends, and saw myself having fun with music and food, and us kids running around absolutely carefree. I dabbed the tears that coated my eyes. The color still showed above the black water. *The quicker the better—the quicker, the better.* I grabbed the stick and quickly drowned all the color in the black water. *There, it's over.*

No more color—just a science project. I left the pants in the dye for half an hour, then squeezed out the dye and immersed the pants in the mud and left it there for a good half day. Then I took them out and rinsed the mud off in the river. The bright colors were becoming different shades of gray. After a few more times of soaking, setting, and rinsing them, the shades faded further. No one in the village even noticed my new pants. All they could see were pants that were not nearly as black as the Black Uniforms' pants. Only my family knew of the rich color they once held.

The rice field behind the hut began to change from green to golden-tipped. The starch was not set completely, but I could not wait. I would sneak into the field and pick the rice stalks by hand, biting on each seed to suck on its sweet milk. Soon after, I realized the rice shells had abraded my tongue to a level of discomfort that I could not bear. I quit that practice and waited. Meanwhile, the field was becoming more and more golden. A week or so later, not every stalk was ready, but some were ready enough. For the next few days, I snuck deep inside the rice paddy to pick the ready stalks and put them into the ends of an old krama that I tied into small pouches. Meanwhile, Em or Kheang were my lookouts. They watched the road in front of the hut and the nearby fields. When I heard them clear their throats, I was to stay still, and when they coughed, I was to come out.

On one of these missions, I heard a noise that wasn't coughing or a throat clearing. I froze and took as many little shallow breaths as I could. The sound was getting closer and closer, and I felt the vibrations through the rice stalks next to me, when I realized that someone else was in the paddy with me. Not knowing what to do, I decided to stay still, thinking whoever was here must not be a Black Uniform. Through the thick rice stalks over my head I, recognized the girl, but she didn't notice me. It was Mr. Savan's daughter, who was the same age as me. She was doing the same thing, stealing from the Black Uniforms. I decided to leave her alone, for she was the most unpleasant among the Savans' kids. She must have noticed me just as I turned away because she said quietly but strongly: "Why didn't you say something? Are you deaf? Or mute?"

Another person besides Pa asking if I am mute! I didn't talk much but, I didn't know that I bothered people. I looked at her and saw the meanest eyes in that girl. I didn't want to give her any satisfaction, so I just turned away and continued in the opposite direction.

In the hut, we would loosen the seeds from their place in the panicle, roast them, and flatten them to get the shells off. Flattening roasted rice is not a quiet job, and we could hear the same job being done all over the village. Even so, Em had Kheang watch the road. If he saw anyone coming toward our hut, we would clear the job site. Thus the whole village could hear what was being done, but none could see who was doing it—except, of course, us and the Savans, with whom we shared the big wood mortar and pestle.

At last Mr. Savan and Pa began talking and laughing in the evenings, just like normal. A new joke in the village was "What kind of animal eats only the head off a rice stalk? Definitely not birds or rats." Another one was "Did you see the new form of rice plant? It is a male rice; it has a stalk but no head." All the rice fields along the edge of the village were eaten by these mysterious animals.

There was a rumor that all of the young men and women from the village were stationed at a rice paddy called Lake Kair. They were having fun, there was music every night after work, and all-you-can-eat meals twice a day. I thought, *What a catch! Can it be true? Are they really having fun? What kind of music are they playing since all the old music is banned?*

I missed my sister, and I hoped that if the rumor was true, she would not forget us.

Day after day in the rice fields, I became increasingly proficient in using a sickle to collect rice stalks. Now that we were in harvest time, we were no longer going to bed with empty stomachs. While working in the field, I often thought of my friends in the old neighborhood, friends that I had gone to school with just a year earlier. Whatever happened to them? Were they in a better or worse place than me? I also thought of the sound of recess at school, how fun it was. My teachers and school—everything was such a sweet world, but now they were all gone. It had been almost a year since the Black Uniforms took over, and I had never heard any sound of children playing, laughing, or horsing around. the Black Uniforms didn't believe in school, so they took most of the school teachers to "reeducate" them. None of the teachers ever returned from reeducation back to their families.

One day after lunch, I heard a soft call coming from across the river: "Em, Em!"

From the thick bamboo wall, I saw someone that looked like Hong. I looked again, thinking my mind was playing a trick on me, but sure enough it was him. He was camouflaged within the bamboo stalks so that he would not be seen by other people in the village. He waved his arms at us. I was overwhelmed with excitement, and my mind filled with questions and answers. *What is he doing? He must have escaped from where he was stationed. What if he gets caught? I must get him and bring him into our hut.*

Pa was nowhere near the hut at that time, so I pleaded with Mrs. Savan to let me borrow her canoe. The water in the river was pretty low, but not shallow enough to walk across. I could not imagine what Hong's plan was, to come home like that, but it didn't matter. First things first.

It was the first time I rowed a canoe by myself. Since I didn't know how to swim, the river looked bigger when I unleashed the canoe. I had seen how people steered and rowed the canoe across the river before, and it didn't look hard to do. But that was not so when I tried. I had to fight the soft current, which was a bit stronger than my arms. I tried hard, rowing up the river to compensate for the current so I could bring the canoe straight across to the other side. The tip of the canoe kept wanting to turn downstream. I fought to keep the tip pointing up the river and at the same time thought that if I could make it, Em would be very proud of me. For a moment, I forgot all about Hong, although I could feel Em's and Hong's tensions on both sides of the riverbanks.

As I got to the middle of the river, the current became stronger and stronger, and the harder I rowed, the more the canoe swayed back and forth. I was scared it would flip over. I heard Em and Hong yelling at me, telling me what to do, but I couldn't make out any words from either of them. I feared that my fire would be put out by this soft river.

"Please, please don't let me go this way," I found myself pleading to the higher being. I tried with all I had, but I could not stop the tip of the canoe from turning and pointing down the river. All I could do now was steer, though I felt I was in much better control than I was trying to fight the current. Fortunately, the turn of the river stopped the canoe from going farther downstream, and I was able to bring the it to shore. Hong hustled along the riverbank through dense vegetation to meet me. Without any time to reflect on what had happened minutes ago, Hong jumped into the canoe and started helping me bring it back to Mrs. Savan's dock.

Hong had doubled his size since he left us, but his face looked more swollen than healthy. He started to cry as Em grabbed hold of his hand while we hustled to the hut. Hong and Em crawled into the girls' compartment, while I was in the common area watching out for the Black Uniforms. Come to think of it, they never walked alone. Through the thatch wall I heard Hong quietly sobbing as he told Em, "My body is swollen all over, Em." He choked up but was able to summon himself to confess his ultimate fear: "I'm not sure what's going to happen."

When he sobbed louder, I tapped on the thatch wall to remind Hong that others may be able to hear. At the same time, I heard Em try to calm his fear, "Don't worry, my dear child. You will be all right. Don't be afraid. If God has eyes and heart, you will survive," Em challenged God to take care of her baby. "For he knows that all the things I have done, I did for my children, and I have never done any bad to anyone. Don't give up, my child. You will be fine."

I wanted to know more of what would happen when a body is swollen, but the truth was that I didn't really want to find out on my own brother, so I kept quiet. As Hong continued to quietly sob, I felt the pain from his heart seeping throughout my body. I felt the tightness of my eyebrows and the soreness of my eyeballs, though not single a drop of tears. My tears had somehow dried up within me. I felt my heart squeeze. My nose and face were tingling—but still no tears. No tears to comfort my brother. No tears to say, "I'm sorry for what you have to go through."

What is wrong with God? This is not fair. Perhaps the Black Uniforms are right: God does not exist. Perhaps I am turning into one of them.

We had experienced starvation, but none of us had had any serious illnesses. Hong looked like a sad version of the Michelin Man, all puffed up and pale. He showed me his swollen legs. He pulled up his pants and exposed his puffy shin and said with some degrees of curiosity, "Little, look closely." With an index finger, he pressed the flesh that covered his shin bone. The flesh sank underneath and around his index finger like foam, and when he pulled his finger out, the indentation remained. As we sat there watching and waiting for the flesh to reform itself, I was having doubts about what Em was saying earlier to Hong. I wanted to say, "Are you really going to be okay?" but I didn't want to scare him. I wanted to say something, but I was not optimistic like Em. I wanted to comfort him, but he would see through me. His breaths were short and fast. He did not look good. I hoped he would come out of it. I hoped Em was right.

Hong told us that he was staying in a sick-house in Chamnaom, a village up the river from French Village. He was sneaking out of the sick-house just to see us, but he had to go back before the Black Uniform nurses made their rounds.

Hong snuck back to see us almost every day. Em was grateful for those days when God brought her son back to her, especially when he needed her the most. She had gone to the medicine man to get herbal medicine to make tea for Hong for the times he came to see us. She also gave him some of the herbal tea to take while he was in the sick-house on the days that he could not come. Eventually, he did get better. Once the swelling was gone, we could see his real, skinny body. I never thought I would be so happy to see his skeleton body again.

While Hong was getting better, Em feared the Black Uniforms would take him away from her again. One day when Hong stopped by, I watched as Em patted the back of her son's head and spoke softly without any expression on her face. "Hong, you have recovered well. I fear that they will take you away again, but I thank God for bringing you back to me." We all knew that sooner or later he would be taken away again.

For three or four days in a row, Hong didn't show up at the bamboo wall. Things were even quieter now than ever. Was he okay? I missed him. Where did they take him this time? Maybe tomorrow he would come home.

Tomorrow came and went many times, but Hong never came back. *When did he leave the sick-house? How he must feel, knowing that we would be waiting for him!* I missed him so much. Em took it hard. She stopped cooking. She stopped eating. She came down with a high fever and many times became incoherent. We were not allowed to stay home and care for her, and they took her to a different sick-house in the village.

Located next to the church, the sick-house was once a home of the village chief. I could not wait to see Em at the end of the long day in the field. Even in her unconsciousness, she gave me strength. Whenever I saw her, I felt like crying, but I felt better. I felt so lonely, so alone. Walking back from the sick-house, I felt as if I was half dead, like screaming to the world. I was breathing, but I had no purpose—just the ugly urge of my physical need to eat. I cried myself to sleep every night in the girls' compartment all by myself, wishing I was dead. I saw, heard, and knew no one around me, not even Kheang and Pa. I didn't remember what they were doing or what happened to them at that time.

Em got better, but she could not walk. She was too weak to stand on her legs. There was only one Black Uniform nurse to care for the house full of sick patients. He seemed like a nice guy and was sweet and soft spoken to Em. He seemed so different from his comrades: he seemed to care. He had lighter skin than most and seemed well educated. He treated Em with science needles, which today we know is called acupuncture. I had never seen or heard of such a practice. I was frightened of the long needles, thinking for sure Em was being experimented on. Somehow, Em was consciously and happily letting the nurse treat her. Em and the nurse seemed to get along very well, confirming to me there was something different about this Black Uniform. A couple of days later, Em was preaching about how good the science needle treatment was, and I was quite happy to see Em getting strong again. In time, Em was able to walk again. Things were almost back to normal.

Em was still recovering in the sick-house when the Black Uniforms came to take me away from my parents. I was gathering rice under the hot sun when I saw two Black Uniforms and the village chief marching toward the field. I shrank down to the ground, wishing I could disappear. I watched them call out a few boys and girls from the field to get in line behind them. Hoping they thought I was too young to go, I turned away from them to put a bundle of rice stalks onto a stack, but it was too late.

They called out to me: "Comrade by the stack, you need to come with us." I felt so light, as if I could float above the ground. As if I was hypnotized, I followed their commands. "You can leave the sickle with the mothers and the fathers here."

I looked for Pa, but he would not let me see him, just like when Chenda was forced to leave. He couldn't bring himself to acknowledge the separation. He continued working as if nothing was happening. I wanted to call out to him, but I was afraid the Black Uniforms would see me cry. The girls and boys were supposed to be happy and grateful to the Black Uniforms for freeing us from the old regime, our parents. I scanned the field, hoping to see Mair and Ouv. When I found them, they looked like they had seen a ghost. In desperation, I locked eyes with Mair, crying the silent words, *Tell my father I love him.*

The Black Uniforms marched us across the field, collecting all the boys and girls before they marched us back to the village. We were told to get our clothes and meet at the church. All alone in the hut, I wanted to run away— but to where? What would they do to my family if they could not find me? I didn't have any choice but to do what I was told. I packed my favorite short-sleeved shirt, a pair of old pants, a spoon, and a plate, but there was no food to pack into the end of my old, sweaty krama. I was hurrying to see Em before I had to leave. I could not think straight, and all the tears that I thought were dried up within me were coming back to blur my vision. I kept thinking of different things. *Kheang—where is he? I want to see him before I go. Where is everybody? I need someone to cry to, but no one is around. I have to see Em; I know where she is. The hut—yes, the hut. I can say goodbye to the hut.*

As I stood by the old fire pit full of old, cold ash, the image of Em squatting by the fire and preparing rice broth came to me. My mind flashed back to so many memories: good, bad, and sad, and to hunger, and to when Pa slapped me. I felt as though everyone in my family was with me. I found myself gently petting the slatted bamboo floor, remembering Pa's skinny body always lying so still in the same corner. *Goodbye hut, I may never sleep with you again.*

At the sick-house, I could not stop sobbing, so many emotions and fears backed up in my mind, ready to be shared with Em, but not a single word could come out of me. Em saw my little bag and knew what was going on. She rubbed the dried mud from my arms, and I hoped that she would never stop. I wished I was sick so I could be with her. I wished to die in her arms. That was where I belonged. Em didn't cry at all. I pleaded quietly in my head, *Cry for me, Em. Please cry. Why don't you cry for me? Em wake up! I am leaving you, Em. Em—talk, please.*

The nurse came over and told me: "I beg you to stop

crying. You had better not let them see you crying. Just think you are not the only one who has to go."

I replied quietly in my head, How could I not cry? I may never see my mother again.

"Maybe you will be with your sister again." Em had finally said something.

The nurse hurried me to leave: "I see them gathering at the church already," he said.

I took a few jerking deep breaths and tried to dry my tears. Em walked me down the wooden steps to be with me a little longer. Standing by a bush at the bottom the staircase, Em's weak knees began to shake and could not go any farther. I cried again. I tried hard not to show it, but I moaned and shocked myself with my own tears and mucus.

Em spoke softly but with no emotion. "Don't cry, my child, don't cry."

Again, I responded quietly within myself. How can I not cry? I may never see you again, Em.

I walked away from Em, never looking back, but I felt that her love was with me and would always be with me no matter where I was. I walked away that afternoon, not knowing if I would ever see any of my family again, not knowing where they were taking me.

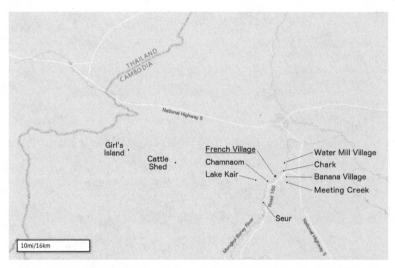

Labor Camps Map—These locations are where I labored under the Black Uniforms. Most of the four-year period, I was confined to a four-mile area in the vicinity of French Village. *(Adapted from National Geographic MapMaker Interactive by K. W. Laux, 2017.)*

Chapter 7

Harvest Season of 1976

The world was so empty; the world was so silent. Everything was gloomy, and I was alone and scared. I felt as though my soul was floating outside of my body as I followed the line of girls led by a couple of Black Uniforms with guns.

I was not sure where I was going, and I didn't care. All I knew was that I was going away from all of the people I loved. We were marching like prisoners in a line. There were many boys and girls, but there was no talking. We were a silent walking line, crossing many golden fields, with the hot sun beating down on us. Finally, I saw some thatched rooflines in the distance. They were situated in the middle of wide-open fields. Not a single tree could be seen, only thatched roofs that rose a bit higher than the fields themselves.

As we approached the complex, I noticed one

longhouse was much larger than the rest. We were led into that longhouse and left alone while the Black Uniforms went into a room in the corner. A man in his forties with black pants and no shirt stepped out of the room, revealing his big fat belly, something I had not seen for a while. He welcomed us to his complex with a speech and a set of rules.

"Welcome to Lake Kair."

Lake Kair. The horror stories of Lake Kair. Many of our family friends from Poipet had been dumped here and had died during the planting season. I remembered the frail woman that visited us in French Village. Her baby died in her arms because she could not produce milk, and her husband died by the fire pit while trying to cook rice soup for her. She had come from this place.

The short, fat, ugly man continued: "You are here because you are big and strong enough to help build our country. From this day on you are the sons and daughters of our government. Thus you are all brothers and sisters under one new parent, our government: the same government that fought for your freedom, rescued you, and freed you from the old regime—the regime that was filled with slavery and labor abusers, and was run by a few lazy fat pigs that called themselves businessmen. Our government will take care of you, and all she asks is that you be willing to help build and protect her. Thus you are also encouraged to turn in any enemies among us. Enemies will show themselves in all different forms to destroy the goal and dream of our government. They will do anything to bring back the old regime."

Freed me from my parents? That thought came to mind when I heard that I had been freed. Nothing made sense. I felt doomed.

While he spoke, he walked in a twisted line that traced a figure eight, with girls in one circle and boys in the other. He added, "Your parents are still covered in crud from the old regime that needs to be rinsed. Thus our government is working on them to make them into better people who will be more committed to helping build our country. You, on the contrary, have not been corrupted by the old regime. Thus our government is counting on you to lead this country to the world. You are the future of our country."

A couple of hands clapped, then the rest of the girls and boys clapped along, with still bodies and controlled manners. We were all listening while seated, quiet and motionless as statues. I felt the man's body stirring the air, but I never knew what his expression looked like for I didn't dare focus on his face. Sitting on the dry dirt floor with my small bag in front of my feet, I hugged my knees for comfort.

"Your duty at this moment is to help gather rice from these fields, and to learn to be a better comrade. Girls must keep their hair short. No hair shall touch your shoulders. Long hair will get in the way of working. Thus you will become less effective and cannot help our government to the best of your ability. Any questions? If not, you are dismissed."

I never thought freedom had anything to do with the length of one's hair. But now that it was taken away, I felt devastated, even though my hair was already short.

The girls and boys were led in separate directions. One of the Black Uniforms led us girls to three empty shelters and told us to grab our own spots. All the girls dashed to stake their favorite spots, as if there was one. Each shelter was just a freshly thatched roof over some posts to support the roof lines. The floor was smoothed out a bit better than the fields around it (perhaps by some men with hearts). I took a leftover spot at the edge of one shelter, but I had nothing to stake it with except my own skinny monkey butt. I watched some girls lay out their large krama and put bags on top of them to mark their spots. Just then, I realized that a good spot would be anywhere in the middle, sandwiched by two warm bodies. As the invisible lines between comrades were stabilized, we were all quiet. Friends were not talking like they were in the fields near their parents, for they were no longer friends. They were now comrades—whatever that meant. As for me, I had not been talking to any of these girls in French Village, so it didn't matter. They were all strangers to me. But now I shared something with them: the quietness, the dead air, the feeling of no feeling, and the thoughts of our parents.

Some girls had to quietly surrender their long hair to appease the devil. As I sat and watched a woman trimming the girls' hair with cast iron scissors, I felt the short-hair requirement was more symbolic than practical as the fat black-uniformed man had explained. I was glad that my hair didn't require trimming.

The sun was almost set when I saw a line of people walking toward the shelter complex. As they got closer, I was excited because I recognized some of them from working in the field near French Village. Could Chenda be in this group, as Em had wished? I watched for Chenda and hoped Em was right. My hope was diminished as the line got shorter and shorter. Most of the girls in my group already recognized some young women to lean on, but I was still hoping.

At the tail end of the line, the young women were walking slower and slower. They were scattered in groups of five to ten young women. Chenda was in one of these disjointed groups. If my heart had hands, they would have clapped. My sister—my skinny, tired sister, who could hardly walk—managed to pull herself together and raise her eyebrows and one corner of her upper lip for me. I felt my heart dancing with joy, happy as heck, but I dared not acknowledge her openly for I feared they would separate us again. I watched her closely and tracked her to three shelters away from me. I found myself repeating in my head, *I am not alone. I am not alone. If only Em knew that I am not alone.*

The triangle bell chimed across the complex from the longhouse, and we were told it was time to go to the longhouse for food. Chenda came and got me. Walking to the longhouse, she told me, "Torheer[13] and Yeeheer[14] are also here." I wished Em could know that though we were away from her, we were all together.

At the longhouse, bowls of fish soup were placed on the dirt floor, ready for us. We all lined up for rice with our own plates and spoons. Once we got some rice, we marched to a soup bowl and sat around it to form a circle of five to six girls. There was a lot of fish in the soup but hardly any water spinach. It was all-we-could-eat rice and soup, and even salt, but we couldn't take

---

[13] *Torheer* is what my siblings call Ee. It means "oldest brother" in my parents' Chinese dialect (潮州 Chaozhou).

[14] *Yeeheer* is what Chenda, Kheang, and I call Hong. It means "second-older-brother" in my parents' Chinese dialect (潮州 Chaozhou).

anything out of the longhouse. We made many trips to the food line for more refills. I watched some girls go to the food line and ask for salt; and salt they were given. A teaspoonful of rock salt was what the woman at the food line gave me. I pretended to nip on some of it every bite with rice, but I held in my left hand all the salt that was given to me. I was thinking of Em, of when she had to exchange some links of Pa's twenty-four-karat blessing waistband for salt. I would save this rock salt for her. I worried about my chance of seeing her again, but for now all I could do was find comfort in saving some salt for her.

The half-dressed, fat Black Uniform came out and marched around us while we were eating. He cracked some jokes for us, and some of the girls even teased him back. The ones who were brave enough to tease him back called him "Father," which gave me goose bumps, making the jokes not funny anymore.

After our meal, Chenda asked me to move to her shelter, and without questioning or thinking, I just grabbed what I had and followed her. Her shelter was a bit more civilized than what I had. The dirt floor was covered with a layer of hay. Her spot was in the same spot I had for my shelter. I wondered how she got her spot, but I was too tired to ask. I thought for sure someone would ask why I was coming to their group, but for some reason no one asked and no one cared. Girls were changing and exchanging places from shelter to shelter. I thought of how lucky I was that the Black Uniforms were disorganized.

No time was wasted. That first night they put me to work. It started off with loud recorded music over the rice cleaning field. It was the first time since the Black Uniforms took over that I heard music on a loudspeaker. The sound propagated throughout the thatch complex and gave me feelings of happiness and sadness at the same time. While the rhythm sounded fun and upbeat, the lyrics were sad and strange to my ears. They were not love songs that I was familiar with. Instead, they were songs for the country, government, and comrades. Words such as "independent," "bravery," "our country," "our government," "our farmland," "our labor," "our soldiers," and "killing the enemies" were used in the songs. The music was our signal to line up and march to the rice cleaning field.

As we marched, electricity lit up the dark sky, which added more excitement to my feeling. It was the first time I saw artificial light since I left Poipet. Like a moth flying into a night-light, I could not help but get excited and anticipate a fun activity. At the rice cleaning field, some young men and women were already working hard. They were singing along with the songs, and some were laughing and horsing around. Of course, they had darker skin than us. The darker their skin, the purer Cambodian they were and the better they were for the government. Our lighter skin told them that we were impure, and that we must have been the lazy, fat pigs that didn't work in the fields to make a living. Even though I could hardly speak a word of Chinese, they called me Big Pocket Chinese Girl behind my back. There were enough lighter skins around that Chenda and I found comfort being near them.

The process of removing rice grains from the stalks was still new to me, so I found it interesting. The ground was prepared to be smooth and tight. It looked and felt as though it was made of cement. Not a single crack existed for a grain of rice to fall into. The rice stalks from the field were placed on the ground in a round shape. Four oxen were connected together by a sturdy yoke. Behind them a man with a whip guided them to walk in a circle on top of the rice stalks to loosen the grain from the stalks. Once the grains were loose, a group of men with pitchforks sifted through stalks, letting the grain fall on the ground and bringing the stalks to the top so that the oxen could march on them again. The process repeated until there was hardly any grain left on the stalks. Then the stalks would be removed and piled into a stack of hay. Another group of men with shovels scooped the grain into baskets for the girls to carry to a different area of the cleaning field for drying on the next day.

Another group of people were cleaning and sacking the previously dried rice. The men scooped the rice into baskets, and we girls carried them to a cleaning fan. Men took turns to manually operate the fan by cranking a pedal with two hands. When the rice poured past the fan, it separated from chaff, small rocks, and pieces of dry clay. We also carried the cleaned grain to the burlap station. No standing was allowed there. Sometimes when things slowed down, we were told to manually re-clean the pile of chaff that was spat out by the cleaning fan. To do this, we used flat woven baskets roughly two feet in diameter with a half-inch lip. I imagined in the past this pile would have been good feed for chickens, but chickens were nowhere to be found since the starving times began. I couldn't remember the last time I heard a rooster crow.

That night we walked back to our shelter with an armful of hay for bedding. I kept thinking how strange it was that I actually had fun working with the group of young people. The songs, the electricity, and the laughing with some of the dark-skinned girls sure did make that night special to me. Earlier in the day, I felt so dreadful and thought I could never again be happy.

Now I felt guilty for enjoying the moment the Black Uniforms had given me, the same Black Uniforms that took me away from my parents earlier in the morning. I wondered if my feelings would last through the nights to come.

Every morning we got up before the sun rose and marched to the fields to gather rice. It took us at least an hour to get to the field, and each day we needed to walk farther and farther as we finished the closer fields on the previous days. The farther we went, the less work we could do. Many days, it was almost noon by the time we got to the field. A group of people was responsible for bringing lunch to us on the oxcart. The meal consisted of rice and salty boiled fish. Day after day it was the same rice and salty boiled fish, but we were always happy to see the oxcart, which was a sign of rest and food. Quite often there was not a single tree in the field, so we would eat in the hot sun. Water was also hard to come by. Sometimes the water team was so late that we were baked dry in the hot sun. When that happened, I could think of nothing but water and remembered the time I spent in Phnom Penh with my aunt in her air-conditioned room. I imagined the chill from the air conditioner on my face.

The dusty heated field was much stronger than my imagination, so I was constantly scanning the area for a sign of an old gasoline barrel lying on an oxcart. The barrel had been modified for easy access with a good-sized opening on its side and placed upward on the oxcart. Whenever we sighted one, all of us would run after it like kids ran after ice cream carts in the old regime. We would all reach out to the water team for the beat-up aluminum bowls of dirty hot water that they gave out. Some girls had bamboo canteens they used to store the water until the next supply arrived. By the look of it, the bamboo canteens were not hard to make, but for Chenda and me, those canteens were a luxury we did not have.

One day, just when I thought things could not get worse, they got worse. I was drying up from the bright, hot sun when the water team finally came. As usual, we all ran to the oxcarts. Some girls were already at the oxcart by the time I got there. I saw them standing around in a cluster, staring at the bowl of water with hesitation and disgusted looks on their faces. I worked my way in and took a peek of what could be so gross. There I saw a bowl of reddish water. Looking closer, I saw that the reddish color reflected from some kind of water bugs as small as grains of sand moving frantically in the hot water. One girl grabbed the edge of her old krama, covered the edge of the bowl, and started to drink thru the fabric. We all solemnly repeated after her. I closed my eyes and sucked the hot water through the critters on the other side of my salty, dusty krama, hoping the edge of the fabric would not give in or tear. Walking back to my working spot, I kept thinking this must be the bottom of hell. I hated being here. I hated all the people around me. Most of all, I hated my instinctual desire to live. For what? I missed Em.

By the midafternoon, the heat had died down, and a warm soft wind started to pick up and gave us all the second wind of the day. Dark-skinned girls started singing again, and dark-skinned boys teased and laughed. No matter how tired I was, the afternoon always made me feel better. I sang their songs in my head along with them, enjoying the rhythm and trying to ignore the meaning. After a while the rhythm took over the meaning, and I did enjoy the songs. I was repeating the words in my head and not even thinking about it. Sometimes I thought about the songwriter. Because the lyrics were refined and articulate, the songwriter must have been an educated man. Therefore, he could not have personally meant what he wrote. No educated man would want any of these things happening to the whole country. That was my excuse to sing the song in my head without guilt. I was certain that most of the dark-skinned girls didn't know the meaning of the propaganda in the lyrics. Those words were the secret message from the songwriters to people like me.

Each day, when it was time to return to the shelter complex, we were exhausted. Our lips and mouths dry and no longer singing, joking, or laughing, we marched quietly to the desolate sounds of our footsteps on the cut-up dead rice stalks lying on the dried earth. Heading toward the oxcart trail, my feet felt heavier and heavier, and I found myself trying to focus on forcing my fingers to grip and hold on to the sickle as it too was getting heavier and heavier. On the oxcart trail, I didn't have to work so hard for each step. I often thought of Cambodian classical music produced by a *Tro*, an instrument generates sounds that go perfectly with the image of desolate open fields filled with warm air. That music, such as "Red Scarf" ("*Konsaing Krawhom*")[15] spoke to my feelings and comforted my soul.

Back at the complex, we were fed at the longhouse and then sent back to work at the rice cleaning field with loud music and a generator for the electrical lights. The next day the cycle started all over again. I kept wondering if we would be sent back to our parents when we finished harvesting around Lake Kair.

About a month after I left Em, I hadn't gotten to take a bath. Not many girls did. Some older girls were

---

[15] You can listen to "Red Scarf" at http://shorthairdetention.com/resources/tro-music.html.

more conscientious about bathing. After an evening meal, they would walk a distance to fetch a bucket of cloudy water and bring it back to the hut. Using the rise of the hut floor as a natural wall, they squatted down, facing away from the hut, and bathed themselves with that cloudy water that looked more like dirty milk. They would wrap a sarong over one shoulder, gather up the hem, leave a small gap under their chin, and stuff the rest of the hem in their mouth. This made a personal portable shower curtain. With one hand inside the curtain and the other hand outside the curtain, trickling the water down the gap under their chin, they washed themselves with a couple of bowls of water. Then they stood up and turned the curtain back to a sarong wrapped over their nothing-there tits and finished themselves off with the rest of the water over their head. That way they bathed and washed their sarong all with a small bucket of warm, cloudy water.

No more than one hour later they would get back to the rice cleaning field for the nighttime job and would get dusty and itchy all over again—way too much trouble for most of us younger girls. We just ate, rested, and hoped the generator would break. For one thing, I did not want to fight for the bucket. There were only two buckets for the group of thirty girls. Another thing was that I didn't own a sarong—a very good excuse. In fact, I was happy that I didn't own a sarong. Otherwise I would have to fetch some water at least once a week to be acceptable to the older girls' club. I just let the air clean me up and the dust soak my sweat away.

My short hair felt like a sticky horse tail when I ran my fingers thru it, which I did often. Doing so, I could almost see my sad face without a reflection, the tears almost coming out, and in my brain a picture of a beautiful and peaceful Em standing in front of me and combing my long hair away from my back, telling me everything was going to be okay. I missed Em. I would do anything to be with her again, to lean my head on her spongy tummy and wrap my arms around her hips and to smell her musty, sweet scent again.

In time, I gave up hope that some special army from the old regime that was stationed deep in the jungle would come and rescue us. I would tell myself: *This is it. This is my life from now on.* I decided to accept it as it was and to try my best to survive and fit in.

I decided to work harder. After a few mishaps, I could do anything a farm girl could, if not faster. The skin under my feet was hardening, and I could walk on the ground that was covered in weeds with hooked thorns just like they could. I could stay in the sun longer than most of them. Chenda, on the other hand, was still slow and seemed to get much more tired than me.

Perhaps her tiredness was because her menstruation stopped completely after we moved to our own hut from the Savan family. I myself had not yet had my first period.

Every day I would line up in the field next to Chenda so I could help her. Each girl was responsible to gather rice from a strip about five yards wide. Together we worked until one field was finished, then moved on to the next field. I worked with Chenda so that there was no lag between us, but not long after we started, we would be left behind far enough that we could not hear any conversation, far enough after a while you could see who the slowest girls were.

Watching Chenda work was torture in itself. She bent over the rice stalks with her knees stiff and her feet planted as narrow as her shoulders. They were not any wider to enable quick movements. She would have tumbled if I had gently pushed her with my index finger. She swung her long, skinny arms freely over the rice stalks. She used mostly her wrists, and hardly her shoulders and elbows. With the jagged edges of the sickle, she pulled the knife back and forth against the stalks as though she was sawing them. Her head was too heavy for her small neck, and she let gravity pull it down as far it would go. When she could not swing her body to reach farther, she would slowly step over and resume the position again. Because she never learned how to hold the collected rice stalks properly, she had to make unnecessary trips to the collection pile. With each slow step to and from the collection pile, she swung her leg sideways as if there was a small boulder in front of her. She was trying to avoid stepping on the freshly cut hay that would scrape her legs. Lines on her brow were always there. Her always-partially-open lips showed her dried, yellowish teeth. She hardly talked. We hardly talked. She accepted my help without any expression, and I gave it without hesitation. There was no Em to complain to about unfair labor, but then there wasn't much of this feeling. I just wanted to help, and I was glad I could.

The hut leader took notice of my hard work. One day she kept me from going to work in the field and sent me to help out the fishing team. I didn't know what to expect, but I knew that I was closer to the food source. No matter how bad the food was, the people who worked closest to the cook always had a good meal.

I was in a small group of six girls. We followed a man who was to lead us to a lake. About an hour later, I could see where we were going. A patch of green was becoming more and more detached from the horizon. As we got closer, I saw that part of the lake was drying up in the sun. The silky mud layer was turning into dry crust, curled up by the heat like pieces of a broken bowl everywhere. We walked toward a different part of lake that had green shrubs and bushes along the side. Still I could not see the water, but I felt cool moisture from the shade of a big tree near the lake. Under the tree was a shack for the fishing team. A fire by the shack was kept alive from the night before.

A team of older men were stationed at the lake. They looked like they had enough to eat. Their skin was shining, tan, plump, and taut with muscles. Their eyes were vivid and full of energy. They reminded me of Ouv when he would stop by our house from his farm to visit Linda. Ouv used to extend his forearms out of his body so that Linda's younger sister could hang on one, with me on the other. Then Ouv would lift us off our feet and sprint up the twenty steps to the second floor of our house. I always thought he was the strongest man I ever knew until I saw these men in the fishing team.

The men had built a dam on one of the inland sides of the lake. Some of the men were emptying water to the other side of the dam, others were knee-deep in the mud and bent down, catching fish with their bare hands. Some of the fish were flipping and flopping on top of the mud surface. As they threw the fish on the dry land, I realized there were a lot more fish already on the dirt by my feet. The fish were covered with mud except their eyes and mouths. They looked more like a bunch of moving pieces of wet clay than fish.

I was so excited to see all those fish moving and jumping as they dried up that I forgot all about the community property of the catch and was just having fun batting and collecting them in a burlap bag. Some of the fish were as big as my thigh. A few were even bigger, but most were small. We caught and took any type and size of fish. Working was fun for me that morning. The leader told us not to take more than we could carry. She was underestimating how many fish could be caught that day. By the time our bags were full, they let some of the water come back into the hole so that the fish could be kept alive to collect on a different day.

We were told to take a break before we returned to the thatch complex. We put our bags of fish in the shade a distance away from the men so we could have some privacy but close enough that if they decided to cook and eat some of those fish, we would not be forgotten. We scraped the mud from our clothes and washed our arms and faces before we rested. It was a luxurious long rest, at least thirty minutes in the shade, but we were too conscious of the men nearby to lie completely on the earth.

Our wish came through when one of the strong men called to us with hand signals to come and have some. Such an invitation I had not heard for many months. We looked at each other, stood up, and tried to not let our hunger overtake our actions as we slowly approached the campfire.

For sure, fish was what the man had to offer, but there was no cooked fish near or around the fire. One man had a big, long stick in his hand. Using the stick, he prodded and rolled out of the fire what looked like a big, stubborn log that wouldn't burn. Out of the coal, the log looked more like clay than wood. Clay it was. A couple of other men with shorter, smaller sticks gently pounded on the stubborn log. Without much effort, the one-inch-thick clay shell cracked. The men used the sticks with skill to peel the clay shell off in sheets to reveal white and juicy fish.

I could already taste the fish with my drooling. It was good. It was too good to talk, too good to do anything but enjoy the moment. My imagination stopped, and all of my five senses were focused on the sweet, juicy white fish. We probably looked like a bunch of hyenas on a carcass, fighting for a good part of the meat, stuffing ourselves as fast as we could. No one thought that there was enough meat to go around until none of us could cram in any more.

On our way back, I paired with a girl who was about my height to carry a burlap sack full of muddy fish suspended from a bamboo carrying stick, one of us on each end. The bag was so heavy that it bent the carrying stick, bouncing and swinging with every step. We were the last pair, and we struggled. It was obvious that I was the one slowing us down, especially for the first couple hundred yards. I pushed her or she pulled me, and the bag between us was swaying in all directions. We had to stop many times to adjust our steps or stop the bag from shuffling us around. Finally, the other girl dropped the carrying stick, turned around, and with a disgusted look on her face, demanded, "Don't fight the bag. Step with the weight."

Unsure of what she meant, I was quiet and looked her in the eyes, waiting for clarification.

Hesitantly, she showed me how to step with the weight. Turning away from me so I could see her back, she pretended that she had the carrying stick in her right hand and held it over her right shoulder. Slowly and carefully, she showed me how to walk properly with the weight. After a few short steps, all I could see was her skinny butt swinging left and right with exaggeration. The urge to laugh summoned itself from within my tummy and melted my muscles. I couldn't help it; I couldn't even stand. Collapsing on the ground,

I felt a spasm with a jolt of laughter that I thought I had lost. Hugging my stomach with one hand and pointing at her with the other, I allowed myself to roll on the ground like a puppy rolling on some roadkill. She looked at me with a kind of "what's so funny?" face, then she chuckled, and soon she too could not stop laughing. I told her to stop and she told me to stop. The more we told each other to stop laughing, the funnier it got, and we laughed until tears flowed down our cheeks. We laughed because we were laughing; we laughed until it hurt to laugh.

Her trick worked. The bag stopped swinging and bouncing wildly, and we stopped pushing and pulling each other. We just walked in that funny rhythm all the way to the thatch complex.

When we got back to the hut, the noon meal was just being served to those who were too sick to go to work that day. Some of them were still finishing their meal. As soon as I walked into the longhouse, I saw Hong for the first time since I had been stationed at Lake Kair. I wasn't sure if he even noticed me. Since I ate fish earlier in the day, I was not hungry, but I tried to eat as much as I could for the next day with the spoonful of rock salt.

I kept an eye on Hong to see if he noticed me, but he would not lift up his face. I didn't think he saw me. Or if he did, he was doing a good job of not showing it. I saw when he slowly stood up that he was thin and frail. I was watching him walk slowly out of the longhouse when I was jerked by a comment from the fat Black Uniform who was not too far from me, lying in his hammock: "I ought to eliminate that guy. He is lazy."

My body stopped functioning. My mouth and throat were stuffed with rice that refused to go up or down. My heart seemed to stop, and my blood seemed to freeze. My eyes opened bigger but then went blank. Loud, slow words started off in my brain. *Oh … dear … God!* I took a deep breath and shook myself out of it.

I have to tell my brother. No, I can't tell him exactly what I heard, but I have to tell him something. Warn him. Encourage him to have hope. Remind him about the song—the hope song that he brought up in our hut. Tell him that I want to see him for a long time. Tell him to live for me. Tell him to live for Em. To try harder and look for the future. Oh, Em, what should I do? Oh, Em, I miss you.

After the meal, we were told to help the cooking team clean up the fish. The fat Black Uniform stopped by and made funny comments, and all the girls were laughing. I kept a smiling face to hide my thoughts and feelings, but I could not laugh with them. I thought about Hong and about how the day started out well. I also felt guilty for eating the fish without Chenda and having a good time with the dark-skinned girl. How could I have fun with a dark-skinned girl? How could I forget about who I am over one good meal? I decided that I would never tell anybody about what happened at the lake, especially not Chenda.

I collected small fish heads that the cooking team threw away and asked if I could keep them. Now that I knew I could keep the small fish heads, I cleaned mostly small fish. The small fish heads kept getting bigger and bigger, with more of the upper body part attached. Fearing being caught, I buried these big heads underneath the good small heads. After a couple of bathroom breaks, I was able hurry to my hut, salt the heads, and dry them on a layer of hay. The sun was so hot that by the time the rest of the girls came back from the field, the heads were dry enough to store in a cotton bag.

As soon as Chenda came back from the field, I told her what I heard about Hong. Her dried face looked even drier, but she didn't say anything. Then she looked right into my eyes with an expression that I could not figure out. It was either as though she was comforting me and saying, "I am sorry," or she was frustrated at me and saying, "What you want me to do about it?" Not sure what to say next, I showed her the fish heads that I collected. She was happy that I changed the subject.

After the evening meal and before rice cleaning field work began, some girls would start a fire and boil some water for herbal medicine. At least that's what they told the Black Uniforms. The truth is the medicine consisted mostly of dried fish, eels, and roasted rice that they somehow got from their parents whenever someone went to the river. For Chenda and me, that day was the first day we had a chance to sit by the fire. We laid a few fish heads over the hot ashes with small, red pieces of charcoal. Needless to say, it was satisfying. The girl from the fishing trip earlier in the day gave me the dirtiest look upon seeing the size of some of the fish heads. I didn't care what she thought. She probably wished that she was as gutsy as I was. Her fish heads were no bigger than her big toe. My fish heads were about the same size, but some included the tails.

That night I stored the rest of the fish heads in a small drawstring cotton bag that I placed by our packages that we used as pillows to sleep on. We were not sure how we could hide them from any sick girl who could not go to the field the next day, but at least for that night they wouldn't get to my fish heads.

In the middle of the night, Chenda and I were awakened by the cold wind. Our hay blanket had blown away from us. I gathered up the few straws that were left and tucked them between my thigh and my tummy.

Tucking my elbows on top of the straws, I tried to keep my body heat within me. The wind continued—not stronger, but eerier. It howled like an unsatisfied spirit moaning. I imagined the airy, thin clouds howling through our unwalled tent. My eyes were wide open, and I didn't want to imagine any more. I sat up and looked out into the open field to see if I could figure out the howling. There was nothing to explain the sound but the sound itself. I was quite awake, and somehow it felt better to sit up than to just lie there on the cold earth. Chenda got up and sat with me. The howling wind started to howl its songs of sadness for us, songs only we understood. Chenda scooted closer to me and I closer to her. Shoulder to shoulder was the best we could do to comfort each other, for I don't remember ever being hugged ever since I learned the meaning of the word. I felt the tightness of my throat, the tingling of my lips, and the heat in my eyeballs, but no tears, for I was more grateful than sad to have my sister next to me. We sat quietly without saying a word to each other. I said to myself, "I shall never forget this night."

I don't remember if the wind had died down or if I was passed out, but I definitely had a dream. I dreamt that some wild animals were intruding on our place, running and fighting on top of us while we were sleeping. I fought and pushed them and screamed. The logical part of my brain told me to wake up and deal with the problem, but the rest of my physical body was too tired to pay attention. I tried to wake up, but I couldn't.

The leader hurried us to wake up in the morning. I was rolling around on the hay when I felt a burning sensation on my tummy that was sensitive to movements. Without further movement, I gently placed my hand on top of my shirt to see if it was real or just a lingering dream. My tummy instinctively pulled back from my hand as I felt raw flesh being rubbed and the burning sensation intensified. I slowly sat up and carefully grabbed the hem of my shirt and lifted it up without letting the fabric touch my tummy. That was when I saw smeared blood along with beads of blood in perfectly parallel lines. These were definitely claw marks across my tummy. It could not have been a rat because the marks were much too large. Whatever it was must have been at least the size of a raccoon. I was shocked and amazed that whatever left this kind of cut on my body didn't wake me up. I scanned every bead of blood along the lines, but I was too afraid to touch and feel them with my fingertips.

Dear God, why did you have to send this animal? Just when I'm beginning to accept this life you gave me, you have to remind me this is an animal's life, not that of a human. What good is there to know, when there is nothing I can do to change my situation?

I showed the marks to Chenda, hoping to get her sympathy. Instead I got a look of fear and disgust. She ran her hands on her tummy and body to see if she may have received the same "blessing," but she was spared.

I found the cotton bag about ten feet away from the hut. It had been torn open with claws or teeth, and my fish heads were gone.

Animal! Stupid animal! If I see you again, I'll make you pay for my fish heads. I'll have you instead. I'll wait for you to come back tonight. I won't be afraid. I'll grab your neck and squeeze it until you can't steal again.

The work around Lake Kair was finishing up quickly, so they moved us to a different place. We were not sure where we were being led to, but this time we were marching toward the river.

Oh, how nice it would be to see Em and Kheang again! Oh, how I missed them! God willing, we would be marching through French Village. Or better yet, we would stay in French Village.

As we marched closer and closer to the villages along the river, my heart beat stronger. Perhaps my prayers had been answered. I felt my blood rushing back and forth between my head and my toes when I spotted the red brick roof of the sick-house.

Would Em still be there? Did she get better or worse? Oh, the thought! How could I forget? When I left, she was weak and shaking in the sick-house. At Lake Kair, I had images only of a strong Em, the Em who was always there to comfort me. How selfish of me. *What if she was not alive anymore? Shame. I hope she is okay.*

My thoughts brought stinging tears to my eyes. When I looked up, I saw the head of our marching line turning away from the red brick roof.

It is my punishment and I must endure, I thought. I didn't love you unselfishly, for whenever I thought of you, it was the thought of you taking care of me, not me for you. I don't deserve to see you. And God wants to make sure I don't see you. However, it is my destiny that I shall see you again, perhaps when I learn to return your love the way you have given it to me. Our love will be so strong that it will wake up all the gods in the universe, and they won't have a choice but to bring us back together. For now, Em, we're still parted.

When we reached the river, boys and girls that were too little to work came out to stare at us. A few old, shriveled grannies situated behind the kids were hunching over and sticking their necks out to spy for a familiar face. There was no excitement, no hurray, only blank faces. How did these naked little children know how to act this way? For sure some of the girls on the team knew some of these village people, but still the silence continued, and only footsteps could be heard.

We marched in a line like a herd of mute cows, said no words, and heard no words. We only followed the footsteps in front of us, and asked no questions.

We were stationed in Chamnaom, the same village where Hong had stayed in a sick-house. They delivered us into a wooden house with a red tile roof along Road 160. The road was in good enough condition to drive on if there had been a car, but I had not seen or heard a car since I left Poipet. The house must have belonged to a decent farmer. Perhaps the farmer would feel better that it was us and not the Black Uniforms who were taking comfort in his house—that is, if he was still alive.

Chenda and I staked out our sleeping spot with our small bags. She then stayed to guard over the spot while I went downstairs to scout for buds on any fruit trees that the farmer had planted behind his house. There was nothing left. Most of the trees were nearly dead and had hardly any leaves on them, let alone buds or fruit.

However, the coconut trees were still good. I eyed the coconuts that clumped together teasingly. How I wished I could get my hands on them! I trotted around the orchard, disappointed, focusing now on smaller and shorter things that I could pick along the ground, hoping to find perhaps berries, herbs, or better yet, a wild potato vine that would lead to potatoes. I came across a big dead tree with not a single leaf left, only dead, brown bark. I heard a sound, as though something dropped from the tree on to the dead leaves on the ground. As I got closer to the tree, I saw something gently moving. I focused closer on the tree bark. Sure enough, the tree bark moved, only this time I could see that it wasn't bark. It was rows and rows of fat, brown, furry caterpillars clustered together on the tree. From a small branch to the big trunk, it was covered with these creatures. In a split second, I checked the ground around my feet, and saw that the ground was crawling, too. Remembering the dropping sound from the tree to the dead leaves, I screamed and twitched my way away from the dead tree. I screamed and screamed, and ran all the way back to the house. *Caterpillars. Caterpillars.* I was certain that at least one of them clung onto my body, or worse, to my short hair. I frantically jumped up and down and shook my body, trying to shake loose anything that might be clinging to me.

"Stop jumping!" a girl yelled back at me. "I can't help you if you keep jumping!"

Stiff but jittery, I tried to stay still for her, but I couldn't control my pathetic crying sounds. She flipped through my tangled, sticky hair and checked the back of my neck and clothes while I stood shaking and moaning with my eyes shut and both of my arms sticking out like a scarecrow.

I had no idea how many of those caterpillars the girl found or if she found any. I was not about to open my eyes to witness it. And I definitely didn't care if my actions made me look like a city girl.

"They're all gone," said this dark-skinned girl, whose name was Tahry—a beautiful name, I thought,—a name that I had heard only in a movie or in a novel. And she didn't change it to satisfy the Black Uniforms. My own name was so ordinary. It used to be Channy in school, Little Girl or Little (*Tuch*) at home. Now it was Comrade Little to my face, and Big Pocket Chinese Girl behind my back. I thought, *When I have a daughter I will name her Tahry.*

Tahry was about my age. She was built bigger and stronger than me. Her dark skin was not so dark; it was a shiny deep brown color. She had a unique and strong face that was not round, nor was it a face with high cheekbones. She was a beautiful girl. Her smile came out from her heart and revealed her strong white teeth. When she smiled, there was no hesitation. She smiled all the way from ear-to-ear. It was hard to laugh in those days, but with Tahry I always found something to laugh about. She laughed as well as she smiled, loud and holding nothing back.

We had been in Chamnaom for about a week, but I had not seen or heard about Kheang or my parents.

Do they even know that we are here, so close to them? They were less than half an hour's walk away, but I couldn't go to check on them for fear of being "corrected" by the Black Uniforms.

I had never seen a person being corrected. How was it done? I didn't know, but I didn't want to find out. The rumor went around the camp that if you were corrected three times, you would be taken away. It didn't take much imagination to guess that "taken away" meant execution. The Black Uniforms often spoke loudly that so-and-so ought to be beaten to death, for he was not worth wasting a bullet. The younger Black Uniforms seemed more vicious. I never doubted the savage threats that came out of their mouths, and I made sure never to make eye contact with them.

One day after our noon meal, I heard a man scream. It was more like a cry for help, the uncontrollable cry of fear, as though he saw the devil coming to get him. Tahry, Chenda, some other girls, and I scrambled out of the house and ran to stand next to the road. At a distance, I saw a group of about ten young men coming our way. They were taking turns carrying a man in a cloth, suspended with rope from the ends of a big bamboo pole. The man in the cloth was moving and screaming frantically, making it impossible for the two men on the ends of the pole to step straight. As they got closer, I saw Ee at one end of the pole, hustling as fast as he could. We exchanged a quick glance, but I wasn't sure he even acknowledged me. Face down and breathing hard in the hot sun, Ee continued on. We could not contain our curiosity. Stretching our necks to take a closer look at the screaming man, one of the girls shouted out the question: "What happened?"

"High fever," a man answered.

It was Hong in that cloth hammock. His head gyrated sloppily from side to side, his hands and arms flopped in all directions, and his knees flapped against each other as he unconsciously screamed and gasped for air. He looked as though something possessed him. Immediately, my head felt light and my face numb. Tahry and the rest of the girls continued to follow the men. I couldn't summon the strength to follow them, but Chenda tugged my forearm gently as if to gesture for me to follow the girls. We followed the men, but not at the same pace, just quickly enough to track their direction. By the time the men turned left toward the river, most of the girls had decided to go back to the house—except Chenda, Tahry, and me. We walked quietly and slowly, tracking the men. Meanwhile I wished Hong could control himself.

Why don't you try harder to control yourself? Try not to scream and act this way. You are going to stand out to the Black Uniforms like a sore thumb. They are going to take you away if you continue to be like this. For crying out loud, for yourself and for us, not to mention Em, try harder, please. Try harder. Be strong. Dear God let him live; if you must take one of us, please take all of us.

When the men turned into the gate of an old elementary school that was now a sick-house, we stopped. I wished I could comfort him and let the world know that I was his sister. But it was only a wish. To do so would definitely mean the Black Uniforms would separate us. At least for now I could still see him.

Tahry broke the silence. "He will be all right now. The nurses will take care of him."

That was the scary part: the nurses were all Black Uniforms. They would not treat him right. I hoped they would leave him alone. At least in the sick-house, he would not have to work, and he could take time to rest. Perhaps when he got better, he could sneak out to see Em as he used to when I was still at home. Somehow in my mind, I always thought Em was waiting to see us again. It never crossed my mind that Em might not be able to survive all of the emotional hardship and sickness.

Chapter 8

April 1976

Not long after Hong was put in the sick-house, the Black Uniforms moved us to a village along the river upstream called Seur. This had been our initial destination when we left Lion Village, but the Black Uniforms had kept us in French Village.

Seur was known as a place where no one starved during the planting season. The Seur river provided its people with fish, and the nearby highland had many fruits and vegetables. It was the birthplace of Uncle Tre's wife. It was a place where I wanted to be. Besides, my aunt was a generous and sweet lady, unlike her sister, Mrs. Savan. I could count on her for food and a smile. She was always good to us kids.

At Seur, the girls were assigned to four houses that were lined up in a row along the river just outside the old pagoda. The old pagoda had several buildings and was surrounded by a fence. The service building, which was the largest building within the pagoda, was used as the eating place. The smaller buildings were raised above the ground on stilts. Once used to house monks, these smaller structures were now used for storing rice on the top floor and for cleaning rice on the ground below. Other smaller buildings were once grade school classrooms where students were taught by the monks, but now they were useless and empty. These classrooms had evidence of looting, vandalism, and chaos frozen in time.

Tahry, Chenda, and I were placed in the second house. Raised above the ground with fine wooden walls and red tile shingles, the house looked like one of the small buildings within the pagoda. Perhaps it was once an overflow building for the pagoda. A three-foot-wide flight of ten stairs led to a nice-sized veranda. A step up from the veranda was an opening to a nicer and more polished wooden floor. There was only one room in the whole place. Perhaps it was a master bedroom for a family or a special room for an older monk. Girls were frantically staking claims to their spots. We would have to stake out three spots in a row for Chenda, Tahry, and me.

As soon as we stepped onto the main floor, our eyes began scanning for the spot. I saw a young Chinese

woman that I had seen around in Lake Kair, one of the
strong Chinese women. She looked more like a man
than a woman. Her name was Lang, and we called
her Bong Lang. It would have been more fitting to call
her Jair[16] Lang, but that would mean that she admitted
being Chinese. Besides, everyone in the girl team was
either Comrade or Bong. So—Bong Lang was guarding
a corner and silently selecting memberships. To reject a
member, she stared out through the corners of her eyes
without any expression until you moved on. When she
saw us, she slightly raised the edge of her lips and gave
a quick, controlled little nod of her head. With three of
us joining the group, Bong Lang could now relax, for
she had just filled up the space along one wall.

A quick scan along the wall made me feel as though
we had made a big mistake joining the group. The second girl in the group was Bong Lang's younger sister,
who was as red and white as her, but much gentler in her
demeanor. The third girl was a Vietnamese girl that I
knew from French Village whose mother spoke Khmer,
which sounds like Vietnamese. Her Cambodian name
was Sopad. During the starvation of the first planting
reason, Sopad's mother was known to feed her family

---

16 *Jair* means "older sister" in my parents' Chinese dialect (潮州
Chaozhou).

with rats that she killed with cyanide. She told Em that she saved some of the powder for her own family in case the Black Uniforms come for them. The one group of people that the Black Uniforms hated more than Chinese was the Vietnamese.

Except for Tahry, the six of us did not look like we were born in Cambodia. Our skin was lighter, our eyes were smaller, and we spoke Khmer without thick villager accents.

Only time could tell whether we would make a good group. We could trade places, but who would want to be next to a big, grumpy Chinese woman? We were doomed. Perhaps we belonged together, except Tahry.

After the remaining girls were moved along to the other houses, some came back. They were loners and looked scared. As they were led around to scout for a spot, we were lying flat on the floor, fluffing up our belongings to fill up the space. Only Bong Lang stood up, again guarding. But this time she was guarding her group, not just empty space. The girl leader walked by without a word, hunting for a less challenging post for the poor loners. Bong Lang automatically became our private leader. Looking closer, I saw that she was at least five years older than I was.

We were lined up like sardines against every wall in the house, even on the veranda. The house took at least fifty girls. The leaders, who were older and darker-skinned girls, took the only room in the house, clumping together just like us six.

That same afternoon, we were told to attend a meeting after dinner. Meeting time was always a "shaming time" for us and a "shining time" for darker-skinned girls. For us, it was always the shame that our parents brought to society: the wheeling and dealing of business people, dishonor for the sake of profit, leading honorable people to do physical work while they sat in their offices, corrupted by capitalism. For the darker-skinned girls, it was time to celebrate their freedom—the freedom from being abused by these lazy people who never set foot in a rice field, like doctors, professors, and merchants, to name a few. Of course there were some gray-skinned people, not so much because of their skin tone, but by their own declaration. Those were the ones who had the option to lay low or declare themselves as dark-skinned girls. For us, there was no choice: we were Chinese comrades. It was only among ourselves that we had our identities and dignity.

There was a sense of importance about this meeting with the leaders. The older, dark-skinned women would take time to bathe, wash their short hair with juice from kaffir limes, and brush their teeth with charcoal powder. They combed their hair and checked their faces with a broken piece of mirror that they shared. With a blackened shirt on top, they wrapped and re-wrapped sarongs that they had blackened, straightening and tightening them around their lower bodies until there were no creases. They finished with a faded, red-and-white-checkered krama wrapped around their neck. They looked almost like the Black Uniforms, except their black was not so black and their red-and-white-checkered kramas were dull and faded compared to the bright red ones worn by the Black Uniforms.

I didn't own a sarong. Not that it mattered. I couldn't keep anything on my waist unless it had elastic or a drawstring. The last time I tried to wear one, I ended up naked in the open from the waist down in front of Mr. Savan. So I wore the only clothes I owned: splotchy gray pants, a shirt, and a cloth that had faded in color from the daily sweat to cover my half–Chinese and half–Cambodian face.

The sound of the new regime's music and songs echoed through the village, signaling that we must start marching to the meeting. I learned to march in a line, watching our own steps only when a leader or a Black Uniform was nearby. As we approached the meeting place, I heard the echo of people talking as though it was humming over the loudspeaker. When we turned the corner into the open space, I saw many boys and girls, many more than I had ever seen gathered together in any one place. Boys were on one side of a temporary podium made out of coconut branches, and girls on the other. They sat on the ground in rectangular blocks, each block associated with their residence. In front of each block sat the leaders, all groomed and polished to their best.

I snuck a few peeks at some of the new girls around us, hoping that our cousins from Poipet might be there somewhere, but I had no luck. However, I knew for sure I would find Uncle Tre and his wife. After all, it was a small village.

The meeting started with a shiny Black Uniform man wearing a bright red and white krama. He greeted us and reported the strength, progress, and independence of the new regime. "Last but not least," he said, "we need to have better organization within our boy and girl comrades. Every boy and girl must belong to a group of three, ten, and thirty, as well as to the whole girl and boy troop. Every night, you must gather for a meeting in the group of three comrades. Once a week you must gather for a meeting in the group of ten comrades. Finally, once a month you must gather for a meeting in the group of thirty comrades. A leader for each group will be selected. All girl and boy troops will be led by one of our comrades here."

He pointed with his gun to the Black Uniform standing next to him. Then he continued: "In these meetings, you must bring out any concern you have during the day, but most importantly, you must take this time to correct any comrade who has a problem following the rules and staying focused on the goals of our government. If the troubled comrade cannot be corrected within three meetings, the comrade shall be escalated for correction to the higher level of the meeting by the leader of the group."

The meeting went on and on, and even the Black Uniforms standing around the speaker could not keep their heads straight. As the sun was going down, I was woken up a couple of times by Tahry, who kept banging her sleepy head on me, and mine on hers. After a while it didn't matter how tough things were going to be—I just wanted to go to sleep. A loud cheer ended the torture.

The next day we started working on something unfamiliar to Cambodians. We were told to pull weeds from the dry-weather rice. The words alone contradicted one another. Rice does not grow in the dry season. In the past, after all the rice had been harvested, farmers spent time doing small jobs around their farms, but mostly visited family in other parts of the country. Now that everybody always had to work, the Black

Uniforms found any kind of work for us, even work that was not worth doing—for example, planting rice in the dry season.

On the way to the field, Tahry gently nudged at me for attention, "Comrade Little, look around you! Look at the scenery!" I looked, and there I saw sweet life hanging from the trees. Mangoes! Big and tall mango trees with fruit swinging teasingly at the ends of their branches. Tahry and I looked at each other with a clever plan in our eyes to get some of those mangoes.

The field was situated along the back of the village. It had more weeds than rice, and caterpillars were everywhere. With leeches, I could control my squirms and jitters, but not with caterpillars. I jumped and shrieked at the creatures. I couldn't stand straight, and I didn't get much done. A few other girls were in situation similar to mine, but not as bad.

The leader called my attention. "Comrade Little, you better stop that silliness. You are disturbing the rest of us from working. Come over here and let me show you something." All eyes were on me and the leader. When I stood next to her as I was told, she opened up her palm under my nose and showed me a handful of caterpillars. They were twitching, squirming, and inching away from her hands and falling on the earth just as I was twitching, squirming, falling, and crawling on the ground while I screamed, trying to get away from them. The whole world was laughing at me as I danced the caterpillar dance off the field and onto the small levee. There I cried, moaned, whimpered, sniffed, and jerked as I sucked for air.

I don't care. I am not going back to that field. I hate her.

The leader was laughing the loudest. She looked at me and turned away, ignoring the fact that I was not working. I sat there until lunchtime. During lunch, Tahry told me I should get back into the field.

"It may be okay with the leader, but if the Black Uniforms see you sitting there on the levee, they won't like it. Why don't you just come and pretend like you are working next to me? I will help you catch and throw away all the caterpillars that come near to you. What do you say?"

I gave in, grateful that Tahry was so nice to me.

After lunch, I got into the field and worked next to Tahry. I watched every rice stalk before I pulled it, and I saw every creature nearby. Needless to say, I didn't let any caterpillar escape my sight, nor did I let them get close to me. Every time I bit my lips and squirmed, Tahry's head was right under my nose. "Where? Where?" she would ask. I would squint my eyes as I turned away and pointed in the general direction of where I last saw the creature. She saved me and took care of me. She let me be a kid as she took me under her wing.

The sun was still high in the sky when we were told to go back to the village. What a nice surprise: our work hours were shorter than at Lake Kair. As soon as we got to the house, all of us rushed into the cool river. Jumping, teasing, and screaming, all fifty of us went to one spot in the river under a big shade tree. We could hear the girls in the other houses down the river were having fun as well. At first I hesitated, but it was too much fun to not participate. I screamed and squealed at the chilled river, laughing at Tahry's wet hair, at the current that was dragging my pants off my hip under the water, at the waves that we made, at anything that floated on the water, at the freedom of laughing. Tahry and I were the last to come out of the river. I believe Tahry was happy to hear me laugh. As we stepped out of the river, I told Tahry with my eyes: "Thank you for being my friend." Without a word between us, she acknowledged.

We went to the service building in the pagoda to have our dinner. After dinner, the leaders came back with stacks of thick, dull, white cotton cloth that opened up to shirts and sarongs. They looked more like flour bags than fabric to put on a body. The leaders distributed amongst themselves this cheap cotton that they later blackened in a feeble attempt to hide the texture. Along with this cheap fabric were two pairs of black rubber sandals that looked nice compared to the homemade sandals with soles cut from tires and strips of inner tube for straps. The new sandals were kept by the two top leaders in the house.

That same night, more leaders were picked among us to run the small girl groups. Tahry was picked to lead Sopad, Chenda, and me. She was trained on how to start a meeting, which she later passed on to us to repeat after her: "I'd like to express my respect to our government. I am grateful for this meeting. I'd like to express my respect for all girl comrades in this meeting."

The second part of the meeting was to bring out in the open any comrade who was not doing the right thing during the day, or to state specifically that you didn't have any correction or recommendation for any comrade within the meeting.

Every day was a working day. After the dry rice planting was done, we were told to build levees. After a while some of us learned how to look busy, to walk slower, to take more bathroom breaks, and to infect ourselves with frequent spells of disease.

I was the best at the art of deception, or perhaps people around me closed their eyes and turned the other way because I was one of the younger girls in the group, and I was the skinniest. When the sun was at its peak, the heat was unbearable. Sopad and I would excuse ourselves and walk a distance to rest under a shade tree and take time to give each other an *air catcher* treatment. This brutal massage was supposed to help you feel better if you weren't feeling well. Between the knuckles of the index and middle fingers, the massager would pinch and pull your flesh, repeating on the same spot until the blood vessels broke under the skin and the flesh would turn purplish red. The same process was repeated on the next empty spot around your neck and your shoulder. Instead of giving each other this massage, Sopad and I would spend most of our time talking and giggling. There were endless stories to talk about. Many times, we laughed so hard our stomachs would hurt. Of course, when other people walked by, we would try to be serious, pinching and pulling the previous day's bruises. Yes, it hurt, but it was better than standing in the hot sun and passing baskets of dirt to the next person while sweating and exhausted, with our heads ringing from the extreme heat.

Sometimes Tahry joined us, but most of the time she would stay in the sun, working hard. Many times I wondered why she worked so hard. She should not have worried so much about being targeted by the Black Uniforms because she had dark skin.

Tahry was good at the *hair popping* treating, a remedy for headaches. This was done by gathering a clump of hair about one centimeter thick, wrapping its length two or three times around your middle finger while keeping about two inches of space between the scalp and your middle finger, pressing the hand with the hair on the middle finger on the skull, then quickly pulling the hair up. It was believed that your scalp would generate a pop sound if you truly had a headache. Otherwise it wouldn't. Tahry could pop any short hair on any head with or without a headache. Sopad and I would laugh at the sensation and the sound it made. We would goofily plead for Tahry to do it again, and fight to take a turn to be treated. It hurt, but the sensation and the laughing outweighed the pain. Sitting on the ground, my back straight, neck stiff, and head still under Tahry's hands, my eyes would squint and my heart pump with anticipation, waiting for the split-second popping of the scalp, so that I would roll out quickly on the ground and laugh with the quick sensation of pain. Once our shadows stretched longer on the ground, we would go back to the working spot.

We found a group of boys that we usually worked with—or more likely, they found us. The oldest one in this group was a man named Tab. Bong Tab was strong and worked hard as he picked up our loads. He was an outgoing man, and all the girls liked him, even the native ones. But he seemed to prefer helping out us lighter-skinned girls. He always made us laugh. For example, he would give us girls about one pound of dirt in our basket and teasingly ask us if it was too much. If he ever saw a grass root in the dirt along his shovel, he would tease us girls. "I found one, I found one." At first we would be mad, thinking this guy was making fun of us, because even while politely fighting for grass roots, we expected a man to give us some dignity. But then he would go on: "What's the matter, you don't like grass roots anymore?" and he would pick it up and start brushing and chewing it as if it was a piece of chocolate, adding with his eyes closed: "If only I knew then what I know now, I would have saved lots of money." We would all burst out laughing with him.

Sometimes there was complete silence for long periods, with only the sound of shovels pecking on the dried dirt and the shuffling of steps to empty the baskets. Bong Tab would start singing out loud the new regime songs. We all tightened our stomachs, laughed under our breath, and gave him a look that asked, What would we do without you? The next thing we knew, the other groups were singing along with him. To me this was Bong Tab's way of saying, "God damn it, I am tired!" But when he was singing every morning like he usually did, it meant, "I am over here, light-skinned girls." And we would reply by never failing to show up.

He would often tell me: "You look sick, Comrade Little. Better go and catch that air before it turns into a tornado." I would smile like I would when a big brother was taking care of me, and off I would go with Sopad, giggling and trying to keep from running.

Speaking of brothers—I had not seen Ee since we were staying in Seur. I didn't know what they were having him do, but I was certain he was okay, for there wasn't any death to speak of recently.

Working with Bong Tab's group, we got to meet two other sisters, Bong Van and Bong Nick. They came from a well-known family in Battambang. I had heard of them, but never met them until then. They stayed in a different house, but we worked together most of the time. Bong Nick was younger than Bong Van but taller and bigger. She and Bong Tab always had clever responses for each other, and they kept us laughing. Knowing the two sisters came from the same city as us made me feel closer to them. I always wondered how they got to the same general area as we did after the Black Uniforms took over, but I never asked. Some things are better left alone. That was one of them, especially knowing both of their parents were taken away to be corrected by the Black Uniforms and never returned.

I saw another girl who went to the same school as me and lived in the same block, but I couldn't say hello to her. Her name was Narith. When she first saw me, she gave me the corner-eye look and quickly turned away with her nose perched up in the air, which was like telling me: "Don't you dare say hi to me." She had changed. I used to go to her house and play with her. With her pretty face, dark skin, and overzealous personality, she had blended into the Black Uniforms well. Narith also had grown into a young woman, not much bigger than me, but definitely curvier. I left her alone. In fact, I was glad she didn't want to acknowledge me. It happened too many times that people turned their friends in to the Black Uniforms.

Later on, Narith's flamboyant personality ended, and she became subdued and somewhat depressed after she became the talk of the pack for losing her rack of white front false teeth in the river.

Another person who changed and wanted nothing to do with me was my very own Cousin Linda. After all, she was darker-skinned than me. She took after Ouv. Linda was always with us on the girl team, but after she was promoted to be a leader of thirty girls, she was a complete stranger to me. Unlike Narith, Linda was passive with her message. Whenever she saw me, she would look at me without expression and turn away.

I wanted to think that Linda had disassociated herself from me because she was fearful of having her past education record exposed. I wanted to say I understood, but deep down inside I was bitter and hurt by the way she disowned me. I didn't have any memory of when Linda came to live with our family in Battambang, but ever since I knew right from wrong, Linda was always with me. She was always sister Linda.

One night I was urinating, and there she was, squatting next me. The feeling I had for Linda was a strange and unfamiliar one. She was like a stranger who knew everything about me, yet I didn't really know what she thought about me. Not knowing what to do, I felt vulnerable. I wanted to walk away from the situation, but I hesitated after I stood up. *Should I say something? Maybe I shouldn't. What if she wants to say something? Maybe I don't want to know.* I waited and waited, standing still in the dark, hoping that Em's love would be strong enough to keep us together. I was ready to be yelled at any minute. Instead, Linda got up and said softly and with great pain: "I can't pee. I haven't been able to pee for a while now. It hurts." Instantly, she was my sister again, just like she used to be. We were bonded together because of Em's love.

Every night before we went to bed, they made us sit in a meeting in our three-, ten-, or thirty-person group.

In our small group, we squatted on the dirt floor in a circle, and Tahry started the meeting with the usual chanting "I'd like to express my respect to our government. I am grateful for this meeting. I'd like to express my respect for all girl comrades in this meeting."

What we talked about during the rest of the meeting depended on whether or not there was a leader walking around us. If they were near us, we talked louder and used words and phrases that were pleasing to their ears. The approved lingo included terms like: "government," "comrades," "capitalism is the enemy of our society," and "freedom from the corruption of capitalism." As soon as they walked away, we switched back to the giggling conversation that teenage girls have. As soon as some other group of girls finished their meeting, we would also finished ours, and we would sing and practice dance steps with the new regime songs. With these songs, I focused on the rhythms and forgot about the lyrics and the meanings. The songs made me feel good. At one point, Chenda reminded me how crazy I was to enjoy and sing such stupid songs. I never felt comfortable singing their songs again because she was right.

I never saw Chenda giggle or smile. She always looked tired and mad, with her eyebrows tied together and lips pouting. Even working under the sun every day, Chenda showed no sign of color on her face. Her completion was more gray than white. She didn't say much and hardly moved. With her dull, black, short hair, she looked frail and vulnerable.

One thing that I enjoyed after the nightly meeting was listening to stories told by one of the oldest girls in the troop, who was at least twenty-five years old. She slept on the veranda just on the other side of the wall where I was sleeping. She told us about her romance with a French guy. Many girls, including the leaders, clustered around her, trying to get even closer. When she told her stories, she would always lie down on her side and prop herself up with a pillow under her rib cage. Under the moonlight she told her story with body movements and arms that flowed back and forth above her like a soft lace curtain.

One day she described how long and beautiful her hair used to be. When she said that, I looked at her closer, and I could see, even under the new regime's short-hair law, she was still beautiful. The desire in her voice along with her expressions and emotions were something I had never seen in Em or any of my aunts. Then she whispered with her head and body perched closer to the crowd: "You know, the French guys like big tits." I was embarrassed to hear her say that, but at the same time I found myself feeling my own chest and thinking, *A French guy would never even look at me.* I always wondered what happened to the French guy and why she didn't go with him. It was strange that a girl with her life experience and age was there in the troop with us. It was rumored that the young woman was once a lady of the night. I wondered why prostitution is so bad for girls but nothing is said to the guys who use them. I remembered a conversation between Pa and Mr. Savan when Pa said, "I would rather have my daughters become prostitutes in other countries than live under this regime."

Tahry loved to tickle me—violently—and I never liked it. Physically, it was always startling, and it hurt at the same time. Emotionally, it made me feel frustrated and angry that she would not stop, and at the same time, I would be laughing because I was ticklish. As time went by I became so sensitive to Tahry's body movements that all she had to do was move quickly and I would jump. When other girls saw what would happen to me, they wanted to have fun, too, so they would startle me with their quick hand movements without even touching me, and I would unconsciously respond as though their hands were all over me. When that happened, everybody had fun except me.

I was exhausted from it all and also angry. I decided I needed to put a stop to this stupid treatment. I was more mad at Tahry than anybody. So the next time she started her trick, I yelled so loud the whole troop in the house could hear me. I threatened that if she ever did it again, I would swear at her mother. That was the worst thing a girl could say to a friend. A girl's mother is her god and angel. We feel her gentle love with us everywhere we are. It is by her love that we never feel alone. It is their love that makes us special.

Tahry immediately retreated and shriveled up into a ball, lying next to her belongings bag. I sat straighter and taller and looked at her. The world stopped for the longest moment, and all eyes were on me. My eyes shifted from Tahry to the rest of the eyes in the room. With my stare I gave them all the same warning.

The next few days, Tahry had nothing to do with me. She didn't talk much to anybody in our small group. One night she quietly cried, and Sopad began sniffling as well.

I poked Sopad gently. "What's the matter?"

"I miss my mother."

I missed Em, too, but lately it hadn't crossed my mind that I might never see her again. My only thought was that I *would* see her, but I didn't know when. Strangely, I found myself unable to cry. Was I growing apart from Em? No, that was not possible. I felt guilty for not thinking of Em every day. I knew I loved her and missed her—but how come I couldn't cry? I could only feel my blood churning in my stomach and the warm sensation that it generated. I felt light-headed and hollow in the heart. I hated these people, the Black Uniforms.

Tahry and Sopad continued to cry until Bong Lang hushed them up. Bong Lang was gentle to Tahry with her words in a way that I thought was impossible to come from her personality as the tough woman.

"Stop crying. It does no good to cry. You don't want them to investigate."

Tahry cried harder, but not louder.

I wanted to ask Bong Lang what she meant when she said, "You don't want them to investigate," but I knew better than to talk about secrets in the night. It was well known that people had been taken to be corrected because their night conversations had been overheard by Black Uniforms who stayed under the house or in nearby bushes to listen for enemy conversations.

The next day I learned that Tahry's father was an old regime soldier who was taken by the Black Uniforms for training. She never saw him again.

One day Chenda and I made a plan to go to look for our uncle and his family. We decided to get sick, and when everybody was gone to work, we snuck out and wandered in the neighborhood. With all the able bodies out working, we walked through a ghost village, taking care to blend in with the bushes and fences.

We saw an old man in worn boxer shorts and a thin, dirty, white T-shirt who hunched as he walked. His eyes were fixed in our direction, and he was trying to hurry toward us. It was clear that he wanted to talk.

"Where are you going?" he inquired.

"We are looking for our uncle and aunt. Uncle Tre and Aunt Cheng."

"Tre who has nine children? They used to live in Poipet?" he asked with excitement.

It turned out that the old man was a distant relative to Aunt Cheng. He had let my aunt's family build a hut on his property next to his red-tile-roof house, hidden behind thick bushes and trees along the river.

Most homes in Seur were built with tile roofs and were bigger than those in the French Village. The residents of Seur were primarily farmers, but the people in French Village were mostly peasants. Many Seur families had already escaped to Thailand.

When we got to the hut, I was surprised to see both my uncle and aunt were home, not reporting to work. My aunt and uncle had not changed the way they look. They had not had to go through starvation. Looking at them, I realized my family's bad luck. We were supposed to be in this village, just like my uncle's family. Pa had a great plan, but the Black Uniforms killed it.

Uncle Tre had become blind, and Auntie stayed

home to watch over him and my little cousins. I learned that my Cousin Ngy was in a girls' labor camp near French Village. My uncle didn't have much to say, but kept smiling. We made a point to let him know that Em and Pa consented to let us go with him whenever an opportunity presented itself for us to escape to Thailand.

Auntie Cheng was so happy to see us. She took us in her hut and fed us. Just as I expected, her generosity and love never stopped. Her most overused phrase was, "Just eat, my dear child, don't think." I never got tired of hearing this phrase over and over. She sent us back to the girls' camp with about a pound of roasted dried rice in a bag made out of an old rag. It was a gift that made me aware that I still had a heart that felt heavy and warm, sad for my own situation, but glad that I was special to someone else besides Em.

The next few nights, before Chenda and I went to bed, we quietly sucked on a mouthful of the roasted rice. It was a matter of mutual respect not to beg for private food among friends, so neither Tahry nor Sopad asked to share. I felt ashamed for not offering my fortune to Tahry or Sopad, even though they didn't offer to me when they had some. However, I felt better when I remembered auntie's advice: "Eat and don't think."

Even though we had more to eat at Seur, we still never had enough. Food was always on my mind. With my skinny body and being one of the youngest in the camp, I took advantage of the situation. I got sick almost every day, and when I did get sick, I was always scouting for food and brought it back to share with Chenda when she returned from work.

I would begin to scavenge as soon as the girls left for work and got back just before they returned. Sometimes I would go with Tahry or Sopad. One of us would climb mango trees and jump up and down on branches to shake the fruit down while the other picked them from the ground. The sound of the leaves and the branch rattling along with the falling fruit in the calm, windless orchard was loud. We were selective of the location within the orchard, the tree size, and the branch before we took the risk. We didn't know what would happen for sure, but we were told that stealing from the government would make us enemies of society. We also knew that the Black Uniforms had only one kind of punishment for their enemies. Still, I stole—I stole from the government that stole from the people. I stole to survive, but never stole from any other girl, just their government.

One time while I was collecting mangoes from the ground, Tahry shook a branch right above me that had clusters of mangoes as well as big, red-ant nests. From the branch twenty feet above, green mangoes landed on me with a dull pain, and my body was sprinkled with red ants. Those ants were not happy, and they bit me, but I had no choice but to stay quiet and hurry to collect the mangoes. After a few more shakes of the branch, Tahry rushed down to help me collect the fruit and leave the crime scene in a hurry.

We hid in a bush with our mangoes, still covered with ants. Tahry stiffened up and looked at me while I was still brushing off the leftover ants on my neck and near my head. Then she started to laugh out loud. "You looked so funny when those clumps of ant nests dropped on your head. I thought you were going to scream, but no, you were doing the ant dance."

"You were supposed to stop shaking when I was under the branch!" I replied.

Tahry was not going to let me spoil her fun. She continued laughing and imitated me until I joined her laughing. We ate as many mangoes as we could and took the rest to Chenda and our small group without being too conspicuous.

At times I got bored with mangoes, and I gathered my courage to explore neighboring villages by myself to look for food. Each village had a cooking shack where people cooked for the whole village. These people were always the leader's family and their favorite comrades. Every day, everybody in a village ate together under one roof near the cooking shack. The days when each individual family had their own ration were gone.

I would search for these cooking shacks and roam around them. Once there, I searched for the woman with the biggest heart. Yes, I could tell how big her heart was through her eyes. Once I found the biggest heart, I waited for the opportunity to offer a helping hand. Almost all of them would start asking: "Where are your parents?"

"They are in French Village."

Even more curious, they would ask, "What you doing here?"

"I am with the girl team."

Thinking I was too young to be in a girl team, they gasped. "Girls' camp? How old are you?"

"Fourteen."

"Does your mother know where you are?"

I wished they would never ask me that last question for it always made me yearn for Em and recall the possibility that she might no longer be with us.

The way they looked at me after they learned more about my situation was frightening. It appeared they didn't think I would never see Em again. Some of them made comments like, "How can you live with only skin and bone?" I had never seen my own reflection since I left Poipet almost a year ago, but I believed them, for I felt pain when I laid down to sleep at night as my bones pinched my skin against the wooden floor.

I always left the cooking shacks with some food that I couldn't wait to show and share with Chenda. I prayed for God to take care of the big-hearted women who were my angels for being so kind and gentle. I never went back to the same cooking shack twice. I'm not sure why.

One time a woman in a cooking shack gave me about two pounds of palm sugar in a Gigo[17] can. It was the first time I had tasted sugar since the Black Uniforms took over the country. My heart was pounding, and I imagined Chenda's excited face as the woman poured the hot, gooey sugar into the can. I don't remember the woman's face, but I do remember the scene just like it was yesterday.

The first anniversary of the Black Uniforms taking control of the country was coming soon. At Uncle Tre's hut, I got to see Cousin Ngy again. She had snuck away from a girls' camp to visit her parents. The temperature

---

[17] *Gigo* is a brand name of baby formula. It came in an aluminum can about four inches in diameter and eight inches in height, with snap-on lids. Most Cambodians who lived in a city prior to the Black Uniforms would feed their infants with this formula. During the Black Uniforms era, this container became a valued possession for hiding and carrying food.

was so hot that the river by their hut had dried up, so we were all scraping the bottom of the river looking for freshwater mussels when Ngy said, "Little Girl, I don't know when I will ever see you again. Probably never." I felt the tenderness of her words, but I didn't share her feeling of sadness. Compared to all the things that happened to us over the past year, not being able to see my cousin again was not the worst thing to feel sad about.

A couple of days later, Chenda told me that Hong was back in the boys' camp. I didn't get a chance to see him because I was sick that day, not strategically, but physically. I was sick with diarrhea, probably from eating too many mangoes. I kept running to the bathroom area, and after a while I didn't have the strength nor time to dig a hole. I thought for sure I wouldn't survive. It was common for people to die within twenty-four hours from the onset of diarrhea. I thought about Em and told myself that I couldn't die. Dying would be too painful for Em to endure. I chanted quietly and softly in my head: *I am not going to die. I am not going to die …*

The day before the first anniversary celebration, I was still alive but very weak when Chenda came to me and told me that Hong and Ee planned to escape that night. She looked worried and sad. When I learned that Hong was waiting at the river to see me, I was excited and wanted to show him I had the strength to go with them. I pushed myself to get up and stepped onto the veranda but realized right there that I was too weak to go any further. I sat on the first step of the staircase so Hong could see me while Chenda went down to him. Even from a distance, I could see Hong's eyes looking right at me. Then he quickly turned away, and I could tell that he was crying. Moments after Chenda and Hong talked, Hong turned away from Chenda. Fully clothed, he walked into the river, getting half of his body wet. He splattered the water on his face. I watched him stand there like a statue, desperate to be rescued. I was scared that people would notice the strange situation and would hurt him and all of us. God heard my prayers when Hong stepped out of the river. Dripping wet, he walked away and never turned around.

Lots of things came into my mind at all once. What was going to happen next? What did I need to do? Where would we meet?

I was still sitting on the staircase when Ee walked up, strong with energy and looking happy. He stood and talked to Chenda under a big, shady tree by the river. Ee kept looking at me. Unlike Hong, Ee was strong and muscular. Somehow he had convinced the Black Uniforms to let him work in the kitchen for the boy team. I was happy to see him. It was the second time I had seen him since we moved to Seur about two months earlier. The first time I saw him, he didn't even acknowledge me. I thought for sure he had been converted by the Black Uniforms and had forgotten our roots and family. Knowing he planned to escape made me feel glad I was wrong about him. The sun was sinking fast when Ee looked at me again, shared the biggest smile, then walked away. I will always remember this last smile, the smile that I hung onto and replayed whenever I missed him.

That night I packed my bag and lay down quietly, without a word to Chenda or anyone else. I wished we were brought up to be more affectionate about sharing our feelings so I could at least hold on to my big sister's hand, but that night we didn't even fight for extra elbow room like we usually did. The night was quiet, but not peaceful.

I thought that Em, Pa, and Kheang would be happy for us. But then I thought, *What if I can't make it all the way to the border?*

Pa had said, "Go whenever you have a chance to leave this hell. I can't help you, and you can't help me if we both stay here."

I thought: How will Ee and Hong let us know they are here? I won't sleep tonight. I will wait for a sign.

When the leaders blew the whistle in the morning, I was about to throw up.

What happened? How could I fall asleep and not hear any signal? Were they here but they got in trouble? Did they leave without me? Maybe they thought I couldn't make it. Maybe I *couldn't* have made it. Was there a change in plan?

The celebration began with music heard all over the village, then speeches on the new regime's progress, then food and a special drink. We lined up for rations from a ladle of ice-cold Coke that had been dumped into a fifty-gallon cast iron pot with a big block of ice. Ee and Hong were nowhere to be seen. The dull pain in my stomach from the night was spreading to my chest, my ears, and my head. My hands and feet felt cold in the middle of Cambodia's hottest season. My breath was short and quiet. I knew then I would never be the same. The Black Uniforms had changed me permanently.

For the rest of the day I asked myself repeatedly: How can my brothers leave me? Are they okay? Where are they now?

The next day, Chenda and I were sick from work, and we snuck off to visit Uncle Tre and his family. I knew there was a good chance that Ee and Hong had gone with Uncle and his family, but we were not thinking straight when we decided to check out for sure. The old man in the same old outfit watched us from his fence. He stopped us from getting closer to Uncle Tre's hut. With his voice shaking, he nervously chased us out, quietly shouting: "Go back! Hurry! Hurry! They are all gone. Nobody there anymore."

Chenda and I quickly turned away. As we did, I saw Uncle Tre's hut in the distance. The Black Uniforms were congregating there. My heart was thumping against my rib cage as I tippy-toed away, feeling blessed and grateful for the old man who had looked out for us, protecting us from harm.

During the next few days, my heart sank deep. I felt abandoned. How could our uncle leave us behind? He was not blind after all. Now I understood why Cousin Ngy told me she didn't think that we would see each other again.

In the field, I overheard people talking about us. Bong Tap made a point to tell us he was mistaken in thinking that Ee had been converted. Tahry and Sopad disassociated themselves from us. I spent the next few days waiting for the Black Uniforms to come to take us away. I imagined what they would do to me. Maybe they would have mercy because I was still a kid. But we were the sisters of the enemies. About a week later, I saw one of Mr. Savan's boys rowing a canoe by the shade tree in front of the girls' camp. He was wearing Ee's jacket. It made me sick.

Chapter 9

Planting Season of 1976 to Harvest Season of 1977

After Ee and Hong left, the Black Uniforms never came around to look for Chenda and me. As time went by, Ee and Hong's escape seemed to slip away from people's minds, and things seemed to get better. Tahry, Sopad, and I were back to normal.

Before the harvest season of 1976 was over, about a month after Ee and Hong left, the Black Uniforms decided our work at Seur was done, so they moved us again. This time, we were moved back to Chamnoam. Because it was a hot and dusty day, they let us rest in a house with a pond full of lotus stems in the back-yard. I was very tired, hungry, and thirsty when Tahry came back from the pond with a lotus stem and leaf in her hand. She sat beside me and said, "Do you know the lotus stem smells sweeter than the lotus flower?" Without hesitation, I leaned over to smell the stem as

Tahry put it between my nose and my upper lip. When I bent close to the stem, she pushed it to my skin and quickly dragged it away. The spikes along the stem grabbed my skin and revealed raw flesh. I jumped and yelled in disbelief that she would do this to me. I gave her a look that said I didn't want anything to do with her again. At first she was laughing, but then the laugh turned eerily quiet.

A rumor was going around that we would be moved to Lake Kair again to work on the field for planting rice. The planting season was not a good time to be in Lake Kair. In the past, farmers would prepare food and take it to Lake Kair to make it last for the whole planting season. Most of Lake Kair would be covered with flood water. The only thing that could be consumed from the field was the wild vegetation. Fish were hard to catch because open flood water was everywhere. Many of our family friends from Poipet had died at Lake Kair during the last planting season.

Besides the fact that Lake Kair was a dangerous place to be during the monsoon season, Chamnoam was closer to French Village, which meant we might get to see Em again. To avoid being moved from Chamnoam, Chenda and I decided to be sick. We didn't eat the rations they gave us. We basically starved ourselves. The next day, when the team started to march again, the leaders let us stay behind and put us in the sick-house where Hong had stayed when he was sick with high fever.

Tahry chose to go with the others, and we never said goodbye. I never saw or heard from her again. I lost my best friend and thought about her a lot. I wonder if she even knew that she was my best friend. I still thought, *If I a daughter, I will name her Tahry.*

The sick-house was in an old elementary school yard with several buildings. Ours was a long building that used to house about four classrooms, but the walls separating the classrooms had been removed to form one long room. The building was covered by shingles and walled with wooden slats. Opposite from our building and separated by an assembly area and flagpole, stood a building of the same size for the sick men and boys. The third building was where the Black Uniforms stayed. They called themselves "nurses."

Chenda and I shared a small bamboo bed that stood above the dirt floor. The bed next to ours was shared by Bong Van and Bong Nick. There were many sick women and girls around us on the beds that lined the walls of all different ages, but no children. The mothers of sick children would never trust the Black Uniforms with their kids.

During this stay we got to know Bong Van and Bong

Nick very well. They shared with us the story of how their parents were taken away. They told us with pride how bravely their mother had insisted that she go with her husband, even though she knew what would happen to her.

Bong Nick loved to tell stories. One of her favorites was about Dracula. She told stories with her hands, facial expressions, and body movements. One time when she was telling me the Dracula story, I pleaded with her to stop because with her pale white skin, big white eyes, and bony face, she looked like a vampire to me.

At night, Chenda and I used to fight for extra elbow room, but when we overheard Bong Nick and Bong Van doing the same thing, we would stop. The next night the routine would start over again.

A Chinese girl was at the end of the room by herself. She always lay on her stomach and would cry for help with her Chinese accent: "Help me, please. Somebody help me. Sisters, comrades, help me, please. It is too painful. Comrade nurse, I need your help now," The Black Uniform nurses told us she had an infection in the middle of her back that was getting bigger and bigger, and maggots were crawling around her.

A new patient came in one late afternoon. They carried her in a hammock and dropped her on the bed on the opposite wall from us. With only a walk space between us, I noticed that she didn't move or make a sound. Many flies were already on her. The next morning, the Black Uniforms covered their noses with their red-and-white-checkered kramas, and with the same cart that they used to carry our rations, and they flopped her stiff body onto the cart and pushed it outside. That was the closest to a dead person I had ever experienced. I couldn't help but think that last night I slept next to a corpse.

The dead girl appeared to have some connection with upper-ranked Black Uniforms when one of them showed up with a rifle (not every Black Uniform carried a rifle) to inspect her body. Chenda and I were watching them, but made no direct eye contact. Then one of them walked toward us and asked, "Is that you, Chenda?"

I did not recognize the devil and neither did Chenda.

He continued, "It is me. Don't you remember? My aunt married your uncle Tre."

Then I remembered him. We had stayed a short time together at Uncle Tre's house in Poipet. He had grown into a strong young man. We, on the other hand, were shriveled up to nothing. How did he get involved with the Black Uniforms? What did he want from us? Apparently nothing—he was just excited to see us. He told us that the girl who just passed away was one of his cousins on my Aunt's side. Based on the way he talked, he appeared to have had a crush on Chenda in our previous life.

Since we were unable to work, our ration was much less than that of our working comrades. We were given a scoop of rice soup with rock salt for lunch and dinner while our working comrades were given thicker rice soup and maybe some fish and a few vegetables. There was no medicine nor any care provided. We were left to tend to ourselves.

Every morning before the lunch ration, we would sit around a fire outside the building to keep ourselves warm. At least that's what we told the Black Uniforms. But the fire was used mainly to burn any insects we might catch. After a while there were not many insects either.

I watched a girl carefully burn the hair off a rope made from cowhide. Then for two or three days she boiled the rope over low heat until it finally turned gooey. She finally tasted it. After a few more bites, she handed it to me. The brown goo and a piece of soggy, hairy string were still on the bottom of the small, beat-up black pot. I took a bite with her spoon, and the smell of an old, dirty, sick cow exploded in my mouth. The texture and the taste of a rotten carcass quickly saturated my body through every open pore, but it was too late, I had already swallowed it. I couldn't throw up even though I wanted to, and I couldn't eat any more.

Soon there would be a school of fish just liked last year, but no one was allowed to fish since all cooking was done in the cooking shack. I imagined fish swam away because the fishing team could not catch them fast enough. I wanted to sneak out of the sick-house, but it was impossible for I would have to roam around in the rain that came almost every day. Then I'd have to sneak back in wet clothes, which would be obvious to the Black Uniforms when they made their round for the second meal of the day. So for at least six months, I was confined to the dampness of the sick-house until the monsoon season was over and the river dried up again.

When the monsoon season was coming to an end, I waited anxiously for the receding river to become shallow enough to cross so I could sneak out to see Em, Pa, and Kheang. I had never been on the road to French Village from Chamnoam, but I had heard that French Village was down the river. Walking around the bushes along the river, I found a spot where the water was shallow enough to cross. On the other side of the river, I continued until the place looked familiar. I got to Mair's place before I arrived at our old hut. When Mair saw me, she grabbed me and took me into her big, tile-roofed house that she shared with the village leader.

With anguish and a sympathetic look, Mair could not wait to warn me: "Don't go to your hut!" She paused to control her emotion and added, "They have moved your family."

"Where are they?" I asked, interrupting Mair and fearing the worst.

"In Meeting Creek (*Ou Chuob*). They are okay. No one got hurt. They were moved soon after your brothers escaped."

Instantly I imagined how distressed and afraid Em, Pa, and Kheang must have been. I was not surprised, but still my heart broke at the sad news and knowing that I wouldn't get to see my family. I asked Mair a favor: "Won't you help me let them know that Chenda and I are okay?"

The Black Uniforms had taken my parents and Kheang away so that Ee and Hong would not come back to help them escape. I learned later that Ee had hired two men to come to our hut and do exactly that. The men were caught in crossfire with the Black Uniforms, and at least one of them was killed.

When I entered Mair's place, I realized that Cousin Linda was staying home with them. Somehow, Mair and Ouv were able to convince the Black Uniforms to let Cousin Linda do that. Linda was a lucky girl. When her parents were in trouble, Em took her in and provided care and education for her. When Em was in trouble, Linda's parents, who could then provide better care for her, took her back. I wished I was that lucky.

Mair gently rubbed my arms and told me how skinny I looked. She cried with her facial expressions and sounds, but without tears. She fed me steamed rice and salted fish. It was a treat that I couldn't wait to share with my sister.

When I stepped down from the house and was just about ready to go back to the sick-house, I saw Linda's younger sister. She was carrying a baby on her hip.

"Who is that?" I asked.

"My sister," she replied proudly.

"What is your baby sister's name?"

"Red Bitch," she answered with a big grin on her face.

Red Bitch was a name that played with words. "Red" usually referred to a newborn, but it was also a disgraceful way of referring to the Black Uniforms based on the more well-known name Khmer Rouge. Red was the most beautiful baby I had ever seen, perfect in features and beautiful in skin color. As I studied her, I couldn't help but wonder how long she would be able to survive. What a name!

Chenda and I rationed the food that I got from Mair's, but it didn't last long. When we could no longer endure the hunger, I would make the same trip to Mair's place. I found myself visiting Mair about twice a week, usually leaving soon after the Black Uniforms made their rounds for lunch ration. When I got to Mair's place, Linda would take me down the river past our old hut to find freshwater mussels. There were signs of a new family living in our hut, the hut we had built with our unskilled hands. I saw the papaya tree that Hong had planted getting taller, but there was no fruit. I asked Linda, "Why does the papaya tree not have any fruit?"

"It's a male papaya."

"Male papaya?"

"Yes, Hong planted a male papaya."

How were we supposed to know a male papaya from one that would produce fruit? Why did no one tell us?

Every time I walked by the hut, the memories of our starving and silent faces stared back at me. I felt comforted and sad at the same time. It was the last place our family had been together.

Linda and I would carry freshwater mussels back to Mair's place, boil them, and remove the shells. After splitting the meat, I would take my portion to Chenda and keep the other half for Linda. I would time myself to be on my way back to the sick-house before the workers returned to the village. Walking through the village and crossing the river, I would hustle to sneak back to the sick-house before the nurses returned to serve the second ration of the day.

Once when I was returning from Mair's place, the Chinese girl saw I was eating mango. She pleaded for some. I couldn't ignore her because she called to me: "Sister! Sister with mango. I just want one bite of a mango, please. It won't keep me alive, but I will die happy."

I couldn't help clean her, and I couldn't help move her because I was afraid of maggots and disease. But maybe I could hand her a wedge of mango quickly enough that the maggots would not get a chance to crawl on me or for a disease to spread to me. I felt embarrassed for even thinking about walking to her. What would the rest of the girls think? Was I stupid? Would they think that I was better than them? No, I just wanted to do something for the girl, and handing her a wedge of mango didn't seem so bad.

So I did. I walked to her without looking on the ground near her in case there were maggots crawling around, not looking anywhere else but at her face. She thanked and blessed me out loud as soon as she saw me walking toward her. Her eyes were bright, energetic, and full of thanks and blessings, more than her words could describe. She continued to thank and bless me for the rest of the night until she tired out. She never pleaded for any other help that night. She died the next day. She had no friends or relatives to know what happened to her. No one knew anything about her or who she was. But I was happy for her, for she was no longer suffering.

After the Chinese girl died, I desperately wanted to see Em, Pa, and Kheang. We were told that Meeting Creek was in the midst of tree lines against the horizon east of the river. It was so far that if we went, we would not be back in time for roll call. I thought about Ee and Hong. What happened to them? Maybe the Black Uniforms did catch them. They always claimed they did when someone escaped. I imagined my love for my family was so strong that they could feel me and they wouldn't give up on me, so they could be strong and we could be together again. Hong told me once that if I ever find myself sad and missing him, I should talk to the moon, the same moon he would talk to. So through the moon I talked to Pa, Em, Ee, Hong, and Kheang. "If you miss me as much as I miss you, look at the moon, and you shall feel my love; talk to the moon and I shall feel your love. They can separate us, but they can't separate the moon from us. The moon you see tonight is the same moon that I can see. Whenever you miss me, look at the moon."

I felt lucky that I was able to continue finding food

for Chenda. I needed her to keep me wanting to beat all odds. She gave me strength. We fought many times over space on the bed, but we never fought over food. Whenever I could find things to eat, Chenda was always on my mind, and I couldn't wait to share with her. I don't remember Chenda sharing any food with me. The only thing she could catch was snails, and the only thing she could climb was the levee because she was very fragile and frail.

The last few times I visited Mair, she was always lying down, covered head to toe. I was worried about her well-being, and Linda would always say Mair didn't feel well and there was nothing to worry about.

Finally, on that one last day, the mussels were nearly impossible to find because the monsoon season had begun and the river was rising again. Determined to find some food to take back to Chenda, Linda and I went to the harvested rice field behind the house to find some mice. We took a garden hoe and a piece of hot coal. In the field, we dug and smoked the mice out of their burrows. We lost track of time, and I was worried about being caught on the trip to Chenda, so we hurried back to the house. While Linda and I were skinning and cleaning our catch, Mair spoke with stiff muscle and an angry tone: "You keep coming here and using up all the wood to cook your mussels, and now your mice. By the time you leave, there will be nothing else for me to use."

I had no reply. She was right, and I was wrong to think she could love me as Em would. My head felt numb and my ears rang. I was embarrassed, hurt, and feeling self-pity. But I tried hard to hold my tears. When I left, my eyes leaned on Linda for comfort. She seemed to understand me, and without a word I told her that I was sorry I had overstayed my welcome. *I am sorry to put you in this situation.* A bit of anger tainted my last thought: *I wish you and your family luck, and I hope I never get to see you again.* Linda handed me the skinned mice, skewered on a string, and kept none for herself. I took them without thanking her and wondered if Em would say to Linda what Mair had just said to me.

I was running late, and the workers had already returned from the fields, so I waited until the bell rang for the workers to go to the eating shack for dinner before sneaking out of Mair's house. There were lots of things going on in my mind. *Where do I go to find food now? How much longer will Chenda and I survive in the sick-house? How can Mair be so mean? The monsoon season has already started with the gloomy sky, and the rains have already raised the river level, so I won't be able to come here again in the next week or so. Why couldn't Mair wait for just for a couple more days? Then I will be out of her way.*

Down the river, I walked slowly to the shallow part. Children were playing in the rising river while their parents were in the eating shack. The water level was much higher than earlier in the day. I could no longer see its bottom where I crossed. The shrubs and bushes along the banks didn't look the same anymore. Some bushes were already covered by the soft, flowing current.

I had no choice but to try to find my way across the river. I secured my small cotton sack filled with skinned mice around my neck, then stepped into the river and felt my way for the shallow part. The closer I got to the middle, the stronger the current worked its way against my legs. The water was up to my chest when the current pushed me, and my feet could no longer touch the bottom. As I bobbed up and down in the river, I cried out for help. I saw children getting scared and running away from me to the riverbank. I cried for help, but I had no hope, for all the adults were in the eating shack. I heard the children screaming: "Chinese drowning, Chinese drowning!" I thought about Chenda. I was breathing a mixture of air and water now. I thought about Chenda waiting for me. How hard would she take this? Then I saw a strong man at the top of the river in a hurry to come down. I thought, *How is he going to help me without touching me? I can't let a man touch me.* I was a shy and starving fifteen-year-old girl.

He tightened the krama around his hip and prepared to jump in the river. Just then I got caught in a bush that was under the water; I grabbed onto the tips of the bush and continued fighting the current when the man yelled at me: "Stand up!" I didn't want to stand up, fearing I couldn't touch the bottom of the river. The man yelled again, louder this time: "Stand up! Before you break the bush and drown!" I followed his instruction and found out that the water was now at about my hip and I was able to pull my way to the riverbank. The man yelled as though he was mad at me even though he was trying to help me. "Stupid girl, asking for death. Don't know how to swim and trying to cross the river during the beginning of the flood," he said in reprimand.

The children laughed at my wet clothes and at the cotton sack that hung around my neck. They danced and chanted to their own made-up rhythm: "Drowning Chinese, drowning Chinese."

I knew Chenda must be worried for me because I was so late coming back to the sick-house. Walking back, I couldn't help but cry softly alone out of self-pity. I couldn't wait to be with my sister and tell her what had happened. I was wet, cold, and shaking when I found Chenda waiting for me by the bathroom. It was a spot where the Black Uniforms would not stroll by because of the stench and maggots, but there was my sister, anxiously waiting for me. It was the first time she ever came out to wait for me. She cried and ran to hug me as soon as she saw me. "What happened to you, little sister? I thought I would never see you again."

I cried back to her, "I almost drowned."

Chenda did her best to comfort me. "You don't have to do this anymore," she said.

We hugged for a long time by the stinky toilet. She wrapped one arm around my shoulders and the other arm around my head, and I covered my face in her bony chest and cried.

When Chenda heard what Mair did, she told me softly: "Tomorrow we will go to find our parents."

"Escaping?" I asked.

Confidently, Chenda said: "We will leave early in the morning before anybody gets up."

I was happy that Chenda made the decision for us to run away from the sick-house to find Em and Pa. I was also scared. What if we couldn't find them? We had never been to Meeting Creek, never even heard of the village until we learned that Pa, Em, and Kheang were there. What if we were too tired and weren't able to walk? What would the Black Uniforms do to us if they found out? Would they take us even further away from Em and Pa? Would they separate us? What would they do? It didn't matter. We had to see our parents again before it was too late.

That night we didn't sleep. We waited until everybody was deeply asleep, and we snuck out of the sickhouse, crossed Road 160, and away from the river toward the east, searching for Em. We couldn't see very well, but we knew we were heading in the right direction. The fields were uneven and mostly muddy from being freshly plowed, which made them difficult to walk across. When the sun came up, we could no longer see the sick-house. We needed to get to the tree lines before nightfall. Chenda looked exhausted, and the more I saw her exhaustion, the more energetic I became to push her to try harder. I knew I could not carry her, and I didn't want to stay in the field during the night.

"Tuch, Jair can't go on any more," Chenda said as she stood in the mud and gave up trying. The trip was too much for her, for she had never stepped out of the sick-house since we were taken in, which had been about a year now.

"No, Chenda, you can't give up. How can I go see our parents without you? I can't leave you here. You don't belong here."

The image of Chenda lying lifeless in the ditch and stuck in the mud was blurring my vision, fracturing a new spot in my heart. I pulled her from the foot-deep mud, led her, waited for her, and watched her shoulders droop and her arms swing slowly but uncontrollably. I knew then that I would have this memory with me forever. How we needed each other to survive! How we encouraged each other when one of us was weak!

Close to the tree line, we met a man sneaking out of work to find fish for his family. He told us where Meeting Creek was. We were slightly off course; we were to walk along the tree lines to the left. The village of Meeting Creek was mostly surrounded by a big creek that was overgrown with wild taro. A bridge over the creek led to the main road in the village. Once we snuck over the bridge, we walked behind the huts and long-houses that were built along the main road. We continued to ask the people we came across for our parents. Finally someone told us exactly where they were. Their hut was at the edge of the village, a good distance away from the rest of the people who were packed together in the longhouses.

It had been more than a year since I last saw Em. The thought of being able to be with her again made me anxious, nervous, and happy. When Chenda and I stepped on the small levee next to the hut, we both froze when we saw Em. She stared at us as if we were strangers until we called out to her. She let out a soft howl and cried with mixed emotions that she had never known could happen all at once: happiness, sorrow, and fear. She took a deep breath and gently felt her heartbeat with her hand, and as she exhaled, she summoned her disbelief. "Dear God," she said, "I didn't even recognize my own children. Like walking skeletons. Like walking skeletons." She reached over and gently stroked our bones with her shaky hands. I felt as though I had been blessed by an angel, and I would have loved to die in her arms.

I was proud to present the mice to Em, but told her nothing about what Mair had done to me.

Meeting Creek was where the Black Uniforms exiled the likes of former landowners, shop keepers, teachers, the Chinese, and the Vietnamese from various villages along the river. Pa and Em met more than one of these criteria. Besides, their sons had escaped. Perhaps they did this to see if we "pigs" could survive without the labor of others. For some, it was the first time to be away from their home. For all of us pigs, this move was punishment for the way we made a living prior to the Black Uniforms. In hope of making things as miserable as possible, the Black Uniforms moved the former residents of Meeting Creek to nearby villages. Only the pigs with hardly any belongings were allow to stay in Meeting Creek.

In the village there was a small pagoda stood next to a school that had no more than five classrooms. The pagoda and the school were wooden structures. They and a wooden house were the only places in the village that had been left undisturbed. Everything else had been destroyed and replaced by new longhouses made from bamboo and grass. These were one way for the Black Uniforms to eliminate individualism and privacy. They were built by the newcomers, most of whom, like Pa and Em, were not familiar with the village lifestyle. Newcomers who were more familiar with farm life helped their less fortunate comrades, and in doing so were able to convince the leaders to build their huts individually and away from the longhouses and closer to the creek.

Pa was able to stay away from the longhouses, but he didn't build an individual hut for Em and Kheang. Somehow, he managed to convince a farmer and his family to share a grass wall with him, where he extended a triangle thatch roof at one end of their hut. The roof sloped down to about five feet off the ground. The place had two exterior thatched walls. Inside, there was a bamboo bed raised a foot off the dirt where Pa, Em, and Kheang slept. This sleeping area was about the size of queen bed. Stepping down from the sleeping area, Pa had lined three to four wood panels on top of logs that were laid on the dirt. This wood panel floor allowed them to make two steps under the roof before they went to the sleeping area. It was where they scraped mud off their feet before crawling into the sleeping area. Still under the thatch roof but in the corner was where Em made her fire on the dirt floor.

The hut was among a cluster of five other huts next to the creek. The most elaborate hut among them was built by a former landowner, Om[18] Leung, with two of his strong, young newly-married sons. Most people married their children off to escape from being taken away by the Black Uniforms to the boys' and girls' camps. The second hut belonged to Om Leung's sister and her family of young children. Their oldest child was the same age as Kheang, and I called her "mean girl." Also living with them were his mother and his brother Nuong, a severely retarded man. The third hut belonged to another farmer with his Chinese wife and her father.

The fourth hut belonged to Om Pad, a former local teacher, and his family. Om Pad's wife was an older sister to one of Om Leung's daughters-in-law, and also the sister of the Black Uniform nurse who cared for Em in the French Village. The farmer who shared his hut with us had once been a Buddhist monk. He lived with his

---

[18] *Om* is a Khmer word referring to someone with respect as in an older uncle or aunt.

wife and a mildly retarded teenage son. His older son, Bong Keal, had a family of his own and lived in the hut next to us. Bong Keal's wife, Lai, was like a sister to me. She didn't have Chinese blood in her, but she treated Em like her own mother, and Em honored her by telling us to refer to her with a respectful Chinese status, Jair Lai. At that time, no one in Cambodia wanted to be known as Chinese, but Jair Lai proudly accepted her Chinese title.

Our place was too crowded when Chenda and I got there, so Pa slept in a hammock lent to us by Jair Lai. The place was basically empty. We had a small blanket that we shared, some old cloth that we used as pillows, and a grass mat to block the wind coming through the bamboo slats underneath us at night. In the daytime, we tucked away our belongings in the rolled-up grass mat that we slept on.

For the next couple of days, Chenda and I waited like hungry chicks for Em to bring us food. Because we were not supposed to be there, there was no food rationed for us, but somehow Em was able to secure rice for us. Without any place to hide or go, we lay down and covered ourselves with blankets during the days. Soon we saw we had no option but to surrender ourselves to the devils. If we were to go back to the sick-house, we would be taken to Lake Kair for sure.

Instead we took a risk and surrendered ourselves to the local girl team in Chark Village, which was down the river from French Village. This village was closer to Em and Pa than for us to go back to our old team in Lake Kair. In addition, Chark was by the river where we would be able to get some fish during the upcoming monsoon season.

Not knowing how we would be punished for breaking the law by deserting our old team, I felt as though I was walking into a torture camp. But it was worth every minute to see my family for a few days. At the time, I didn't fear for my life. I only imagined and readied myself for whipping and starvation as punishment. Perhaps that was because I trusted that my sister would get us out of the situation. She was the one who was going to have to speak for us.

No questions were asked, and no punishments were given by the leaders of the new girl team. They just took us in. It was not the leaders we had to worry about, and it was not the black-skinned girls that we had to deal with but the way we felt about ourselves. This time we were away, not just from our parents, but from any familiar faces. I felt as though we were being judged and discriminated against by girls having all different skin types. In time, I would get to know these girls better, and we would be okay, but I knew I was not going to find another Tahry in this crowd. I missed Tahry. I lost the urge to try to find extra food and just ate what they gave me and did what they told me. I stopped fighting with Chenda for elbow space. And I stopped talking or looking anybody in the eye, not caring what kind of eyes were around me.

One cold, windy, and rainy day, we were building a levee. I couldn't move let alone carry mud in a bamboo basket for the levee. I stood under the pouring rain, my legs deep in mud and my body shaking uncontrollably. I thought about Em and wondered if she could handle another loss. I didn't think I could make it any further. I thought about Pa, about how I didn't want him to feel bad about the way he treated me. A big, tight hug tried to stop me from shaking. It was Chenda. She whispered, "You're going to be fine. You are going to be okay, I promise you."

The scene attracted the attention of those who worked close to us. Soon we were surrounded by boys and girls who didn't know how to help us. One of the leaders yelled at Chenda with his strong, loud voice: "Why don't you take your sister to the village? Stupid girl."

Chenda propped me up and guided me through the muddy field in the cold and windy rain to the village. Sitting next to the fire with my sister's arm wrapped behind me, I started to feel better. But she had to go back to the field in the rain. My sister hesitated before stepping into the sheets of rain falling from the sky. She was going back to cover for me, to take my place so the Black Uniforms would leave us alone. I wished we could be free to be with our parents again. I thought about the leader who yelled at Chenda to take me into the village. I was sure that the leader didn't want me to die. I remembered overhearing he was a former taxi driver and I was certain he would rather have been a taxi driver than a leader for the Black Uniforms.

An old woman who was the owner of the fire start talking to me after Chenda left. "You feeling better, honey?" she asked in a weak and shaky voice.

"Yes, thank you," I replied.

She was in her mid sixties. It was strange to see a woman as old as she was surviving the hardship.

"Where are your parents, honey?" she asked.

It was a hard question, and I couldn't answer. I felt the depression in my chest as soon as she asked.

"How old are you? Where were you before the liberation?"

She kept asking questions and was able to make me talk until I felt like we were old friends. She left me alone for a few minutes, and when she came back out from the rice bin that had been converted to her living space, she said, "I have something for you in the bin."

Feeling my hesitation, she coaxed me along. "Go, get up there and you'll see."

I got into the rice bin with my clothes still wet. I saw a plate of steamed rice and a bowl of squash soup sitting in a corner as though they were offerings to one's ancestors. I turned around and looked into her eyes for confirmation. She replied, "Eat it, my dear grandchild. Don't think about anything." When she said that, I automatically thought about Em and longed to be next to her. The soup was cooked with pork meatballs and dried shrimp, just like the way Em used to make it for us. It had been over two years since I had a taste of pork or dried shrimp. Carefully and slowly, as if I was afraid of the unpredictable emotions that the taste of the soup would provoke, I took the first sip. I was choked by the sweet memories of our happy family at our dinner table. A tear softly flowed down my cheek, and I could no longer breathe without sniffing. I felt blessed and self-pity at the same time. As I ate, I hugged myself into a ball and imagined the sweet old woman putting her arm around my back and telling me that she understood and cared for me. I realized then that I had never cried from hard labor nor from starvation, but I cried for love and compassion. Little did I know at that time that the old stranger woman was one of my many angels. I thought of Chenda and could not eat the meal alone, so I snuck some dried shrimp, a meatball, and a squash under my waistband to share with my sister in the field.

A couple of weeks later, a small group of us were moved further down the river to Water Mill (*Rohat Tuek*) Village. The more they moved us, the more we became like animals. We had no friends that we could trust. We worried only about our own stomachs and survival. And the feelings of sadness and lost hope were worse than starvation. I wanted to see Em again. Every day all I could think about was a plan to see Em again. Finally, Chenda and I snuck out to find our way across unfamiliar muddy fields between Water Mill Village to Meeting Creek, searching for Em again.

This time Em took both of us to meet with the village leader who in his former life was a Buddhist monk. She requested permission to keep us in the village so she could treat us with some herbal medicines and promised to return us back to the girls' camp when we regained our strength. "Please have a heart. Look at them. I am afraid I will lose them," she pleaded.

The village leader looked at us with a sad and dried face, and sighed. "It is not up to me to decide. You have to go to the District Boys and Girls authority in the next village. However, you will have a better chance to be granted permission if you request for only one girl. You have to understand, you're not the only mother who has had her children taken away."

Back in our little hut, time was running out. We needed to go back to the girls' camp before we had to walk in the field during the night.

"I can't keep both of you with me. I wish I could," said Em.

I was happy to know she had a plan to keep one of us. I was scared to find out what it was, but couldn't wait either. I knew whatever Em decided, I would gladly accept, and I had no doubt Chenda was thinking the same way.

Em spoke softly to Chenda. "Since your younger sister is skinnier and much smaller than you, it is most likely they will let her stay." Nothing else needed to be said. None of us liked the decision, but it had been made, and Em had to decide for Chenda to sacrifice. Em packed dried fish and roasted rice for Chenda to take back to the girls' camp. This time she went back by herself. I hoped she would get there before it was dark and that she didn't feel sad and abandoned.

Paternal Grandparents, 1968—Grandmother Ly Chiv Heang (李秋香) and grandfather Chhi Yong Hao (徐永孝). My grandmother was a Chinese descendent born in Cambodia. My grandfather was born in Putianzhen (埔田镇), a town in the Guangdong (广东) province of China.

Em and Pa, Honeymoon, 1956—This picture hung prominently in the living room of our house in Battambang City, greeting everyone who walked into our home.

Uncle Khemm, 1973, Phnom Penh—His graduation photograph after earning a bachelor of science in economics. During the Black Uniforms era, Em kept this photograph among her possessions, risking persecution, as it exposed our past social standing. The photograph was in prime condition when the Black Uniforms began their reign.

Aunt Nay Hak and Cousin Ou, 1979, Paris, France—Em, Chenda, and I would not have been able to escape to Thailand if Aunt Nay Hak had not paid our way in gold. Cousin Ou saved us from dying of dehydration during our first attempt to escape.

Aunt Sareth, 1963—Em's half-sister. She was like a mother to me.

Cousin Pros and Aunt Sareth, 1983—Visiting family in Kampong Chhnang, Cambodia. Pros was fourteen years old.

Little Chenda, 1965—Fashion design and makeup done by Aunt Sareth.

Ee and Hong 1976—Their first week after arriving in Lincoln, Nebraska. The picture was taken in the back yard of Mr. and Mrs. Mark Hammer.

Afro Ee, 1979, Omaha Airport—My oldest brother, who had become very Americanized. His extraordinary hairdo froze my emotions when I first saw him.

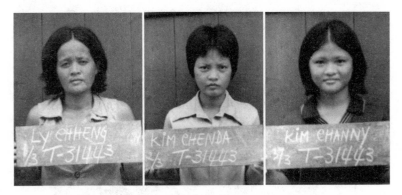

Our T-Numbers, 1979—Chenda and I continued to use the last name that Pa had changed from Chhi to Kim to evade being discriminated against for having Chinese heritage. We changed it back to Chhi when we applied for American citizenship.

Omaha Airport, June 20, 1979—Emotional Em, supported by Ee just outside the Jetway. Ee is holding Em's broken handbag and the UNICEF bag that contained all of our documents. Hong ran into the Jetway behind Em and Ee to receive Chenda and me. The photo was taken by Mr. Don Howe.

Our Family, June 1979—This picture was taken the first week after Em, Chenda, and I arrived in the United States, in front of our apartment in Lincoln, Nebraska. Left to right: Hong, Chenda, Em, me and Ee.

Em Cooking, July 1979—Em loved to cook. She was making spring rolls for our new friends, Norman and Shirley Sandager.

Our Family, 1981—Back row: Me and Chenda. Front row: Hong, Em, and Ee.

Ouv and Mair's Family, 1987—The photo was taken in Big Mountain (*Phnom Thom*), Cambodia, with a rice bin in the background. Left to right: Oun (Linda's sister), Red, Ouv, Mair, Linda, two little friends, and Linda's son Visal in the far right.

Becoming a US Citizen, July 3, 1986, Omaha, Nebraska—I was so proud, but unexpected emotions struck when I had to swear to renounce allegiance to Cambodia.

My Wedding, August 27, 1988—Left to right: Hong, Chenda, Em, Me, Kent Laux, my sister-in-law Cathy, and Ee with their daughter Rita Chhi.

At a wedding dinner in 1993 with my husband, Kent.

Eagle Scout Ceremony May 25, 2013—Me and my son Richard Laux.

The Lauxs, August 20, 2015—At my daughter Natasha Laux's USC School of Pharmacy White Coat ceremony. Left to right: Richard, Natasha, me, and Kent.

Chapter 10

HOME

Planting Season of 1977 to Harvest Season of 1978

I never knew how Pa felt about having me stay at home instead of Chenda. I knew deep down that he would have preferred Chenda to stay. *Why did we have to make such a choice? Can I still say I love my sister, even when I valued my comfort over hers?* I was a weak human being, and I was not proud of myself.

Before I could stay home, however, I had to get an approval from the District Boys and Girls authority in Banana Village. How would I do this? I didn't want to do it because it would require eye contact with the Black Uniforms. Whenever I saw a Black Uniform at a distance, I put my face down and shrank as close as I could to the ground, either by bending down over my work or sitting low to the ground and looking busy. Never, not even once, did I let them see my Chinese skin color and features, nor my scared eyes. When they walked past me, my breathing nearly stopped. Short and shallow breaths passed through my nose, never deep enough until they were gone away from the corner of my eyes. The thought of going by myself to where the Black Uniforms lived and asking for permission to stay home made me feel light-headed, cold, and wanting to throw up. I just wanted to go back to the girls' camp where I could be with my sister. It would be easier there.

That morning, before Em, Pa, and Kheang left for work, Em encouraged me: "Don't be scared. Anybody who sees the way you look will feel it in their heart. Most people have no motive to hurt children. Be sure you tell them that as soon as you feel better, you will go back to the camp." She told me to change my shirt to have short sleeves. Without asking why, I knew what she was thinking and did what I was told. With short sleeves, people could see my bones better. I wondered if I was really that skinny—like a walking skeleton.

Em's encouragement for me to showcase my rack of bones scared me. It reminded me of people's comments and reactions regarding the way I looked. I started to believe what they said—that I wouldn't be around much longer. For that reason alone, I thought perhaps the Black Uniforms would use me to build their good karma and gain favor from God by granting me my last wish to be with Em.

Pa said, "If you are afraid, you have to get closer. Do you know what that means? You will have a better look into their eyes. Perhaps they are not as bad as you think. If they are, they can't hurt you as much as they may want to. A knife at close range can't hurt as bad as a knife at a swinging distance."

Oh my God—Pa wanted me to be with him. Em was right when she told me, "I have never known a parent who doesn't love their children."

Pa's encouragement alone made me determined to do my best to be with my parents again. If Linda could stay with Mair and Ouv, then I, a little walking skeleton, could find a good soul who would help me to find a way to be with my parents again before I die.

I went to the District Boys and Girls authority in adjacent Banana Village, the same village that Em and Chenda went to scout for food in the first starvation season of 1975. I asked people along the way how to find the leaders' place. They all offered guidance, but all gave me a strange look. When I got closer, it was obvious which house was the leaders'. It was the only house where Black Uniforms were still roaming around instead of being out in the fields. They wore shiny black uniforms, and some had guns strapped to their shoulders. My heart pounded against my rib cage so strongly that my voice rattled when I asked one of them: "May I please speak to the leader of the house?"

The Black Uniform looked at me as if he saw a ghost and asked, "For what?"

"Asking permission to stay home to be treated by the well-known medicine man of this village, and to have my mother help me until I get better so I can go back to the girls' camp."

He went up the wooden stairs, then came back and said, "You have to come back later. He is in the field."

My courage was growing. I said, "If it is okay with you, I would rather wait." To him it must have seemed like my last wish, and it is bad karma to not grant a dying person their last wish. Judging by the look on his face, he wished he had never met me. Based on the way he talked, I was already a ghost spirit. He gestured for me to wait for the leader on the veranda.

I sat as low as I could on the wood floor, watching Black Uniforms come and go. None of them asked me why I was there or chased me away. I sat perfectly still from morning to late afternoon, without food or going to the bathroom. I was determined to wait for the leader. I went from being scared to being bored. I replayed all the words that Em and Pa told me earlier in the morning. When I saw some people coming back from the field, I was nervous again and recited what I would ask the leader. I imagined the leader as a big, strong, tall man with a gun on his shoulder. When the bell rang for the people to go to the eating shack, I concluded that I would never get to meet the leader. After sitting all day in one place, I quietly slipped out, thinking that the leader saw me but ignored me. What would I do?

I knew Em and Pa would be disappointed with me. But I didn't know what to do. I didn't want to see them, but where could I go? When Em saw me, she was so anxious to find out, she immediately asked, "Do you have the paper?"

"No, but the leader said I can stay." I don't know why those words came out of my mouth, but they did and they didn't sound so bad.

"No paper?" Em's voice conveyed disbelief.

"Nope," I replied as confidently as I could.

Em took a deep breath and looked stressed out. Pa said, "That's because they don't know how to write."

Em stared at Pa, and Pa smiled.

The next day Em took me to the Meeting Creek Village leader. Together we squatted in front of him, and Em explained to the leader that I had permission to stay. To my surprise, the leader didn't even ask for the paper. The leader's wife sat by him, smiling gently at me. They had a little girl about my age. She was strangely healthy, and her expression was like that of her mother and father—gentle. They were Black Uniforms, but they were sympathetic.

My condition got worse. In addition to my skinny appearance, I started to have the same breathing problem as Em, and it left me feeling exhausted. The medicine man gave me one of his remedies, and I had no choice but to take it. I was forced to take a tablespoon of gasoline to help with my wheezy breathing. I believed that the medicine man was a lazy old man who didn't like working in the fields so he claimed his own magic out of nowhere. Gasoline was not easily accessible, but for medicine's sake the man found a way to get some to cure me of my breathing condition. A gulp of the gasoline made me choke and cough until my eyes bulged out. A couple of weeks and about a quarter of a liter of gasoline later, I had not gotten any better.

The medicine man changed his treatment: This time I was to drink half a cup of a slimy concoction extracted from chopped raw snails, spearmint, and water. The medicine man was crazy, and I thought for sure that he wanted to kill me. I held my breath and drank the slime, but it never got too far. My body ejected it right back out. The medicine man would say, "There you go! It brings out all of the bad stuff along with it. Now you can breathe better." I hated that man—never wanted to see his face. None of what he gave me worked.

We heard about a kind of bush (*klack*) that, when you dried it and smoked it like tobacco, it would help you breath clearly again. However, the plant itself is poisonous if eaten fresh.

Em and I tried it. At night, we would smoke the dried leaf of the plant. Em taught me to take a deep breath and hold the smoke in for a few seconds and release it. I felt buzzed afterward and coughed all the mucus out. I felt that I could breathe again, but I keep drooling like a shaggy dog in the hot summer.

Pa and Em fought about my condition and the way I was treated. It seemed to me that I always gave Pa a reason to not like me, from conception to birth, and since then I had never brought him peace, happiness, or prosperity. I started to blame myself and became less mad and angry at him. I wished it was different, but I couldn't control it.

During this time I really believed in my heart that Pa loved me. At night, Em and I would have problems breathing. We wheezed and coughed until we got so tired we passed out. Pa never complained about the cough and the restless nights. Instead, every night he made us fire and placed the hot coals under our bamboo floor where all four of us shared the small blanket that we brought with us from Poipet. Em slept between Kheang and me, and Pa was next to Kheang.

We were made fun of for having hot coals under our bamboo floor where we lined up like smoked fish. Many times I feared that the bamboo floor would give in and we would be lying in the hot coals, but we didn't have any option. Without the hot coals under us, we wouldn't be able to sleep during cold rainy nights since we had only ragged clothes and a small blanket to share between the four all of us.

I still have that blanket with me today. The smoky smell has since vanished, but the smoke stain is still there. The last time I held it in my hands, the memories were too much to handle. So I put it away, and I am not sure I want to feel it again. Maybe I will, but only when I am alone because I don't think anybody can understand what it means to me.

Even with her breathing problem, Em still had to report to work where she sifted rice every day. I was too weak to do anything. Even walking to the eating shack took too much from me. So at lunchtime Em would bring me food. I would wait for her like a chick waiting for its mother. Sometimes Jair Lai would take food for me and her son, whose name spoke for the way he looked: He was called Premature Lizard (PL).

PL was a four-year-old boy. He looked like a skinny Buddha with a big belly, which was the biggest part of his body. He never had clothes on. He never cried or talked. He slept most of the time, and when he was not sleeping, he would sit up, waiting for his mother with flies all over his nose and eyes. He didn't even bother to shake his head or swat them away. All he did was blink his eyes and twitch his nose. The flies would move a little, then come back and insist on being on his face. It was a despairing sight.

I recognized PL's condition from when I was in the Chamnaom sick-house. Once people were too tired to chase flies away from their face, they didn't last long. I prayed I would die before becoming like that.

Jair Lai and Em took turns bringing food for me and PL. Day after day, PL still sat there and let the flies pick at his eyes and nose. One day, his teenage uncle, who was mildly mentally challenged, made a remark to PL that was unkind, but what he said was exactly what I was thinking: "I think you're going to die soon 'cause you're not strong enough to chase the flies." PL didn't care. His eyes were getting dimmer and dimmer.

From that day on, I made it my job to keep PL's face clean. When Jair Lai came home that first day, she saw hope in her son, and she was happy. She tried harder to find food outside of the eating shack to feed her son. In the process, she gave me some, too. Both PL and I got better.

Em decided that I should volunteer to get back to

work. So there I was, back in the field and planting rice again. Since all the girls my age were in a girls' camp, I found myself working with older people and younger children.

One of the kids was an outgoing little girl, a group leader's daughter. All the other girls seemed to be her entourage. They followed her, listened to her, and did what she said. She didn't like me nor the fact that I was staying home out of my age group, or perhaps she was intimidated by having an older girl around. So she was determined to make my life miserable. At first, I didn't think that this little girl could do anything too damaging, so I ignored her, but that became impossible. She followed me around and made fun of me to the rest of her clan. She talked about the awkwardness of my bathroom habits, which was somewhat true but mostly exaggerated for the good laughs. She accused me of being lazy and not being honorable to the Black Uniforms because I snuck around and found food while others were working hard. She also made fun of the monstrous way I devoured small creatures that I found in the fields. I felt scared and embarrassed by these accusations because there was some truth to them. When I got so tired and hungry, I didn't give a damn about social etiquette.

I felt isolated and depressed by the idea of staying

home because of this one little girl. It was the first time I felt personally condemned and humiliated by society for the way I talked, walked, ate, and everything else that I did. This child made me look over my shoulder constantly.

Every planting season is a starving season. All of the crops that were harvested over the dry season were shipped out as soon as the burlap bags were filled. When the monsoon season came, we were fed with rice soup again. Every village in the area was told to switch from steamed rice to rice soup. How thick the rice soup was depended on how big the heart of the local leader was. The Meeting Creek leader was a former monk, so he provided us with the thickest rice soup any village could ask for. Any thicker and it would not qualify as rice soup.

Every day in the field we were always on the look-out for the food delivery team to bring us rice soup and salt. At the end of the day we waited patiently by our hut for the feeding bell to chime, then would hurry to the eating shack with a plate and a spoon in our hands. Pa's hearing was getting worse. He couldn't hear the bell very well, so he would wait for us to let him know. Pa's knees were also not very strong; they bothered him when he walked. We would slow down and walk with him on our way to the eating shack. Little kids in the village liked to tease Pa with his hearing and some-times his limping problem. They would sneak up and limp along behind him, chanting a makeup rhythm: "Old-Man-Mak[19]! Tak Ting Tak! Old-Man-Mak! Tak Ting Tak …" Pa would not respond, partly because of his hearing problem and partly because he loved children so he ignored them.

Em was so bothered by it that she would chase them away, which made it more challenging and exciting for them. It was not so much the kids that bothered Em—it was their parents that did nothing to teach them the proper way to respect the elderly. Em thought it was rude to allow little kids to call grownups by their name.

Every day when I walked behind Pa to the eating shack, all I could think of was fear that he might not be with us much longer. I wished I could let him know how much he meant to me.

At the eating shack, the whole village ate together. Like animals we fought our way to be the first to get our stomach filled. Since Meeting Creek was not situated along the river, there was little chance of catching fish like people along the river could. Every day we were served with a blob of thick rice soup and a bowl

---

[19] *Mak* is my father's nickname. His full nickname is Tor Mak, which means Large Eye in his Chinese dialect (潮州 Chaozhou).

of prahok broth with a few cooked maggots floating on the rim of the bowl. It was always Em's job to skim the cooked maggots out. I would rather just eat the rice soup alone, but I found myself sipping on the broth to help down the thick rice soup and because I craved its saltiness.

Since the bowl of prahok broth was supposed to be shared by five or six people, we were always joined by an old lady and her son who was single but too old to join the boy team. He was not pleasant to look at. His hair was very curly and stuck out of his head like a set of black curly wires. He was called Worthless Curly, and the lady was called Worthless Curly's Mom. We always squatted in a circle with a plate of rice soup in our hand, a simple bowl containing the cloudy broth in the middle, next to our muddy feet and wet clothes. Sometimes we dripped rainwater from our wet hair. Curly's Mom was assigned the responsibility of babysitting little ones so their parents could report to work in the fields. She often received some dried fish from the parents. Occasionally, Curly's Mom and Em would secretly hand us small, salty dried fish pieces, and we would discreetly nip on them between the rice soup and the broth.

When we didn't have anything to add to the menu, Curly's Mom would openly share salty hot chili paste unwrapped from a banana leaf. Unlike salty fish, salty hot chili paste was somewhat acceptable, and the leaders would look past this minor crime.

Whenever we had salty hot chili paste to share in our circle, people would come over and beg to have some, too. I always wondered why people did that. Why didn't they make their own salty hot chili paste? Was it because they forgot it at home? Were they too tired? Too lazy? The salty hot chili paste was simple to make. It consisted of salt, hot chili, and green tamarind that had been pounded with mortar and pestle until all ingredients were mixed into a uniform paste.

Anyway, Curly's Mom was always kind to us, but not to those who pleaded for the salty hot chili paste. To those beggars, she would be grumpy and speak her mind, but still they continued to ask her again and again every day because Curly's Mom would always let them have some, even when she was harsh with her words. One time she told us not to eat the salty chili paste, but she pleasantly let the beggars have as much as they wanted. You should have seen the response on the beggars' faces after they took a bite. After that, we were hardly bothered. Curly's mom had spiced up the paste. It was at this time that I built up my tolerance for spiciness.

Curly's Mom was older than Em, but I could imagine

how pretty she had looked when she was younger. She was also elegant in the way she talked and the words she used. She had definitely seen some good night life in high society in her younger years. Later on, I learned she used to make a living running a brothel. I was disappointed to know that and wondered why Em and Pa could be good friends with someone who had made a living that way. However, Em, Pa, and the lady respected each other, had fun, and enjoyed each other's company. She made Em and Pa laugh at a time when Em and Pa hardly talked to one another.

Everybody in the village loved Em. To this day, I never met a person that didn't like her. She was a hard worker, always putting others' needs before her own, smiling every time she talked with people, and never saying a bad thing about anyone. If she agreed with you that someone was not being fair, she would smile instead of adding fuel to the fire. In our tight family, she would be frustrated but never mad. In a way, Kheang took after her. This quality alone had saved Pa's life, for all of the leader wives found comfort in Em and they all took care of her. They would give fruit and vegetable for Em to take home.

One day in the middle of the planting season, Ouv came to Meeting Creek for food. Em and Pa gave Ouv all of our stash. I saw Pa talk to Ouv in the most affectionate way. I was confused with Pa's kindness since the last time I saw the two men together was when Ouv had taken Linda from us, and they didn't get along. As I watched Em pack food for Ouv, I relived the last thing that Mair did to me in French Village. I thought that if Em knew what Mair did to me that last time, she would not give all that food to Ouv. As soon as Ouv left, I told Em what Mair had done to me and shared with her my feelings.

Solemnly, Em told me, "You have to remember the good things as well, not just the bad things." Referring to the Black Uniforms, she added, "They bring out the worst in all of us."

What I learned from Em and Pa that day would last me a lifetime. It was not so much what Em said after she learned about Mair, it was her action toward Mair and Ouv. It was how Pa and Em were willing to forgive and forget, to help those who were in more need than we were, and to not forget the good in others.

Kheang was eleven years old then, but without enough food he looked much younger. He was tasked to look over the cattle. It pained me to watch as he reluctantly left the protection of our little hut and walked into the monsoon rain every morning. Each morning he would get up and stand by the edge of the hut and piss into the rain. Then Pa would take a turn, except the hut was not high enough to allow Pa to stand up straight. Em and I would hold on to our full bladders until we had to step out into the rain. We sat quietly like a group of soaked monkeys and listened to the rain and sometimes Jair Lai's kids crying. We watched the rain and waited for someone brave enough to step into the morning rain, usually someone from Om Leung's family who would walk by and yell out, "Come on, let's do it!" Kheang would put on a hat, take a deep breath, and step into the white sheets of rain and onto that muddy ground, and head into the field of water next to our hut. Then Pa followed Kheang, mumbling "motherfucker." Then Em and I would step into the rain, squat down on the muddy ground not too far away from the hut, and empty our bladders. Then off we went. I hated living in hell. *When would it ever get better? Would it ever get better?*

Em's work allowed her to be sheltered from the rain because her job was cleaning rice with the leaders' wives and a few other women. They performed this task under a wooden house on stilts. Herding the cattle allowed Kheang occasional protection under a tree. Pa and I were always in the open field and exposed to all the elements—cold, windy, and wet. Pa's task was to carry bundles of young rice stalks to us girls, women and children alike, to be replanted. I watched Pa stumble every day while plunging and plugging his feet from the deep mud under the sheets of water with fifty to sixty pounds of weight on his shoulder. I never missed seeing him when he stumbled by. I looked for Pa every time I had a chance to stand up, and every time I wished I could do something to help. The pain of watching my father suffer every day will stay with me as long as I live. I heard rumors that some people were so exhausted they fell down and died in the field. I was afraid that kind of horror might happen to Pa. He was so skinny that his stomach touched his backbone and his rib cage was sharply defined; his cheek muscles were not strong enough to hold his white lips shut, and his eyes had lost their sparkle. I wanted to take care of him. *I will take care of him.* I wondered if Em saw what I saw, but I was afraid to ask her. *What good would it do?*

Pa always spoke his mind, just short of challenging the Black Uniforms to respond to his comments. One day Pa stumbled along the narrow levee behind the planting line where all the women and girls were bending and spreading our legs to stretch as far as they could to cover more planting ground. I stood up and found him standing there, looking at the planting line and chuckling. He said in a loud voice to ensure that he could be heard, "Lady comrades, please don't spread your legs too wide, and don't bend too low. You are making us nervous." He amused himself and laughed out loud as he turned away.

The group leader who was working not too far away from me was not amused. In an eerie voice, she said, "That man—he has to be corrected."

My ears quickly plugged with the wind of fear. I couldn't hear anything else but my own heart drumming. Why does Pa have to say things that offend the leader? Could this be the comment that gives them the reason to take him away to be reeducated? Why does he have to be so clumsy?

Under the Black Uniforms' rule, everybody was created equal. Women have equal rights with men, children have the same right as their parents, and all belong to the Black Uniforms. There was an unspoken rule: Don't say anything that might make someone in the leadership role upset with you because you will be corrected in public. After that, if you do not improve, you will be relocated from your family for reeducation. Pa had just challenged the unspoken rule by not respecting the opposite sex and upsetting the leader.

On that same day after lunch, the village leader finished with her daily meeting and asked if anybody had anything to add to the meeting. The group leader, who was a level lower than the village leader in terms of leadership ranking, stood up and spoke out.

"I'd like to express my respect to our government. I am grateful for this opportunity. I'd like to express my respect to all comrades, men and women, boy and girls alike."

She paused, then summoned herself to continue. "I'd like to take this opportunity to correct the behavior of comrade Old-Man-Mak. This morning he made a remark that was disrespectful to the lady comrades." It was not an everyday thing for someone to be deemed in need of correction. My heart sank when the village leader straightened up her composure.

"What did he do?" she asked.

She tried to be calm, but the group leader got excited and couldn't wait to blurt out her anger in a shaky voice: "When we were focused and working hard planting, comrade Old-Man-Mak told us not to spread our legs too wide and not bend too low. It makes him nervous, he said!"

The group of about fifty to sixty people were quiet and motionless. What was going to happen now? No one had ever been brought up for correction in this village before. I felt the thick rice soup thrusting its way back up for a chance to be regurgitated, but then I saw an angel in the village leader's face. She couldn't control her giggling any longer and blew up laughing out loud. Everybody else followed suit, laughing hard and wiping away tears of joy. In the next second I went from so much fear that I almost threw up to laughing with great relief. My frustration toward Pa turned proud and happy that he still had the charm that always made people around him laugh. I couldn't wait to tell Em what happened.

Once she was able to contain herself, the village leader calmly said, "You shouldn't mind the Crazy-Old-Man-Mak." From that day on, my Pa was known as the Crazy-Old-Man-Mak. The story was told again and again for a good laugh in the field and by the rice cleaning team and the cooking team. Many women in the field repeated what Pa said for a good laugh and to remind themselves how they looked to the men who were working behind the planting line.

In the eyes of the Black Uniforms, all the people who were relocated to Meeting Creek were "pigs." Relocating was their way of punishing the pigs. Their thinking was: Let's see how the pigs survive without maids and their belongings. This fact alone made living in Meeting Creek very safe for us pigs. It was the best thing that could have happened to Pa and Em. Neighbor did not turn neighbor in to the Black Uniforms. Even so, Pa still got in trouble with one of the group leaders when they were working together getting firewood for the village kitchen.

The group leader was a young man in his mid-twenties. He claimed that Pa was lazy and still leaning on other people to do his work. Unlike the woman leader who corrected Pa openly, this man was vicious in his spirit. When I overheard how he complained about Pa and the kind of words he used, I feared for Pa's life. Soon after I told Em about the situation, the man was in an accident—killed by a falling tree.

Em made a point to tell me that this was not the first time Pa had been threatened. There had been another leader, also a wood cutter in French Village, who had tried to take Pa to be reeducated. Soon after Mair informed Em of what was going on, this leader, too, was involved in an accident and was killed by a falling tree. "An angel was looking out for your father," Em said, feeling blessed as she told me.

One of the residents at Meeting Creek was Pongrit, Hong's high school teacher. The village leader spared his life in exchange for his emptying toilets for the whole village. He and his toilet comrade would carry oozy tubs of excrement every day, empty them, mix them with ash and rice shells, and let them dry up to be use for fertilizer. One of my jobs was to spread the disgusting caked up and crusty fertilizer in the field. The teacher hardly talked, but always gave me the biggest smile, so big that I always smiled back in shock. Em would refer to him as "nephew" to express her kindness and understanding. Pa, on the other hand, always called him "teacher." This was another one of Pa's ways of giving the Black Uniforms the middle finger and giving the teacher the respect he deserved.

As the water receded with the latter part of planting season, we were able to find more fish to supplement our daily meals. One night Jair Lai and I went out to find food using a net that was cut from an old mosquito net. Jair Lai held one side of the net, and I stretched it tight and held its opposite corners. Between the two of us, we made a nice rectangle net to scoop any creatures there were out of a ditch in front of the hut. We walked in the ditch, dragging the tightly spread net along the bottom of the ditch. The water was up to my hips, touching my ear as I bent down, and dragged the net along the bottom. Every fifty feet or so we would slowly lift the net as gently as we could. Sometimes we got some fish, but most of the time on that particular night we didn't get much, only a few small shrimp and tiny moving creatures. Suddenly I was so frightened that I couldn't even scream for help. All I could do was make weird sounds and drop everything. Jair Lai was scared, too, when she saw me acting crazy. "What's going on?" she screamed.

"I don't know. Something is in my pants. I don't have underwear. It's moving strong. Hurry, hurry!" I cried for help as it felt like a big snake trying to get out.

"Quiet! People can hear you!"

She got her hand in between my crotch and whatever it was that was moving and grabbed onto it. "Get out of the water, quick!" she demanded.

I got out of the water as quickly as I could while she was hanging on to that thing. I could still feel it moving, and at the same time I felt relief knowing that she got ahold of it and it had not yet hurt me. I imagined that if it was a poisonous snake, it would have bit me by now. Once we were out of the water, she quickly pulled the thing out of my pants, and without even taking time to look at it, she slammed it against the dirt road. I ran away as fast as I could and then I heard Jair Lai laughing hard but quietly. She held onto her stomach, laughing and walking to me. I found myself laughing with her, knowing that whatever that thing was, it was not a snake or something that could hurt us. She leaned her wet body on mine. I almost fell. She said, "It's a frog. A big frog. You scared me for no reason. God must have eyes."

Curious, I asked, "Now God is good?"

Still smiling, Jair Lai responded, "Yeah, tonight he is. Let's go home. This frog is good for my PL tomorrow."

It was the biggest frog I ever seen. We finished netting for fish early that night.

One time after a good night of netting, I hid one

small fish within the grass wall of the hut so I that could satisfy my craving for a solid prahok. I also took some salt from the family stash and began to salt the hidden fish to ferment it. Every day I would check on it, and to my surprise, no other wild animal took the fish. However, every day I felt guilty for keeping the fish to myself. Every time I checked the fermented fish, I ate a little bit of it. Finally, a week later I finished the fish. My craving for prahok was gone, but not the guilt I had for hiding food from my family.

It had been at least three months since Chenda went back to the girls' camp. She had not been back to Meeting Creek, and we had not heard from her. Em asked me if I could find my way back to the girls' camp in Water Mill Village. Even though I was unsure of the route, I felt I could find my way to Chenda. I tried to convince Em to let me go. After much hesitation, she decided to let me go with Kheang. Part of her decision was based on the fact that having two kids roaming the fields was better than Em or Pa trying to find Chenda. Even the Black Uniforms were more lenient toward children.

We left the hut before the sun came up and before people left for the fields. I felt responsible for making sure we wouldn't get lost and would be able to come back to our hut at a decent time. Kheang was close behind me all the way to show that he didn't want to slow us down. For a shortcut, we walked across a wild mango patch on cemetery grounds. We had heard many haunting stories about this place, but we didn't have any better options. When we got closer to the cemetery, I asked Kheang if he knew any prayers to keep the spirits away from us. He gave me a wide-eyed look and quickly shook his head with the slightest move. I felt the tenseness of his spirit and told him to repeat the words *"Puto Ackrahang"* in his head. This Buddhist chanting phrase blesses you and calms you down. I made sure our foreheads were not covered, just as Em had told me to do before I left the hut: "If you feel scared of any spirit, don't cover your forehead. Your own spirit will be stronger than others' if you allow it to show through your forehead." "Others" referred to the spirits of the dead.

Pa added, "And don't run. If there is something suspicious, turn around and look. Let your spirit shine into it." Quietly Kheang and I held each other's hands and we walked as fast as we could without running.

Beyond the cemetery was a big field between us and the tree line that marked the river. Estimating my direction, I led Kheang to a set of dense tree lines because I knew Water Mill Village was one of the big villages along the river. The water level in the fields was still high enough that most of the levee was covered, so we walked in the fields of water and the growing green rice stalks. It was exhausting, and we were afraid to rest since we didn't know how much time it would take us to cross the fields. Without talking, we kept marching to the larger cluster of trees. I knew that I picked the right cluster of trees when I saw the red roof of the building I used to stay in with Chenda.

Between the field and the red-roofed building was a good-sized ditch. Clear, calm water covered both the fields and the ditch. Em had packed dried fish and roasted rice for Chenda. I wondered how we were going to cross the ditch and keep the food dry. We were already standing in the water up to our belly buttons. Neither one of us knew how to swim or even how to tread water.

After long hesitation, we began to search for a spot that would be shallow, but it was hard to tell the depth of the ditch. I was a little bit taller than Kheang, so I went in first, sinking deeper and deeper with every step into the ditch. I turned around and looked at Kheang's face when the water was touching my armpits. Then I took the next step that might be the step that took me under the water completely or the step that raised me back up. By then I was in the middle of the ditch. That last step I sank deeper, but didn't know how deep because

I panicked and struggled. The next thing I knew, I was on the other side of the ditch and had managed to keep the food dry. It was the first time I felt I had to be strong and not let my emotions show: I was responsible for supervising my younger brother's emotional and physical safety. With confidence on my face, I stepped back into the ditch, extended my arm, and convinced him to do the same thing on the other side. When our hands touched, we counted to three, and when I pulled, he pushed, and we both got across the ditch. With a sigh of relief, I smiled for my little brother as I pulled him up along the bank, feeling proud of him. I knew he was scared, but he didn't complain the least bit.

I snuck Kheang into the girls' place and found Chenda's little sack in the same spot that she and I had shared before. Both Kheang and I sat in wet clothes and waited for Chenda to come back. Not knowing when she would return, I became concerned about going back to Em before the day was over. *What if Chenda didn't come back until the end of the day?* I couldn't leave the food there and go back home. She wouldn't know where it was from, or worse yet, the sick girls who were all around us would steal the food, and Chenda wouldn't even know we had stopped by. If we stayed until she came back from the field, the rest of the girls would know. At least for now, only a few sick girls knew

Chenda had visitors. What would happen to us if all the girls knew? Where would we sleep that night? What if they kept both Kheang and me and refused to let us go back to Em? How was Em going to feel? What was I supposed to do?

I didn't even think about these questions until then. I was faced with a decision that could change both Kheang's and my futures. Before I could think any further, I asked Kheang to lie on the wood floor with me next to Chenda's belongings to disguise our presence among the sick girls. I wondered how Em and Pa could send me here without a plan to handle this situation.

But God knew our plan, and he had made Chenda stay home sick that day. She was not very sick, so she was able to walk to the eating shack for lunch, which is why she wasn't at her place. I was so relieved to see her. Once again I started to believe in God. Chenda introduced us to a sick girl nearby, and it appeared the girl would not snitch on Chenda, so we were able to sit up and talk to Chenda about our trip. She stroked our wet clothes as she asked about Em and Pa. We told her how scary it was to cross the ditch, but still felt too spooked to tell her about walking through the cemetery.

Chenda was more sad than she was happy to see us. She was happy to see us, to know that Em and Pa were doing fine, and to have some food from Em, but she was sad that we had to walk a long way and that we couldn't stay very long. We sat on the wood floor and sadly gazed at each other's faces. No happy or sad words were spoken, but the mixed feelings were strong. Chenda encouraged us to eat a full portion of the food that we brought for her so we would be strong walking back home. We ate as little as we could even though we were very hungry, and left as much as we could for our sister.

Less than an hour later, we had to leave Chenda and head back home, a place where we were loved, cared for, and protected at all cost, a place where we could be next to Em.

Chenda walked us back to the ditch behind her place. She looked so sad and distressed. I knew she wanted to cry if she could, but she didn't. I showed Chenda how I crossed the ditch. It was easy without the food: just push and glide to the other side when the water was above my belly button. Kheang did the same thing as Chenda and I proudly watched him.

In our soaked clothes, Kheang and I stood quietly on the side of the ditch opposite from Chenda. It was harder to say goodbye than I could have imagined. Silently we stood and stared at each other across the ditch. I tried hard to release the tightness of my chest and said, "We will be back soon, now that we know how to get here."

She tried to smile with her lips and hide her sadness as she encouraged us to leave. "Go, so you can be home before dark."

After a long hesitation, Kheang and I turned and walked away from our sister. When I left home in the morning, I was scared but happy with the thought of seeing my sister, and I was imagining how happy and proud she would be of us. But I didn't anticipate the sad and agonizing goodbye that no words could express. I hated what happened. What had we done in our past life to deserve this torture? We kept walking away, looking back and waving goodbye to our sister, who waved back to us until the trees swallowed her. I hoped she was able to cry after we left, for I felt the same pain she was experiencing, but I had Kheang and I was going home, and she was left behind all alone.

On the way home my mind was saddened by thoughts of how Chenda must have felt when she had to walk on these same fields back to the girls' camp by herself. I wished she wasn't so sad when we left her.

I was interrupted by a snake on a small termite mound. Its body was about two inches in diameter, stretched about five feet long. With the first glance at the snake, we backed away, but then I noticed it was moving very slowly. My eyes focused on the snake, and I asked Kheang to hand me a stick. Again and again I asked Kheang to hurry, but he didn't even try to find a stick. "What's wrong with you?" I said as I finally gave up and the snake moved away.

He looked at me with gentle eyes. "What if he bit you? You don't know what kind of snake it was."

"You should have listened to me. I knew I could get him before he got me. He was moving slowly!" I exclaimed.

My gentle little brother shared his view. "He was scared of you. Don't you feel sorry for him?"

In that instant I saw a sweet and beautiful person in Kheang. I had a flashback to right before the Communists took over when Kheang and I were in Phnom Penh, the capital city. Because it was during the Chinese New Year celebration, we were allowed to play cards all night long with our cousins. The next morning, the winner was supposed to buy everybody a bowl of noodles. Kheang was the winner, so I went with him to the front gate when we heard the calling sound of bamboo thumping to let us know that the noodle delivery was in the neighborhood. We called out to the boy who was thumping the bamboo and told him we wanted five bowls of noodles. He was happy, running back and forth between our front gate and his master's portable noodle cart, bringing a bowl of noodles every time he returned.

When he gave us the last bowl of noodles, Kheang asked him, "Why do you have to work?" Meaning, for such a young boy. "Where are your parents? Where do you live?"

The boy was about the same age as Kheang, who was nine years old at the time. He told us that he was a refugee from a village that had been destroyed by the war. His parents were killed, and he lived on the street with his grandmother. I was so taken by his story that I gave him a good tip, but Kheang gave the boy his bowl of noodles. The boy hesitated at first, but then he ate. Kheang kept asking the boy all kinds of questions. He watched the boy eat, and in his expression, I could see he wished that he could do more to help.

Kheang was always gentle to all living things.

Walking away from the termite mound, I kept thinking about how compassionate my little brother was and how proud I was to have a such sweet person for a brother. Kheang never brought anything home from the fields for Em to cook. At that moment, I understood why. I couldn't imagine Kheang grabbing a frog and smashing its head against a rock, nor could I imagine him twisting the head of a small fish. Instead, he would always bring home wood and fetch water for Em.

Before we could see the wild mango patch of the

cemetery ground, we were in a field that had many snails and crabs. I searched and caught them, and Kheang was right behind me, placing them in the cotton bag. Thinking Em would be very proud of us, we spent time to find more snails and crabs on the adjacent fields. All of a sudden the sky turned from shining to purplish and gray, just as it always does when it is about to set into the edge of the earth. Kheang and I panicked when we looked for the mango patch cemetery and realized that we were far away from where we should be. By the time we were by the cemetery, the sky was dark, and the wind seemed to blow stronger between those mango trees and was howling gently. With one hand squeezing Kheang's hand and the other hand securing the bag filled with little crabs and snails, I told Kheang not to run but to walk as fast as possible. I felt cold and empty as if the only thing I had was my head for thinking, and no other part of my body mattered to my existence. In my head, I prayed and asked for forgiveness for intruding on this resting place.

We walked out of the cemetery and continued to walk fast until our backs stopped feeling the chilly air from the cemetery. The fear of haunting by mean or teasing spirits left my memory when I remembered that Em must have been worried sick about us. We continued to walk as fast as we could, but we needed to walk around the edge of the village for fear of being caught. By the time we got near our hut, I saw the soft silhouette of Em standing and anxiously waiting for us. She walked toward us as soon as she noticed us. I thought for sure I would be scolded, but all she said was: "You are killing me. If I have to endure any more of this agony, for sure I will not be able to survive." As she wrapped her arms around us and pressed us against her chest, I knew then she was pleading to the higher being to stop testing her.

In school I learned that each year has three seasons: hot, raining, and cool. However, as a teenager working in labor camps it seemed as though there were only two seasons: the starving season, which happened during rice planting time in the monsoon, and the rice harvest, when we no longer went to sleep on empty stomachs. After the rice was planted, I could hardly wait for harvest time.

While waiting for the harvest season, I was told to work in the orchard. I planted tobacco and worked with seedlings for the garden. I was also told to clean rice, which allowed me to work with Em and listen to the women tell dirty jokes. It was fun to see the women laughing, even though I had no clue about the punch lines.

After many odds tasks, the harvest season of 1978

finally arrived. This year it was special. Em was able to secure a chicken; she let it lay eggs under the bamboo floor of our hut, right below the bedding, which protected it from the elements and wild animals. Little did we know that having a chicken under the hut floor was not like having cows under a wooden house. The chicken nested about a foot below us. Little chicken mites came up to our bedding, and they liked us as much as they liked the chicken. I felt them crawling all over my body, but I couldn't see them. It was itchy, and there was nothing we could do but learn to never do that again.

We were allowed to raise chickens as long as we promised to hand them over to the government when they were big enough for slaughter. In the past, a chicken would lay about ten eggs per nest, but after the Black Uniforms took over, they would lay four to five eggs at most. By the time they were ready to be slaughtered, only two or three per nest survived the wild animals and were left to be shared with the whole village.

We ourselves were among the wild animals that snatched the chickens and their eggs. We cooked them in the tea kettle since we were not allowed to own a cooking pot.

The first time Em asked me to slaughter a chicken, she asked: "Little, are you brave enough to slaughter a chicken?"

I didn't know how to answer such a question. I had seen it done before, but I never thought I would have to do it myself.

"It's okay, you can do it. You won't receive any bad karma because you're doing it for your need to survive. Pa and I are too old to do this kind of thing."

I knew what she meant. Because I was younger, I would have plenty of time to recover from my sin of taking a life. It was not the case that we valued chicken over fish or any other lives. It was just that the red blood squirted out when their throats were slashed.

Em helped me prepare for the ceremony. She told me how to step on the feet, clasp the wings and pull them and the neck backward, pull the feathers around the protruding neck, and line up a bowl to catch the blood. Then she gave me a sad but encouraging smile and handed me the knife. "You are blessed for serving your parents," she said.

When Em turned away, I got so nervous that I found myself asking God for forgiveness for the action that I was about to take. I sliced the chicken's throat and let go as soon as its throat was opened. The dying chicken was kicking and flipping over the catching bowl on the ground in the process. Blood shot up in the air in all directions and sprayed on my face and body before the chicken finally gave up jumping around and lay there, kicking softly on the dirt. I forgot all about the guilt of killing the bird. Instead I felt bad for not being able to catch the blood for cooking, and thought for sure that I would get in trouble with Em. She was disappointed, but she didn't scold me.

That night Pa refused to eat such a good meal in the dark, choosing instead to eat the chicken near the fire pit while we all guarded the road to the house. He said: "Let it be known that if they kill me, it was because I ate the chicken that I had raised myself. Don't leave the hut to guard the road for my sake." He wouldn't listen to Em, but he listened to Om Pad, who told him to be discrete about the meal and more understanding of Em's fear. Om Pad was the teacher who lived near us. He had good rapport with Pa. Many nights Pa and Om Pad would talk late into the night.

Pa complained about how the country was moving backward while the rest of the world was advancing. "We replaced cows with humans to work the fields, while the rest of the world was replacing animals with tractors." He would stress the end of his statements with the phrase "motherfuckers." Even though I was scared and wished they would stop talking about things like this, I still listened to them and contemplated what I heard. When Pa said that in America farmers were using airplanes to fertilize their crops, I didn't believe him and thought that he was exaggerating. I was mad at myself for listening to a couple of old men who were mad about everything and couldn't find anything good to talk about.

Pa's voice would get louder and louder because his hearing problems were getting worse. Em was worried every time these two men talked. Many times Om Pad would gently tell Pa: "Let's not talk anymore. Nothing will change. We're only worrying the ladies." This would soften Pa's temper toward the Black Uniforms. Om Pad was one of the few men in the village who treated Pa with respect and love. Om Pad always laughed when Pa tossed off one-liner jokes. Pa had many expressions and broken phrases for jokes. I didn't understand any of them.

During harvest, not only are the fields ready with rice, but the orchards are filled with many kinds of fruit. Life seems to rejuvenate in the harvest season. After a long day of work, I would go to the orchard and sneak around to pick guavas, dig potatoes, and cut bananas and anything else I could reach and pick with my hands. When I brought them home, Em would tell me to stop stealing before I got in trouble with the Black Uniforms. Pa would say, "Don't listen to your mother. You are not stealing from anybody. It is the Black Uniforms who are stealing from you." I choose to ignore Em's concern and continued to grab whatever I could, mainly because I saw other people doing the same, and it was a matter of my getting to it before they did.

One time after breaking loose a cluster of about ten bananas, I heard someone coming. In a panic, I left the bananas and hid away behind another banana bush. Lying close to the ground and away from the scene of my crime, I was safely concealed by dense undergrowth. While lying motionless, I saw that a sugar man[20] had discovered my bananas. He looked around, grabbed my bananas, and carried them away, walking quickly to a bush and stashing them away. He then whistled and coolly marched away with empty hands. As soon as the sugar man was out of sight, I approached the bush where he had hidden my treasure. I wanted my bananas back. Beside my bananas, I found a jackfruit and some coconuts. Jackpot! I knew he would come back to his stash at dusk, so I hastily moved all of his stash to a new location within the orchard. That night I made three trips between the hut and the orchard. I didn't feel guilty for stealing from the sugar man, just as I didn't think I was stealing from the Black Uniforms. Being the sugar man was the best job in the

---

[20] A man whose job was to climb palm trees to collect palm nectar to be reduced for sugar.

village, for he could always get his hands on any fruit at any height. Pa was proud of me, and he thought it was funny. A few days later, the sugar man stopped by and told Pa and Om Pad what had happened to him, I tried very hard not to laugh.

As time went by, I became bolder with my actions. Nothing was unreachable. If I couldn't climb to it, I would pry it down, shake it down, or throw sticks to knock it down. I even got the coconuts down without climbing the tree. Nothing Em said could deter me from this behavior, and it was becoming a bad habit more than a survival skill because we were not starving at that time. Nevertheless, we were always hungry.

What happened under one purple sky did set me straight. I stepped on a dead branch and fell twenty feet from a feroniella lucida (*krawsankg*) tree. When I landed on the hard ground with many old dead branches, a thorn punctured the base of my right-hand index finger. I was aware of everything around me and scared that I couldn't move and would be stuck on the ground through the night. After a few long minutes of lying on the ground, I was able to lift the punctured hand and carefully pushed myself up to sitting position without pushing the thorn deeper into the finger. I tried to remove the thorn, but it broke off deep under my skin. Hardly any blood came out, but half of the large old dead thorn was inside my finger. I waddled back to the hut that day without much to show. I didn't tell Em, Pa, or Kheang what had happened.

That thorn was never taken out and is still embedded in my finger to this day. The sore and swollen area with the thorn would occasionally flare up and bother me for at least ten years afterward. Just like the thorn in my finger, my experience in those years will always be with me. However, it can't hurt me as much as it used to. Eventually the pain may completely disappear, and my experience will become nothing more than just a story. When that day comes, I shall be free from the pain.

Jair Lai's family and ours grew to know each other well. We cared for each other like our own. Like me, PL's health was getting better. He was getting more mobile until finally he could walk again. He was so cute with that brown naked body of his and the protruding stomach protecting and hiding his private parts. One day, PL got up from the hut and started picking up pieces of corn on the ground, stuffing each one in his mouth, first one, then another, then another one as if someone had dropped a line of bait for an animal. It turned out that someone did drop the pieces of corn, but they were not bait and they were not fresh pieces of corn. They were undigested pieces of corn that had oozed down the leg of Nuong that lived two huts away. Poor PL.

Nuong was really mean. He mumbled all day long and every now and then spurted out angry words. In our small patch of huts, only his hut had two buckets that could be used to carry water from the creek. One of Kheang's routine tasks was to fetch water for Em, but to do that, he had to go to Nuong's house and borrow his buckets. Many times Kheang would come back to Em, tormented, with a tight face, and crying. "He hits me on my head with the carrying stick," or "on my back," or "on my shoulder," or just, "He did it again." It agonized me to see Kheang so tormented. I hated that mean guy.

Nuong also scavenged our place for any cooked dried fish that we saved. We would hide the fish within the thatched wall, and he would still find it. One day I caught him in action. He had our fish in his hands and was smiling at me with ugly teeth and our fish in his mouth. There was nothing I could do, but I did think about whacking him in the head with the carrying stick so hard that he would bleed. I imagined that would be the only way to stop him from tormenting Kheang.

Thinking back, I always enjoyed the first few weeks of harvesting rice. The stunningly beautiful golden color of the rice fields made me feel good to be out in the open. Everyone was in good spirits. The weather was not too hot, and we were finally fed steamed rice again. We were confident we would live for at least another four months until the crops were cleaned and taken away from us. Until that time came, we were the hens that nested in the grain bin. We were the termites in the rainy night, flying by the electric lights. This precious time was intense and short. It was during this time that people sang in the fields while working, telling jokes and laughing. Even though I didn't understand many of the cryptic jokes, I was enjoying the atmosphere.

It was during harvest that I first heard one of the former peasants complain about the Black Uniforms. She said: "In the past I used to slave for people, but at least I ate what I wanted and always had new sarongs after harvesting. Now I can't even find scraps to mend the holes of my musty old sarong."

I began to realize that once we all hit bottom we were not so different from each other. We were all afraid of one thing, but, we were not sure what it looked like or smelled like. We all had our own different ways of referring to it. Some called it the government, Pol Pot, the Red Khmer, the Khmer Rouge, the Red, or the Black. I call it the Black Uniforms.

With plenty of food, young couples were soon expecting babies. In our small cluster of huts, Om Pad's sister-in-law was expecting her first baby. I was fifteen years old at the time but was clueless about how babies were conceived and how they were born. Mair told me a while back that when a baby is ready to come out, the mother's stomach explodes, and a midwife or doctor stitches the stomach back—hence the stretch marks. At the age of fifteen, this story no longer made sense to me, but I had no one to talk to except one of the Chinese girls named Moy. She was the same age as I was. Moy stayed with the old people because she claimed she couldn't see very well. She wore thick glasses. We were both quiet, so it took us a long time to open up and talk to each other. We talked about babies.

With a smile, I began, "Moy, I heard that if you love a man, you'll get pregnant. You think that's true? What do you do if you have a feeling and you can't control that feeling? Could you get pregnant that way?"

"If you don't talk to them, then you won't have the feeling in the first place," was Moy's solution.

"What if they talk to you?" I replied, still smiling and with my eyebrow raised.

Moy responded sternly, "That's why you're supposed to ignore them and not look at them. Pretend you don't hear them."

With even more curiosity, I said, "Moy, I heard that if you let a man touch you, your breasts will swell up and the rest of the world will know."

"Don't talk like that!" She was embarrassed, and I reached over and grabbed her arm pretending I was a man. She squealed and we giggled.

Finally, I had to ask, "Moy, do you know how babies are born?"

Moy was uncomfortable and hushed me up with the tone of her voice. "I don't know."

"Did you ever ask your mom?"

She pushed back with a smile. "You ask your mom!"

I told Moy about Mair's story of how a baby was born. She was disgusted with the story and couldn't believe that I even contemplated such things. She was confident that her story was more reasonable, when she told me, "It comes from the mother's shit hole." I wondered why Moy had to say such a word, regardless of whether it was true. At the same time, I thought it was funny. I laughed hard until Moy got mad at me, but at the end she was laughing, too, because my laughter became contagious.

Moy spoke Khmer a with thick Chinese accent, and many times she chose words that were descriptive but inappropriate, especially for a young girl. To her I was a Cambodian girl because I knew all of the Khmer etiquette and I didn't speak Chinese, but to Cambodian girls I was Chinese because my skin was too white. I corrected Moy's Khmer and asked her, "How can you be so sure?"

"One time I heard a mother say she had a very easy delivery. She thought she needed to go take a shit, then when she pushed, the baby came out. No pain, she claimed."

Moy was confident her explanation was more logical than that of the exploding tummy. But both of us felt disappointed and grossed out. "But how can that be? Babies are much bigger."

Moy's reply was, "Maybe the baby expands after it feels the fresh air." We both were uncomfortable with that idea. Then we turned to push each other to find out more.

"Why don't you ask your mom for sure?"

"No! You ask your mom!"

A few months later, Om Pad's sister-in-law was in labor. When I got back from the field, I saw many old women trying their best to help the family, but all they could do was make sure hot water was available. Then one by one they dispersed, and as they walked by our hut, I heard one of them say, "There is not much hope. She is not pushing anymore." Later in the night, I heard her husband screaming and begging for his wife not to leave him.

Cambodians believe that the spirit of a woman who dies with an unborn child is very unsettled and will stay around a long time to haunt people. So her death changed the atmosphere in the field. No one dared to talk about it after she passed. People also became more sensitive to the spirits that were believed to be around big trees and large termite mounds.

One time our work took us far away from the village, near an isolated patch of wild bushes and trees. One of the biggest and tallest trees among the growth was a tamarind tree. It was known to the locals that not too many years ago a young woman had hung herself from that tree. During lunch breaks, I was always scavenging for food to take home after work. I forgot all about the tamarind tree, but when I came face-to-face with the tree, I felt a chill in the middle of the extreme heat of the day. Between the tree and me there was an empty patch of land about twenty-five feet wide. I was afraid to search for the branch that the young woman had hung herself from, even though I wanted to. I felt as though she was looking down at me. Without looking up, I scanned the trunk and saw some dried tamarind on the ground. Pa asked for forgiveness from the spirits for cutting the trees in the cemetery ground in French Village, and I thought that I could do the same. I asked for forgiveness, picked as much tamarind as I could from the ground, and proceeded to climb the tree. I asked for forgiveness again and again as I picked as much fruit as quickly as I could.

At the same time, I thought that perhaps the same branch where I stood was the very one she had used. I was on the tree for less than five minutes before I couldn't take it anymore. I thanked the spirit, got down, and walked away slowly and lightheaded. With some distance between us, I looked back and noticed the tree was mostly brown and covered with fruit. I took a bite of the tamarind and realized it was a sweet tamarind tree. Not many tamarinds are sweet, but this one was. The women at the field thought I was crazy. They were afraid of me because they couldn't figure me out. One woman said: "The Chinese kids don't believe in spirits. They don't know better." I played along and never let them know how I really felt.

Every harvest season it was clear that the Black Uniforms took rice away from us in burlap bags, but I never saw it happen. However, one day during this third harvest season I heard rumbling and roaring. Then large trucks drove past our hut to the rice cleaning field nearby. The men on the truck were in dark green khaki uniforms with one giant red star in the middle of their caps. They parked their trucks and waited for them to be loaded, then drove off with almost all the rice we had harvested. They were men from Communist China.

Many people came down with malaria during the harvest season. I contracted malaria toward the end of the harvest. Every day I woke up in the morning tired and weak. When everybody was out of the hut, I waited for the cycle of symptoms to start.

The fist symptom was shivering cold. Just as the shadow of the thatched roof hit a specific spot on the ground, I started to get ready by grabbing the only blanket we had and going off to sit in the hot sun, covered with the blanket. The chill within me reached the point that even in the middle of the extreme heat of harvest time, the blanket could not keep me warm. My body would shake uncontrollably, my teeth chattering. Then I would crawl back to the hut and lie on the bamboo floor, covering myself with everything we had and waiting for Em. At lunchtime Em would come and sit on top of me to control the shaking. Unsure of her action, Em would say, "I think if I don't sit on you, you won't feel so sore and painful afterward." I would plead for her to sit on me because when she sat on me, the shaking was not so violent, and I felt better.

Then Em would go back to work, and I would pass out, only to be awakened by high fever. The fever was so high that I cried uncontrollably for help like a baby. I felt as if my internal organs were on fire. My eye sockets felt like they were steaming. I felt pain and burning from the inside out and howled, just as others before me who were strong enough to howl did. I knew I could die from malaria, but dying was not in my mind. I was just responding to pain. Em would leave work early and show up just in time to cover my entire body with a gooey mix of crushed neem leaves and water, while I was gasping for air. I felt so much better and felt the steam escaping my body.

After the fever, I must have passed out again, only to wake up with a different kind of pain: a throbbing headache, like someone stood there pounding on my temples with the back of an ax. My eyes felt like something was pulling them out of their sockets. I tossed and turned and begged God to stop—stop sooner, please.

By the time everybody came back from the field, all my symptoms were mostly gone except muscle ache and joint pain. But then I was confronted with hunger. For this reason alone, when someone was going through malaria, the Black Uniforms would say we have "psychological fever," which meant that we were faking our sickness. In their eyes, psychological fever could only be treated by head removal.

My malaria lasted for at least a month. Every day from about ten o'clock in the morning to five o'clock in the afternoon, I had to endure a cycle of cold, shivering, hot, pain, headache, and hunger. Only when I was not enduring the pain was I thinking about the possibility that I may not survive it. It was a reality, but somehow it didn't scare me, perhaps because I was next to Em.

Chapter 11

Harvest Season of 1978

Kheang was a beautiful boy with strong yet gentle facial features. Even when food was scarce, Kheang looked strong, not so much in a physical way, but more in his demeanor and spirit. He was tall, good-looking, and twelve-years old when the Black Uniforms took him away from us.

Before they took him to the meeting, I watched Em cut his hair with dull cast-iron scissors that she had borrowed. Combing his hair slowly and gently with her fingers, a wrinkle lay between her eyebrows, and tears were in her eyes, but not enough to form a drop. As she wiped her eyes, then wet his hair, her body shook from the uneven breaths she took while trying to control her emotions and to be strong for her baby.

I watched them like a sad scene out of a play. There was nothing I could do; it had to go on. I didn't want to do anything because it was their time to bond with words, expressions, comfort, and emotions that they would keep forever and that I should not interrupt. Kheang cried quietly but surely not from the dull scissors yanking on his dirty, tangled hair. Perhaps he was crying because he wanted the time with Em to last or because he knew the worst was yet to come.

Em spoke, "Dear God, for all the good things that I have done, please grant me one wish: let me see my baby again."

The next day we found out that the Black Uniforms had decided to keep the boys in the village where we were. So Kheang was only a field away from our hut, in a wooden house with many other boys of similar age.

Em was so happy with the news, but Pa's response was: "Sooner or later they are going to take your baby farther away."

After about a week, Kheang began sneaking home every night. Em always had some fish or rice for him to nibble on—not a lot—just enough to munch on a few bites. Kheang needed food as much as he needed to be together with us. He would tell us what happened during the day. He told us a story about the Black Uniforms making boys take turns guarding their place at night to protect their comrades from the enemies. From this experience, he had learned to sleep while sitting up.

Pa asked him what he would do when the enemy came at him. "I'd ask if they can take me with them," he responded. Pa smiled proudly.

"Jair Tuch, today I ate roasted worms for a snack," Kheang told me, grinning.

"What?" I said.

"Yep!"

"Seriously?" In a split second, my expression changed from disgust to sympathy that my little brother had fallen so low as to eat worms. Then I remembered I had eaten rat when I was in the Chamnaom sick-house.

"They were banana worms, not the ordinary ones," Kheang said.

That's what I told people about the rats I ate. They were field rats, not the ordinary ones.

"They are in the cocoon of a banana leaf. They are white and hardly move. We just toss the whole leaf into the hot coals. They taste okay."

You're okay, and I love you no matter what. I hate what the Black Uniforms have done to us.

Kheang was growing taller and stronger right before our eyes. Four years younger than me, he was as tall as I was. Sooner rather than later, they would take him away to the older boy team.

Em said, "I am afraid you will forget where we came from."

Kheang quickly reassured Em, "I will never forget noodles." Kheang loved all kinds of noodle dishes. Prior to the Black Uniforms takeover, every time Em asked us what we want for dinner, Kheang would say he wanted noodles. It had been three years since we last had a taste of a noodle.

About two months after they took Kheang away, Em and Pa thought that I should return to the girl team. Em said to me, "Little, you are getting stronger. You know sooner or later they will come to take you away again. You can wait until then, or you can volunteer to go back and choose the girl team that is in this village."

The expression on my face must have been begging for more explanation when Em continued, trying to convince me. "If you go back to the team in this village, you are likely to be one of the leaders because you would be one of the oldest girls. The current girl leader has been complaining that she needs help."

I listened quietly but was not sure why Em wanted me to leave her.

Em continued uneasily. "In that role, you could help influence other leaders to keep your brother close to us. He acts very mature and looks too tall for his age, and they are going to take him away any day now. But the truth is that he is still too young to be away from us. He will be so afraid and will do everything they tell him. He will be brainwashed."

I thought, What if the opposite happens? Both Kheang and I will be away from you for sure.

I would have rather waited until they came and took me away, but it was a sacrifice that I had to make, just like Chenda did for me. Now I had to do it for my little brother. Chenda left so I could stay. Now I would leave so Kheang might get a chance to stay closer to Em and Pa a little longer. Unlike Chenda, I would at least be in the same village as Em.

I readied myself to leave the hut with a bag of my essential belongings in my hands—a spoon and a plate, a pair of patched old pants, and a long-sleeved shirt— but I didn't want to leave without saying something or hearing words of wisdom from either Em or Pa. There was nothing to be said. Pa broke the awkward silence by walking away without even taking a glance at me. I knew then that it was not so much Em's idea but Pa's, but I was not mad at him. I knew Pa was always proud of Kheang, just like all of us. It would be a final blow to Pa if they were to move Kheang away.

The girl team leader was an easygoing young woman. She didn't care or give us a hard time if we stayed home sick. Although she was not mean and we didn't have much in common, we did have a good rapport as Em was hoping for. Every night she would flirt with the boy leaders, laughing loudly and yelling when she talked to them.

At night, while our team leader was out flirting, I was tasked to look over the young girls. They were not as brave as the girls in my previous team. They were much younger, scared, and very quiet. Many of them still wet their bed every night. They did what they were told. There was no individualism within the group. They had no interest in each other and left me alone. I felt lonely and out of place. Through the night my task was to wake up girls to do their guard duty. Many nights the guards team slept through the night while guarding. Other times they would wake me when they thought their time was up, so that they could go to sleep in their spots, and I would have to wake up the next team for guard duty.

The good thing during this time was that I got to see Em more than ever. I was stationed in a pagoda building, and Em was working under the building, sifting rice. So every time I did not report to work, I got to see Em during the day whenever I came down to the eating shack or to the bathroom. I got to hear her laughing with the women, telling jokes that only older women would understand. Sometimes I would look down between the wooden slats of the floor and watch Em working. Somehow, watching her repeating the motion of sifting rice made me feel content. It would silence the world, and I thought about nothing else.

One day I went to do my number two job in the orchard, where cassava grew in rows. Every time I was there, I checked the plants to see if there was a sign of baby roots forming. Finally, on that one day, I saw not the roots themselves, but a sign that some-one had been pulling a plant out for its roots. I turned my head and checked around like a wild animal in a farmyard, then I sat still as if I was just bending my legs. My fingers scratched the earth that was cracked from the bulging baby cassava root. I looked around again before I committed, then quickly broke the plant and pulled out a baby cassava about the size of a baby's wrist. I walked away from the crime scene to a line of small trees along a dry, shallow ditch where I could hide between the trees and eat the sweet, raw baby cassava root. Suddenly a man in a black uniform stepped out of the tree line and asked me, "What you doing?"

I knew I was in big trouble. What was going to happen to me?

The man started to recite the law of the land and threatened to take me to the official. I begged him and promised him that I wouldn't do this again. I was not an enemy; I was just hungry.

He said, "Such a shame to have a beautiful girl like you commit such a terrible crime." He grabbed my arm and pushed me toward the ditch between the rows of small trees and bushes. I fell into the dry ditch, scrambled to get back up, and sat on the edge.

"If you want to live, you have to do what I say."

"What do you want from me?" I truly did not know what he wanted. I knew that he probably wanted to rape me, but what is *rape*? I had heard of the word, and knew that it was a terrible thing that could happen to a girl, but not how bad it could be.

"I want to lie down next to you," he said.

I knew enough to know that a man and wife sleeping together was how women got pregnant. "If you lie down next to me, I will get pregnant. Then they will cut my head off. How about we just sit down and you can touch my breasts?"

He chuckled. I felt better, not so scared.

"I won't make you pregnant, and I won't hurt you," he said.

He started to caress me, then again forced me down into the ditch and began to pull my pants down. All my life I had never even looked at my naked self. Now this ugly Black Uniform man had pulled my pants down and was rubbing his naked body against mine. I prayed to let it be done soon, for if someone found me with him like this, it would be worse than stealing cassava root.

Before he let me walk out, he told me that he wanted to see me again, that he would wait for me at about the same time the next day. I told him what he wanted to hear.

When I got back to the girls' place, I went straight to Em and squatted next to her. "Em, I need to talk to you." She saw that something was wrong. She stood up and walked me away from the women—not far away, but far enough that they could not hear our conversation. When I looked back, I saw eyes were on us.

"I was raped." Tears started to come out as soon as the words were spoken.

"Stop crying, you'll let them know," Em said.

In my head I said, I am the bad luck child. I bring so much hardship to you and Pa. Now this shame. I am not a good daughter to you.

Em doubted me. "Why do you say that? When and where did this happen?"

When I told her, I saw disappointment in her face in a way that I had never seen before and watched the pain engulf her whole body. As I told her more, her poor soul was tortured. In a split second, she summoned herself and tried to lessen the impact. "This happened to one of your aunts, too, when she was a teenager, but that did not stop her from having a good family and future. You will be okay."

I felt the opposite of what Em was hoping for when she told me that. I felt sad and didn't realize this could affect my future, but it made sense now.

"Let's not talk here anymore," said Em. "Come to the hut after supper."

I went up to my place, lay down, and replayed what had happened. What could I have done? What was going to happen to me? Would I get pregnant? What would I do if I got pregnant? How many days and months would it take before my stomach stuck out? I felt sick to my stomach. I could not wait to talk to Em some more. I skipped supper and snuck out to see her.

Outside the hut and away from prying eyes and ears, Em was already waiting for me.

She started off by saying, "Tell me every detail of what happened."

I answered her without any expression. "No, he was not one of the boy leaders in the village. He was one of the Black Uniforms. No, he did not carry a gun, but he wore a black outfit and had a long machete with him."

"How can you be sure he was one of the Black Uniforms?" Em asked.

I started to doubt myself. Why did I assume that?

By then, many of the former farmers and peasants had started to wear black clothes. I would not have been so scared of him if I had not assumed this. I could have run away. But what if he whacked me with that machete? Maybe that would have been better.

Em went on to ask, "Was he one of the people in this village?"

I responded, "No, I've never seen him before. He was Khmer, with an old and mean face. He was about thirty years old."

Em asked, "Are you in pain?"

I wasn't sure what she meant.

"Are you physically in pain?" Em clarified.

I replied, "No he didn't hit me or bruise me."

Without saying a word the thoughts came to my mind. He forced me, but not that hard. I could have fought, but I didn't. Why didn't I? I wish I had. This is too painful, Em. It's all my fault. I let it happen so easily.

"Are your private parts in pain when you walk?" Em asked, putting the same question in a different way.

"No," I replied, and thought, *Should I be in pain?*

Em seemed perplexed and frustrated. "Then what do you mean when you said you were raped?"

With a calm voice, I told Em, "He pulled my pants down." But with pain and anger I thought, *Isn't that bad enough, Em?*

I saw Pa walk toward the hut, and I asked Em, "Does Pa know?"

"Yes," Em replied softly.

When Pa walked by me, I looked down at the dirt by my feet. I was not sure whether I was avoiding his anger or his pain. As he walked by, I heard him say under his breath, "Unlucky motherfucker." I felt the beams of his eyes burning holes in my skull. I stood still, feeling hollow. I looked at Em, turned away, and walked back to the girls' place. Em didn't stop me. I felt she was frustrated and not as understanding as I was hoping for.

On the way back, I felt naked—exposed and in the open, like the whole world knew what had happened to me. I had no one to cry to. It was the worst thing that could happen to a person.

I replayed the whole thing over and over. The more I thought about it, the more I felt that I could have escaped if only I had known what was going to happen to me. I started to blame Em for not telling me to be careful with these things. I didn't even know what he wanted or what he was going to do. But maybe knowing or not knowing made no difference. *Not only am I an unlucky child, now I'm going be an unlucky wife. Will I be an unlucky mother or grandmother? No, I won't let these unlucky things continue. I will change it for good. I won't marry any man.* I had to see Em again because there were so many unanswered questions. The main one was whether I would get pregnant?.

The next day I went to see Em again. Before I could say anything, she already had questions for me. But she looked mad this time. Maybe she thought that I could have gotten away easily.

"Tell me *exactly*—what did he do to you?" Em asked.

"He made me lie on my side in front of him. He pulled my pants past my crotch. Then he did it. Then I felt wet and warm."

"You just lay there?" she asked in disbelief.

My heart was breaking into many pieces, "I was scared."

Em persisted. "Why didn't you fight or scream for help? Or run away?"

I had no answer. The question squeezed the tears out of my heart. I wished I was dead.

"Your father wants to know if maybe you wanted it too," Em blurted out.

Oh, that was it! He thought I wanted it. But no, I didn't want it. And how can you ask me this kind of question, Em? I couldn't answer Em.

Em took a deep breath and tried to calm down for her next question. "Were you bleeding?"

Pleading and desperate for support, I replied, "No.

I felt wet afterward, but no blood. Am I going to get pregnant?"

She asked me again about the wet and warm fluid that I felt. We both were terribly uncomfortable about going into detail, but I had to be as clear as I could in hopes that she could tell me whether I could be pregnant.

"Was he inside you?" Em asked.

What? I wondered. I had not a clue what Em was talking about.

Em asked again about the pain, "Did you feel tight-ness or pain in your crotch when that happened?"

Still, I had to know the answer to my question. "No, I didn't feel any physical pain. Em, will I get pregnant or not?"

Em replied softly, "I don't know for sure because your body just started to change recently."

"When will I know for sure?" I asked Em again in distress.

She answered solemnly, "In the next few months."

In that moment, I made up my mind, and told Em: "I will commit suicide if I get pregnant."

Em looked sad and fearful, but she didn't respond to my threat. We stood quietly and stared into each other's eyes, knowing that committing suicide would be better than being decapitated in front of people in a meeting where they would force Em and Pa to watch.

The shame, anger, and embarrassment made me walk away, ready to be on my own and never wanting to see Em or Pa again. How could they doubt me? But maybe they were right. Maybe it was my curiosity more than fear that kept me quiet. No, it is not possible, I hate that man. I'll never forget that dark and ugly face. He ruined my dream of having a good family of my own someday.

In my mind, it was clear what I had to do. As soon as I know I am pregnant, I'll go to French Village, where there are steep riverbanks. I'll try to abort the baby by making myself fall. If this doesn't work, I'll hang myself. Maybe I will come to say goodbye to Em. Or maybe I won't. If it turns out that I'm not pregnant, I'll never get married.

For the next couple of weeks, I would go to work and not stay at home, even when I felt sick. Staying home meant I would have to go to the bathroom in that place again. When I did come back from the field, I would not go to see Em and Pa.

One night when I came back from the eating shack, I saw Em standing by the stairs, waiting for me. She said, "Just want to make sure you are okay." I had never seen or heard of any mother who came to the girl team and waited to talk to her kid. When I saw her there, all of the barriers that I placed between me and her were melting away. Somehow, I was happy that she was taller than me. I felt her hug without touching, and her love without saying a word.

The following month, I made myself fall every opportunity I got. Every now and then I forgot about my problem, but it haunted me and made my stomach sick when it returned.

I missed my friend Tahry. I wished I could see her again and tell her what happened to me. She would understand. I missed Moy, my Chinese girlfriend. I missed talking and laughing. This episode changed me more than starvation or hard labor. But it was all going to get better because I had Em with me. I hardly talked to anybody besides Em and Kheang. But that was okay because Em loved me.

A couple of months after the cassava root incident, a high-ranking official came to visit our camp. He came with an entourage. They walked in a perfectly straight line to make themselves look bigger and stronger than they really were. Their leader looked at me and continued to turn his head to track me as he walked past me. At that moment I felt like I should have hidden behind the wooden slat wall, but it was too late.

I had already prepared myself when my leader approached me the next day, and in a soft, sad, quiet voice she told me that I had to leave the camp. I didn't ask for a reason. I was either too old to be in the kids' camp, or not pure enough to be the leader, or both. I didn't want to say goodbye to Em. I didn't need to see her. *What for? It was just another goodbye.* Why should I torture myself and give them the pleasure of seeing us bleed?

With my small bag, I followed the leader down the wooden stairs. The young girls' eyes were all on us. I imagined all the mothers' eyes under the house were squinting at us as well since all the noise associated with grinding, pounding, and fanning the rice had stopped—all except for one person sifting alone. The unique and uneven solo sound continued, sifting the rice by itself, sending me off with blessings and prayers that someday we would see each other again. I imagined Em's eyes filled with sorrow, staring aimlessly at the sifting basket but didn't know for sure because I didn't want to find out. With the sound of her solo rice sifting, I felt her arms around me and her hand pressing my head to her chest.

The leader stood at the bottom of the stairs as a gesture for me to go and say goodbye to Em. I stood next to the leader and looked away from the sound. I saw and felt nothing, but I heard every grain of rice Em tossed and dropped onto the sifting basket. The leader slowly and gently led me away—from Em.

The faint sound of Em's sifting finally gave way to the silent world as I was led away from Meeting Creek. I regretted having to leave Em and Pa for a sacrifice that led to no reward. I felt that I had failed them. We were too smart for our own good, for that alone I felt shame and embarrassment. I thought about the cassava root incident and the happy time I had had with my Chinese girlfriend Moy and wished that Em never asked me to leave her.

I was taken back to the Chark girls' camp for the second time. The first was when Chenda and I had surrendered ourselves after we left Pa, Em, and Kheang in Meeting Creek. This time I felt lonely and desperate. I was in a world that I had never experienced before. Even with so many boys and girls around me, still I was alone, with no sister, no brothers, no cousins, no friends, not even a familiar face. I was in the same Chark camp but with a new team and different leaders. None of the girls knew what my family looked like or anything about me. Nor I about them.

I missed Chenda. I had not seen or heard anything from her since Kheang and I took food for her in Water Mill Village about six months ago.

After a couple of weeks at the new girls' camp in

Chark pagoda, I felt that I could not endure the loneliness, so I started to plan my escape. I packed my ration of mushy, steamed brown rice with its musty smell into a small cotton pouch with some dirty rock salt. All I needed was two days' rations. I imagined that if the leader hunted for me, she would come within the first two days. After that, Em would know what to do.

In the middle of a moonlit night, I crawled down from the pagoda building and snuck out from the camp. As I passed the edge of the village, I recalled my crime in the cassava patch that resulted in a scar on my life when that devil took advantage of my situation. *What would I do this time if a similar thing happened? Would I kill a man? Possibly, but not for sure. One thing was sure: Either he or I would die fighting.* It was dark, and I was more afraid of such devils than I was of the Black Uniforms or ghosts. I was grateful for my blessing, for was not pregnant.

Finally, I was far away from any village. I felt free, walking in the dark through the uneven fields—free from rules, laws, and torture. It was just me and the sound of the creatures of the night. After a while I started to worry that the sun would come up and I would be exposed in the middle of an open field. So I hunted for a good tree to climb and hide in when I was at the edge of Meeting Creek. As I climbed up a tree just outside the Meeting Creek Village, I asked the keeper of the tree that was in the middle of a termite mound for permission to use the tree as a sanctuary for the day and for forgiveness. My request rambled and turned into a plea to the keeper of the tree to help me and protect me from the evil within mankind.

As the sky began to change color, I realized that I was not too far from the grave of Om Pad's sister-in-law, who had died from child labor and been buried with her unborn child. Not too far away was another fresh grave for her friend who had died from the same cause a week later. I felt my blood rushing to my heart, leaving my feet, hands, and my head to be chilled by the early morning sky. *Please don't haunt me,* I pleaded.

My heart pounded when I heard the sound of footsteps plodding through the water along the edge of the creek. *Please don't haunt me*, I pleaded again. To my relief, a man's profile emerged from the thick bushes. He had a small bamboo basket hung over his shoulder. Even within the thick leaves of the tree, I felt vulnerable and exposed because I could see him, so there was a good chance he could see me. He was definitely committing a crime: finding food for his own family and not for the whole village. He continued to plod along, unaware that he was being observed. After he was gone, I felt confident that the tree was a good hiding spot.

I heard rustling from the village as the sun emerged over the edge of the horizon. Soon after, a line of old, tired, and ragged people emerged from the tree line along the creek and into the field. I had no clue which field they were going to work on that day. The line slowly turned its head toward me, moving uneventfully under my position. I don't think I was breathing at all.

I wanted so much to go to our hut, but I needed to stick with my plan. My hope was that if the leaders came and couldn't find me, they would forget about me. I wanted to come down from the tree, but I was afraid to be seen. So I stayed on the tree, bored and tired and contemplating all kinds of things. *Would Em be happy to see me? Am I causing her trouble? What would be her reason to keep me this time? Should I sneak back to the camp?*

An army of black giant ants was invading my musty, mushy brown rice. I tried to salvage the rice, but there were already more ants than rice. When I opened the pouch, ants were oozing out of the pouch and were all over me. Moreover, the musty rice turned into a sour and mushy rice ball. I emptied the spoiled rice and tried to salvage the cotton pouch instead.

Before the day was over, I found myself hiding near our hut by the creek. I'm not sure if it was my hunger, my curiosity, or both that pushed me to go to our hut. Watching quietly in a thick bush by the creek, I saw hustling around our hut. Four or five Black Uniforms were there. One of them was the new girl leader, wearing her pitch black sarong looked as if it was pressed. Her voice was calm and determined. Some of the neighbors were answering the Black Uniforms. I didn't see Em or Pa nearby. Somehow I was not afraid. My heart was content while I watched the whole thing unfold as though it had nothing to do with me. I had no plan but was confident that they would not find me. It was a strange feeling. I think people were more scared for me than I was scared for myself.

Suddenly I was startled by a man who appeared nearby. He shouted as he claimed his prize. "I found her! I found her!" Then he demanded: "Come out! Come out! now!"

I stared at him as if I didn't understand him. In those split seconds, I decided that I would not do what they told me. I didn't care about the consequences. The man grabbed my arm and yanked me through the bush. He threw me to the ground, and I felt an angel's soft arms catch me. Angry voices were around me, but the angel patted my head. I felt a dull pain on my ribcage and my head, the ripping of my arm from its socket, the scraping of my body, but I felt the angel hover over me. A lady's voice screamed in agony. I heard the same voice pleading for them to stop. I felt the urge to comfort her, to tell her that I was okay, but I couldn't move or see. A loud, strong voice yelled into my ear: "You can't do this to your mother! You are going to kill her!"

Oh no, I thought, *Em mustn't see me like this*. I said goodbye to my angel and fought to get on my feet, to stop the girl leader from yanking my hair, to stop her from torturing Em's baby. Finally able to see again, I saw Em. She was shaking and frantically pacing the hut like a mother hen watching a weasel snatching up her chick. I heard Em pleading for the devils to stop hurting her baby. I saw the man with that same strong and deep voice that brought me back to reality. He was comforting Em, saying, "Everything will be okay now." To the Black Uniforms he said with that deep, calm voice: "She is young and stupid and doesn't understand the goodness of our government. She has learned her lesson." I still heard Em crying the dry-tear cry as I continued to walked away from her.

I knew that they would punish me, but I didn't know how. Often when a person was escorted by the Black Uniforms, she or he was punished or even eliminated. I thought about Em. *How will she go on, knowing her baby will be tortured one way or another?* I thought about Kheang and how my actions would affect him and his relationship with other boys. I was sorry that I made their life miserable. I was selfish. When I thought about

Pa, I was sure that he was proud of me for having the guts to stand against them and ignore their rules and law. Then again, I thought about Em: How many more stabs to the heart could she take?

At one point on the return trip, there was a turn on the road. There was no hut to be seen and no one nearby when the Black Uniforms told me to stop. I thought about how they would execute me: a blow to my neck without letting me know, or would they make me watch the executioner? I imagined that the girl leader would take pleasure in executing me. She had what Cambodians call the "eye of a wild hen," the kind of eyes that chill your bones when they scan you. They were eyes that were untamable. They never experience love.

One of the Black Uniform men tied my hands with a rope. I said to myself, "It's okay. It will be quick." But then I remembered that I once saw a man walk by our hut with his upper arms tied behind him. Em told me that when the arms are tied behind the back, it's definitely an execution. Since only my hands were tied in front of me, maybe I would not be executed.

The man handed the end of the rope to the girl leader. She walked me to and through the camp like a dog. I was an example of what could happen to anyone who ran away from the camp. At the end of the day,

I was back at the Chark pagoda girls' camp the third time. I should have been grateful that I was still alive, but instead I felt embarrassed and ashamed.

I was now an outcast. People tried to avoid me; they didn't want to be seen with me. "It's okay," I said to myself. "It's not their fault; I understand."

Chapter 12

PROMISE

April 1978

I decided that I would never try to go to see Em again, at least not from this girls' camp. I never heard from her nor she from me. But I was sure that no news was good news. If I had been executed, the village would know and so would she. My life was spared, but I was broken. I forgot how to smile, not to mention laugh. My heart was physically squeezed every time I thought of Em. She was the only person in the world that could feel my pain.

I reported to work every day, and every day I worked hard to give them no reason to eliminate Em's girl. All the weight that I had gained while staying with Em at Meeting Creek was shedding away from my body. I began to look like a walking skeleton again. People started to treat me as if I were a walking spirit. Some girls were scared to even talk to me. When I could no longer get up for food, they took me to a sick-house. I was cradled in an old krama and suspended from a bamboo bar. A team of men took turns carrying me to the Water Mill sick-house. I knew they had given up on me. But I couldn't give up. I needed to see Em again. When I saw her again, *then* I would give up. I wanted to die in her arms, not alone.

The Water Mill sick-house was a pagoda before the Black Uniforms took over. All the sick people were lined up in the worship house. There was a young woman in the sick-house who wouldn't leave me alone. She was at least five years older than I, and her face showed the beauty of her past. She always asked me how I was feeling and what bothered me the most. I just wanted her to leave me alone. "I don't know," I would tell her. Every day she would tell me how she was in a worse condition than I and that they had already given up on her, but she was getting better, and I would too. Then she would rub her bald head and brag: "I made a promise that I would shave my head if I survive."

The shaved head and the way she bragged about it made me smile again. I was thinking, *To whom did you promise? God, of course, but no one dared to use such a word. It would insult our government.* Every time she bragged about her bald head, something inside me just wanted to giggle. But I was too exhausted. All I could do was twitch my lips and tighten my stomach. I said to myself, "I shall make sure to not make such a promise."

I can no longer remember her name. For the first few weeks of my stay, every morning she would prop herself up, hunch over, and slowly walk with her cane to my bedside. Her voice and her mind were the strongest part of her. They attracted all kinds of girls. Those who weren't bedridden would roam around like her entourage. Even the Black Uniform nurses liked to hear her stories. Many stories were funny, but most were girl talk. Today I think of her as my angel. She made me laugh again and not as sad from missing Em. However, one time she told us that a girl without pubic hair is a bad luck girl. Another mark against me. At least this one was hidden. That worried me for at least two or three more years.

When I regained my strength, probably just from resting, I looked for my sister Chenda. However, I was told that her team had been moved to Dang Trang. I had never been to Dang Trang, but I heard that it was close to Meeting Creek.

The Water Mill sick-house was overflowing with sick people, so they moved some of us to Banana Village sick-house. I felt blessed, for I would be closer to Em again.

The Black Uniform nurses in the Banana Village

sick-house were strict compared to those in other sick-houses. They treated us patients as if we were enemies. We were processed prior to getting a bed. While standing in line, waiting to be processed, I thought of how I would answer each question that I overheard. The two questions that made me nervous were:

Why are you here?

What school grade were you in?

These nurses would not like my reason for being here. If I were to tell them I'm just tired, they would label me as having psychological illness—which is not good. If I were to say I don't know, they might try to diagnose me, and that would not be good either. I had to find a better reason quickly.

The second question was purely to assess my family status prior to the Black Uniforms time. For that reason alone, Em had told all of us to lower our grade if we ever got asked. I remembered that I was supposed to be second grade, but I feared no one would believe me.

The line moved faster than I wanted it to while I searched frantically for the right answers to the two questions and tried hard to hide my fear. I said a prayer to God and my ancestors one last time before I stepped forward to stand in front of the table with a Black Uniform nurse behind it and a second nurse standing next to the table.

"I have *marring*," I said. The nurses responded with expressions that were somewhat subdued and not as vicious as before. *Marring* was like a cancer to the Black Uniforms and to the people who lived in rural areas of Cambodia. The word described lumps that form behind the ears and eventually became swollen and infected. They believed that marring is incurable and that the infection recurs; thus, the victim weakens with frequent fever and eventually dies from the disease. Out of curiosity, the nurses took turns checking my neck, and they could feel and see the scars that were left from the infection I'd had while I was in French Village. I told the nurses of my recurring symptom, and they seemed satisfied with my reason for not reporting to work. The truth was I had some recurrences of these lumps swelling and becoming sore, but then they went away and were never bad enough to cause a fever.

I felt the intensity of their x-ray vision when they stared at me, but decided to move on. One of them asked: "What was your grade at school?"

With little confidence that they would believe me, I tried hard to cover my fear and said, "Second grade."

The nurse behind the desk looked mad at me. Clearly she did not believe me. She slammed the pen on the paper and shoved it to me. "Write your name down," she demanded. My angel made me reach over with my left hand to write my name. The nurse quietly stared at me, and was disappointed that my writing was ugly. To try and remove any doubt from her, I said, "It has been a while since I last wrote." With hesitation, she decided to go on with the rest of her questions and then dismissed me.

The second nurse led me to a small bed. I lay down on my new bed and quietly said thanks to the angel who had helped me with the second question. My tears flowed softly as I lay there, struggling to release all the fear that I had been trying to contain.

The next day the nurses came around with needles and syringes in their hand, offering shots to patients. The shot was supposed to help patients gain strength. The same needle was inserted into one patient after another. When the syringe was emptied, they refilled it with a liquid that was stored in an old classic Coke bottle.

In my head I thought, I would rather die in the field than take that shot. But what do I do? How do I get out of this? I pleaded to God to help me.

When the nurses came to my bed, one of them said, "A medicine man is coming this afternoon to treat you."

As the nurses walked away, I gave thanks to God. At least I was safe for the moment. Later that afternoon, when the medicine man came, he rolled up cotton into three tiny balls and placed them behind my left ear while I was forced to lie down. After he said his magic, he proceeded to burn them. I was still grateful that I did not have to take the shot but was able to endure the burn without any resistance.

Days later, after learning the routine of the nurses, I went to see Em and Pa. They had been moved from that small thatched hut nearby Om Pad to one of the longhouses. Two thatched walls separated them from their neighbors, and a half-wall gave them some privacy from the main dirt road in the village. There was no back wall, so Em planted some sugar cane on the back of their compartment for privacy. The government allowed its people to have a garden as long as the produce was brought to the community kitchen. Those who were too weak or had small children didn't have energy or time to care for a garden. Those who were lazy became best of friends to the government because they volunteered to make sure that the produce from gardens was properly shared. It was as though the government helped those in need, punished those who produced, and rewarded the lazy ones. In addition to privacy, Em grew the cane because it made her feel good to see the fruits of her effort and to take her mind away from all the problems that she had to endure.

I wasn't sure if this new place was the punishment

for my running away from girls' camp, or if Pa did something to piss them off. The Black Uniforms preferred to move you around if they didn't like you. The more you moved, the fewer possessions you had and the less opportunity to hide things from them. Also, they watched over you while you were packing and rushed you if you took too long. "Why should this take you so long? You should have nothing except for a couple of sets of clothes, bedding, spoons, and a plate. The government is taking care of the rest of your needs."

At least twice a week I would sneak out after lunch to visit them in the longhouse. Most of the time I hardly saw Em or Pa, but I always managed to find some mushy rice in a Gigo can they had hidden for Kheang and me. More often than not, Kheang and I showed up in the longhouse at the same time. We sat face to face like two little mice, quietly taking turns passing the can. Em told me that Chenda had been sneaking out to visit her too, but our paths never crossed. I never emptied the can by myself, nor would I ever find an empty can.

A few weeks later, additional patients arrived at the sick-house. These new patients were frailer and thinner than any of us. They had wide eyes and a vicious way of looking at us. They had lost trust in humankind and in God long ago. Some of them spoke with a Vietnamese accent, and others had strong accents that

I was not familiar with. One old woman with a strong Vietnamese accent told us that she had lived through months without rations. The government had left them alone to fight among themselves for food. She told us, "Where I came from, humans eat humans."

We all stood up and dispersed. I had no doubt she was telling the truth, but I was feeling sad for her. I didn't want to know what happened to the rest of her family.

The next time I saw Em, I shared the Vietnamese woman's story. Em told me that there were changes in the village as well. A new group of Black Uniforms came from the eastern part of the country. One by one they were quietly replacing most of the old Black Uniforms. They called themselves "Eastern Comrades." They had lighter skin and seemed to be more friendly toward people. And yes, they had the Easterner accent.

One day, Em was in the longhouse while I was there. I showed her the bedbug bites from the sick-house. Her gasp scared me more than I already was. I was afraid that I would have the same problem as the young Chinese girl in the Chamnaom sick-house who had died from an infection that she couldn't even see. I knew my bites were bad, but I couldn't see them because the infections were all on my butt, the only flesh I had left. The itching turned into pain and oozing a mix of blood

and other gunk. Em took one of her stomach prescrip-
tion pills that she had saved from Poipet, ground it into
white powder, and sprinkled onto the infected area.
The next day—literally—all the oozing stopped.

The sick-house was infested with bedbugs. Every
day I would place my straw mat in the hot sun, roll it
up, and give it a quick and strong pound to expel little
creatures out of the mat. The very first knock, many
would fall out and scramble for shelter. I tried to smash
as many of them as I could, but most crawled away
quickly and blended in with the dirt, especially the
small ones.

Sometimes Kheang would stop by the sick-house
and drop off food for me from Em. The Black Uniforms
took everything from Em and Pa, including the kettle
for boiling hot water. Nevertheless, Em found a way to
give me a cooked egg once in a while. She would bury
an egg in warm ash until it hardened within the shell,
just like a boiled egg.

Kheang would come to my bed by a window, drop
off the food, and quickly leave. I wanted him to stay a
little longer with me, but he always left so soon. I confronted him with my frustration. His response made
it clear that he was a young man and not just my little
brother any more. Even in this harsh environment, he
stood out as being good-looking and kind. He was shy

and conscientious in the way he acted around the girls in my sick-house. I saw the way those girls checked him out, and batted their eyelashes at him, even in their sickbeds. Needless to say, I felt special to have him as my brother.

The last time Kheang stopped by the sick-house, he looked pale and worried, not wearing the grumpy look he usually gave me.

What happened? I silently asked him with my expression. He tried to answer, but all I saw were his red eyes and tightened face. Without a word, he turned and walked away to the back of the sick-house. I met him a few minutes later in the thick banana patch.

"Why are you crying?" My words were more harsh than comforting, conveying that someone might become suspicious of his actions.

"I am leaving you," he spurted out as he looked softly into my eyes as though he was trying to comfort me.

His words shook my heart instantly. My hands and feet were suddenly cold.

"Don't cry, my dear little brother. Everything will be all right." That was the first and last sweet thing I said to Kheang.

He sobbed in silence, his face down and his tears pounding the earth with anger and pain. I stood inches away from Kheang, but could not do anything to help him.

"Don't cry, they might see you."

He wiped his tears and nose without a sound. He wanted to tell me something else, but I signaled him to stop talking. Still, he managed spit out the message: "Pa wants you to come home as soon as the lunch bell rings."

Not long after Kheang left, I walked thru the graveyard behind the Banana Village to Meeting Creek. I was still hoping Pa would take me, too, even though Kheang said he was leaving me. *Maybe Kheang was not being clear. Maybe I was fooling myself. I was Pa's least favorite kid. I was the bad luck child. He had told me that himself many times. Why would he take me with him?* I felt worthless.

But it is okay; Em loves me. Is Em going with them? Probably not because she can't walk that long distance. What about Chenda? Will she be at the longhouse today? If it is the case that only Pa and Kheang are leaving, then all the men in my family are leaving us. What are we to do? When are they leaving?

At the longhouse, I didn't see Chenda nor Em, but Kheang and Pa were there. The village was so quiet. Everybody was in the eating shack celebrating the third anniversary of the new government. Pa told me to go to our old hut and bring him a bag from Om Pad, our old neighbor.

"Be careful with the bag," Pa warned me.

On my way back from Om Pad's hut, I took a peek into the bag and found two brand new pairs of the Black Uniform shoes. My heart dropped. I knew for sure that this was real and that Pa and Kheang were going to leave us. The thought of being abandoned sadden me, but then it did not make sense for Pa to try and take Em along for she may not have been able to endure the hardship of trekking through the jungle. For that last thought alone, I felt better. I tried to convince myself that Pa was going to leave me behind so I could care for Em and not because I was the bad luck child that might curse his escape plan.

Many thoughts with different possibilities occupied my mind, but the feeling of being abandoned persisted. I resented the fact that Pa asked me to help with his escape but gave me no option to go with him nor an explanation as to why he did not want me to come long. I also remember thinking that I didn't want them to go. We were not starving like during the first monsoon.

Why did Pa have to go? Maybe I should take these shoes and go back to the sick-house. When are they leaving? Today? How long ago had Pa planned this? Maybe his timing had to do with the arrival of the

Eastern Comrades, and the third annual celebration of the Black Uniforms.

Back at the longhouse, I shared the mushy rice with Kheang for the last time. Not a word was spoken between us. I still didn't know when they were going to leave, and I was afraid to bring it up. I imagined we were waiting for Em. The quietness made me feel cold and shaky and gave me the urge to urinate. I stepped down from the longhouse into the sugar cane bush to urinate, but I could not completely let it out, nor could I completely finish. I squatted longer than I wanted to. Then Kheang spoke to me. I stood up quickly to be next to him. He began to address me calmly and clearly, but ended with a shaky sound from his heart.

"Jair Tuch ..." He paused as I listened intensely. He tried hard to control his emotion, as my crushed heart plugged my ears with the rushing of blood. Finally he was able to summon the rest of the message: "I don't want to go." The thought came to my mind, *Dear God, why are you so mean?*

"Why, you are crazy? You are lucky that Pa will take you," I said to encourage him.

"I'm scared," he whimpered softly.

I reached over to grab and squeeze his cold fingertips. It was the closest to hugging I could give him without being noticed.

"You take care of Em," he choked as he stared into my eyes. Tightening his lips, holding his breath, and squinting to control the tears, he added, "Please be gentle with her."

My baby brother, so thoughtful and caring. What a beautiful thing you are. You take care of yourself and don't worry about Em. I will take care of her no matter what.

My throat and lips were too tight and stiff to let any more words out, so I squeezed his hand tighter and nodded in reply.

I felt Pa waiting for us, and I turned and painfully climbed back on top of the bamboo floor, all the while wishing Kheang would not follow me. He could decide for himself and walk away, but how could a twelve-year-old boy decide anything like this for himself? He was too young, and I was not helping him.

Again we sat in complete silence. Kheang sat next to me, and Pa was facing us a couple of feet away against the opposite thatched wall. Just then I noticed both Kheang and Pa had on their best clothes, with only a few patches on them. The clothes were dry and clean with not even a speck of mud on them. I knew for sure: today was the day. Any minute now they were going to leave. Where was Em?

"Go wait for Pa at the place," Pa said, urging Kheang

to leave. He handed Kheang a small, tightly wrapped sack. Kheang grabbed the sack, and with one foot off the bamboo floor, he stopped and turned around to look at me one last time. I hugged him with my eyes. That was the last time I saw my baby brother's face.

I sat still as a statue as I watched Kheang pull away from me until he disappeared into a patch of trees at the end of the village. He was gone.

Pa was squatting on the bamboo floor in a fetal position, hugging his knees to his chest and leaning on nothing and no one but his own heart. He focused his eyes gently on mine. He was more beautiful than ever. He had made up his mind. He was calm, peaceful, and gentle. We had many sweet conversations in those last few minutes without the distraction of words.

Yes, I will take care of Em. I will be fine. Yes, I know you love me, and I love you too. I understand, but I don't want you to go.

I wanted to hold him and tell him that he was special to me. I wanted to bow to his feet to show him how much I respected him and to ask for forgiveness for all the bad things I had invoked for him to act harshly toward me. Most of all, I wanted to beg him for his blessing and beg him to make me a strong person so I could take care of Em.

All of a sudden I knew exactly what I wanted to tell

Pa, and it had to be quick because Kheang was waiting for him. Pa needed to know because it was good. I started to tell him:

"Last night I had a dream. I was in a shipwreck, but I survived. However, I was devastated because I couldn't find you and Kheang. I cried and wandered in the thick woods along the beach, looking for you and Kheang. Not too far away from that desolate beach, I found a small brick worship house that was peacefully quiet and filled with paintings lining its walls in chronological order, describing the story of Buddha and his enlightenment. My wet clothes dripped on the beautiful tile floor, but the keeper of the place kindly encouraged me to continue viewing and learning about the paintings along the walls. I wept and mourned as I learned about the story of Buddha. I empathized with him and his only son for the separation and torture they endured, inflicted by the greedy beggar.[21] I kept thinking that it was just like a story of you and Kheang. My sorrow came to a halt at the last few paintings. The Buddha in the

---

[21] Growing up I learned the story of how Buddha reached enlightenment. In the story, Buddha's practice of detachment was put to test by a greedy beggar, who begged for everything that Buddha had, including his children. The beggar's test resulted in both Buddha and his son having to endure painful separation, but eventually Buddha was able to reach enlightenment.

paintings looked more and more like you, Pa. And the Buddha's only son looked more and more like Kheang. In the very last painting, where Buddha reached enlightenment, you were in the orange monk wrap, sitting on a rock under the bodhi tree, and Kheang was standing next you in the same monk wrap."

Pa looked at me and calmly said, "The meaning of your dream is very good, my child. It is a peaceful and happy ending. It is a blessing for the trip."

I was happy and proud that I had told him of this good dream for his trip. But that feeling didn't last. Pa looked at me lovingly. I was convinced from that last look that he loved me. He wanted the best for me. I wanted to hug him so much. He was only a couple of feet away from me. We sat directly facing each other, but I couldn't even hold his hand although I wanted to. I wanted to say something else. But then Pa took a deep breath and he turned his head away from me and never looked back.

No … No! I am not ready, I yelled and cried silently within myself. I wanted to tell him to wait, but I knew I shouldn't.

Maybe the Black Uniforms were right that there is no God. For if God exists, he wouldn't allow us go through all this intense misery.

Don't cry, don't cry, I demanded to myself. *People will*

know. But softly and silently my tears flowed down my cheeks. I let them be so I would never forget the moment.

I situated myself so I could continue to see Pa as long as possible. I watched him walk away from me, watching every step he made until he disappeared into the same patch of trees that Kheang had gone to.

They were gone.

I crawled into the bedding corner and lay there waiting for Em. What would I tell her because she was late? They were gone already. Would she be able to control her agony and suppress the pain? She had to be able to; she didn't have a choice.

Em never came to the longhouse that day. When I could not stay any longer without getting into trouble with the Black Uniform nurses, I left too. I had to leave Em all alone when she needed help the most. It was probably the first time in her life that she spent the night alone.

On my way back to the sick-house, I thought about Kheang. I already missed him. But then, for a split second, the animal within me wedged a thought into my mind: *But now I can have all of the mushy rice to myself.* Oh, how terrible I felt even before the thought was complete! It came out of nowhere, and I was glad it was gone as quickly as it came.

I also thought about what was going to happen to us. From now on, it would be just us girls: Em, Chenda, and me. In this man's world, we would be dismissed and looked down upon without any regard or reservation. What was going to happen to us? What were they going to do to us? I wondered if Chenda even knew what happened on that day.

I always wondered if Kheang had confessed to Em that he was afraid and didn't want to leave. If so, what did he tell her? I never asked Em, nor did I ever tell Em or anyone else of my last conversation with Kheang. It would be too painful to relive.

That night at the sick-house, I sat outside with a couple of other girls, but I was not paying attention to them. It was a cool night. I was free to think. I imagined all the things that were happening to Em, Pa, and Kheang.

Em, sleeping by herself, must have been praying for Pa and Kheang's safety and reflecting on what Pa must have said to her, questioning what she should have or could have done and said to convince Pa to stay or keep Kheang with her. Remembering the gentleness and caring that she may never have again from either one of them, I was sure she was lashing out to God and begging him to take her life instead of making her live with this torture. Would this be the last strike she could handle? I yearned to lie down next to her.

Pa and Kheang—had they crossed the river yet? They needed to pass the river before the night was over. Kheang—he must have been thinking of Em. Pa—would he be okay walking? He always had problems walking straight because he was weak, and his knees always bothered him. Who were the people with Kheang and Pa? Who was leading them? Would I ever see them again?

I wished I had more time to say goodbye. The moment had happened too suddenly and was then gone too quickly. There had been too much to say. But my dream had a beautiful ending: They would make it. I prayed to our ancestors, the angels, and the keepers of the jungle to protect Pa and Kheang.

Chapter 13

LOVE

April of 1978

As expected, the next morning there was unsettled air in the sick-house. Quickly but quietly, everybody seemed to know the news: There were escapers last night. Someone frantically whispered, "They're escorting the fugitives' wives and kids. Look, they're coming by the sick-house." I ran to see it with my own eyes. The families of the escapees were paraded through the village for all to see. I believed if Pa and his friends had seen this, they might have been hesitant to leave.

I saw Em. Even though I expected to see her, I was not ready to see her as a person who lost everything. She was the last person in the line. Her dull, thick, short hair stuck out of her head like tangled wires, set as wide as her shoulders. Her grayish long-sleeved shirt was too big, and her dark gray pants were too short. In her hand she carried an old sarong that she turned into a makeshift sack to hold her belongings. On her bare feet, she walked as if she was floating on air. She looked at no one and saw nothing. Right then and there, I knew I could not let Em be all by herself. I wanted to be with her.

While the girls were mesmerized by the parade, I snuck back to the sick-house, packed my own little bag, and hustled to the bush near the trail ahead of the parade and away from all prying eyes. Hiding in the bush by the levee, I waited for Em to come by. I watched Em from a distance and had time to contemplate. It was a good thing that they walked her by the sick-house. I would rather die with her than experience the torture of living without her. She would not die alone.

For a quick second, I reflected back to the story about Bong Nick's mother, who had refused to let her husband be escorted alone. Now I understood. Love has no fear. I knew exactly what I was doing. I understood the possible consequences. I was exactly where I wanted to be—with Em. The world should know that Em's daughter loved her so much that she was willing to comfort her even when it meant giving up her own life.

One of the women in the line was the wife of Om Pad, the man that I picked up the shoes from. She had her three little children with her. The oldest of her children was no more than five. A second woman I had not met. She held an infant in her arms and a tiny boy walked by her side.

When they walked past me, I emerged from the bush and slipped into the line next to Em, who continued to walk as though she was expecting me. She accepted me without any expression on her face. All she said was, "Come close to me."

I wanted to tell her: "I am not afraid, Em," but there was no need to stir her emotions. It felt right just as it was. I was surprised but relieved that she did not push me away. Even more surprising, the two Black Uniforms did not even pretend to be aware that a new person had just joined the line. I imagined how they would execute us: a blow with a bamboo stump. I imagined how I would be next to Em. I hoped to hold her hand when that happened.

They walked us toward the river and into Chark Village and left us in an abandoned brick worship building of the same old pagoda where the girls' camp was. It was getting dark, but we could still see a larger-than-life Buddha statue sitting peacefully against the wall at the end of the emptied room. The government did not believe in religion, but the Black Uniforms were afraid to destroy or disrespect a worship house, so they just left it empty. Em whispered for me to pray to Buddha. I privately hesitated, for he had done nothing so far. However, I shared the Black Uniforms' fear of his power.

Em added, "God is helping us. He brings us here. He will be with us and watch over us."

I felt the thick, cold air brushing my neck. I prayed, "Dear God, please give the Black Uniforms a heart and let them see the goodness in us. Help us get through this alive so my sister Chenda will not be alone."

My prayer was interrupted by the Black Uniforms, who showed up with food. I had instant goosebumps. I turned to the statue on the opposite wall. There he was, but this time I noticed his smiling face. *Thank you, God, I believe that you are with us.*

The children kept the ladies busy with tending to their present needs rather than worrying about the future. Em held on to the unknown woman's infant as if he was hers. I imagined she was reliving the memories of all her children. She looked into the distance, softly cradled a sleeping baby, and hummed a lullaby ("Em's Lullaby")[22] for us, so loving and beautiful, but so sad.

That night we slept in the worship house. The next day we were moved across the river, left at an empty rice bin, and told to report to work the next day. The

---

[22] "Em's Lullaby" as I remember it can be listened to at http:// shorthairdetention.com/resources/em-lullaby.html.

empty rice bin was our new residence. Once again, our lives were spared. Perhaps the Meeting Creek leader had convinced the Black Uniforms to spare our lives. Perhaps that's what Pa was counting on when he decided to leave us.

The rice bin was built two feet above the ground and had a grass-panel roof. Its walls and floor were made from bamboo plastered with a mud and rice stalk mixture. We were to share the place with the unknown woman and her two little children. Having a rice bin as a shelter was one small benefits of not having enough rice to store. Although it had only one opening, it was one of the best places to protect us from the elements. It was tiny but felt large for the five of us since we had hardly any belongings.

The unknown woman's name was Stubby (*Tek*), which described her perfectly. We had never met before because she had lived in Banana Village. Her husband was the one responsible for Pa and Kheang leaving for he was the one who knew the trail through the jungle to Thailand. He had been on the same trail many times before the Black Uniforms took over.

It had been two nights and three days since Pa and Kheang left. Isolated and scared, we confined ourselves to the small bin with an opening, which allowed us a glimpse of the field through a line of bamboo bushes about fifty yards away. Our men must have passed by that field when they had to leave us. Without saying a word to each other, Em and I sat by the opening and looked past the fence. I thought of Pa and Kheang. Where were they now? I envisioned them walking and hiding in fear. What agony and anguish they must suffer when they think of us! I thought of Em and all the things that must be on her mind, the emotions she must endure and suppress. I said quietly to myself, "I love you Em."

Stubby's baby cried nonstop that day. I wondered how she had the energy to cry so much. It was rare to hear a baby cry because most of the women could not conceive in such a harsh environment. I imagined that she was crying for her father, and I wished I could scream like her. At least I was free to think.

That night I lay down and shared with Em the same blanket we had shared with Pa and Kheang many nights. With the baby crying in the background, I reflected on Em's life. She was an orphan by the time she was fourteen. Her only brother, younger than she, was separated from her. Her best teenage friend died from complications giving birth to her first baby. As a girl, Em had moved from house to house. Some people adopted her but treated her like a maid. However, when Em needed a mother the most, a rich and powerful lady in town took her in and treated her like a long-lost daughter. The lady's name was Ly Tang Lai. We called her Great Aunty. The love that Great Aunty gave Em had encouraged Pa's mother to propose a marriage between Em and Pa. After nineteen years of marriage, Em finally lived in prosperity, but then the Black Uniforms came, and piece by piece, they took everything from her.

That night I promised myself that if I ever made it out of there, I would make sure the world remembers Em and how much she meant to me. I would take care of Em as much as I could, no matter what. I did not yet know how, but I prayed to God to show me a way: "Dear God, please help me to be a strong person and guide me down a path so I can provide and care for my mother."

My prayer was distracted by my own desperate reality. I couldn't grow anything in the monsoon season by the river. And just like our first monsoon three years ago in French Village, there was nothing to eat until the schools of fish arrived, which last for only about a week. How could I help Em? I didn't have any fishing tools. Suddenly an idea came to me: Salt. I needed to get back to the girls' camp. They always gave us salt with rice soup.

When I shared my plan with Em the next day, she didn't have much to say. It seemed that I had no option but to return to the girls' camp. After a woman came by to take Em and Stubby to work, I reported back to the girls' camp, which was a five-minute walk across the river. This was the third time I had been to Chark girls' camp. I told the leaders that I had got better and left the sick-house to come back to be with my comrades. As expected, no questions were asked.

Both Em and Stubby were assigned to clean rice, one of the fortunate tasks. At least they wouldn't have to be exposed to the elements. I was sure that Em's skills and personality helped her to land this task. Stubby was allowed to stay away from field work because she needed to be near her infant baby.

My driving force had reversed. Before, I always told myself I needed to survive for Em, but now she needed to live for me. I knew for me there was no meaning in life without her. I feared she could not handle losing her baby boy.

I did what I could to show Em I could take care of us. Maybe she would try harder if she saw that I didn't give up. Every day after work, I went to see Em, Stubby, and her kids. I would save my salt ration from the girls' camp along with little creatures from the fields and would give them to Em and Stubby. They used the salt sparingly and kept most of it to exchange for fish.

Em and Stubby shared the same goal: Every day

they worked hard to keep Stubby's two children alive. Em told me that sometimes, after a long day of work, she and Stubby would leave the two little kids by themselves and go out to try to find some little fish. Em would stabilize a floating bucket while Stubby filtered small fish along the banks of the ditch using a small net that they borrowed.

Occasionally Em would open up and share her feelings of self-pity. "Water came up to my chest sometimes." Her phobia of leeches caused her to dump the bucket many times, but still she and her new friend Stubby continued to dip themselves into the leech-infested fields to get something to eat. Up until then, Em had never stepped into a flooded field.

Em and Stubby became best friends in short period. Em always told me that she found comfort and forgot her troubles every time her new friend sang. Stubby would sing songs with lyrics chosen by our government, but with the old music. All Em could hear was the beautiful old love songs, and they allowed her to ponder and reflect over the love she felt for her children and Pa.

Every day I snuck around to see Em. On the way to the bin, I would pass by the hut of the old woman who had shared the squash and pork soup with me about a year ago, and I wanted to tell her that Em was now in the same village too. But I never saw the old woman again.

Chapter 14

ON MY OWN

Planting Season of 1978

A few weeks after I returned to the girls' camp, I was selected among a few girls to be relocated. It happened on one cold early morning, too early to see clearly, and much earlier than usual. The leaders just woke us up and told us that we had to move to a new place. A few minutes later we were marching across the river and out of Chark, westward into the rice fields. There was no chance to say goodbye to Em, even though she was only a few minutes away. I felt lucky that Em was with Stubby, especially her babies, for they kept Em busy and gave her the chance to be a mother again.

As usual, we never knew where we were going until we got there. Usually they moved us along the river or to the villages east of the river, but never westward. We marched in the rain through flooded fields, with the water in some areas rising above our knees. It was around noon when I noticed a huge, new wooden complex situated on top of the highland, poking up through the trees. With a sigh of relief, I anticipated having a lunch break and getting my feet out of the water. Instead we were forced to continue marching through the flooded fields and muddy levies.

As we marched past the wood structure on the highland, I thought for sure that the place must be Syhsamon. I had heard that Syhsamon was an isolated area where, prior to the Black Uniforms era, farmers would camp and work the nearby fields. Besides Lake Kair, Syhsamon was the only place west of the river that was allowed to be occupied. However, only the Black Uniforms were to allowed stay in Syhsamon because it was very close to the Thai border.

Exhausted and hungry, we came across a broken, newly built levee. The break in the levee created a large gap that allowed water to flow between the fields with a strong current. Many girls swam to get to the other side of the gap. The strong currents landed them on the other side of the gap and away from the levee. A few of us clustered up just before the gap, with water above our waists, hesitating to take further steps into the gap that was bigger than we could glide through. I knew sooner or later we would have to cross, but I was hoping someone would walk across the gap and show us how deep it was. Perhaps if the leaders knew we couldn't swim, they would create a line of people to help us walk through. Nice wish, but no luck.

I heard the leaders yelling, and I was pushed from behind. I lifted up my foot to balance myself, but the pressure from behind moved me deeper and deeper into the gap. The deeper I went into the water, the faster my heart beat. Finally, my feet were not touching the mud any more. My instincts took over, and I started to kick and grab on to nothing but water, breathing some water thru my nose. My heart pounded in the cold water, and I feared for my life.

Dear God please stop torturing Em. Let me live for her sake. Then I felt the mud on the tip of my toes. I wanted to cry but couldn't. I should have thanked God for hearing my prayer, but I just didn't want to.

With my belongings in the small, wet sack strapped on my back, I walked thru the softer currents and thought about Kheang and Pa. I knew they needed to travel west, but did they have to go through a flooded field like this? Like me, Kheang did not know how to swim. I knew Pa's plan was to leave before the monsoons came, but this far west the seasonal floods were already taking place. Maybe the field just flooded a couple of days ago and not when Pa and Kheang left. I was thinking about Em. Could she feel my fear? Would I see her again?

It was almost dark on that same day, when we arrived at a much smaller farm camp called Meeting Creek, the same name as the village where Em and Pa had lived not too long ago, but this Meeting Creek was in the middle of nowhere. There were patches of trees with some small fields scattered between them, but they were not rice fields. They were emptied, uncultivated bald spots. I was not exactly sure what the old farmers used to do in these fields. There was nothing habitable or familiar in the area. The only thing man-made was a cattle shed.

Exhausted, wet, cold, and hungry, we were told to build our own shelter to sleep in for the night. A group of young men that came from the river with us were chopping bamboo and cutting vines. Some of them were not much older than Kheang. My heart ached for them, and I missed my little brother. It hurt to have feelings. We helped haul the bamboo and vine to the cattle shed, but then there was nothing else for us girls to do but watch the men build our sleeping rack under the same roof of the cattle shed and above the unsettled cattle. At each end of the long shed, a ladder was built for us to climb up to our sleeping rack.

We went to sleep without having any food all day.

The rain kept coming down harder and harder all night. Although I was exhausted from the long journey, I couldn't sleep. All I could think about was my brother and father. *Did they make it? Are they in this same rain as me?* I missed Em, for she would comfort me and make all the troubles go away. But for now, I was on my own. There was not a soul nearby who cared about me or knew what I had gone through just a few weeks ago, nor did I care about them.

Miserable wind brought rain into the sleeping area from all directions, sideways and through the poorly built thatch roof. I covered my head with my small sack and an old, torn cotton krama and tried to ignore the persistent and heavy rain, but the constant wind chilled my bones through my thin wet clothes and kept me shaking and awake. The odor of the cattle and their disgusting poop and urine in the rotten mud fermented the air. Someone was peeing through the cracks of the freshly built bamboo rack onto the cattle. Startled, they mooed and rattled the shed in protest. I feared the whole shed would collapse, and we would be trampled.

Lying down, I suddenly felt exposed and vulnerable. I sat up, hugged my small sack between my empty stomach and my thighs, and wrapped my arms around my shinbones. Resting my chin on my knees, I realized the stench was mostly from my own muddy feet.

After that night, we were awakened every day before we could see each other's faces and were forced to march to the edge of the jungle to clear shrubs and fallen tree branches to prepare land for planting rice. These shrubs and trees were very different. Some I had never seen before, and even the ones that I recognized had developed an eerie characteristic that made me imagine I was destroying someone's sanctuary. Every day before I began to work, I asked for forgiveness from the spirits of the place and the caretaker of the jungle.

The flooded land at the edge of the thick tree line was so dense that my feet didn't sink into the earth. The water was crystal clear, so I could see my bare feet underneath. The land had definitely been untouched for many, many years. One time I was sure I saw a small piece of a dead branch moving in the water. A second glance confirmed it was something moving quickly. After I picked it up, I realized that it was a big, old crab, but I couldn't eat it. The shell was thick and hard, with long, hairy green algae growing on it. Then I realized the little bumps with green and long, hairy algae that were scattered on the flooded land were not rocks but snails.

The experience with the strange creatures made me think of Em. I couldn't wait to see her again and tell her what I had been through. I reflected on my life's journey. Reality reminded me that I was in a jungle, and the jungle was not as romantic as I had imagined when I read about it in stories.

Every day, by the time we returned from the long day of work, the sun had already sunk past the edge of the earth. With wet clothes, plate and spoon in our hands, we lined up to receive rice soup. Away from the food line, we squatted down in the ankle-deep mud in circles of four to five girls, sharing a bowl of soup planted in the center. It consisted of wild-grown vegetation and some fish. With the glimmer of dim light from the food line, we could hardly see the bowl of soup, let alone what was in it. We took turns dipping our spoons into the soup. The pieces of fish and vegetable seemed to swim away from each spoon with a swirling current. Even in this time of hard labor and starvation, peer pressure still existed, which enforced acceptable behaviors. Fishing and chasing for the meat and vegetables in the shared soup bowl was not acceptable. Every girl had to wait for her chance and only one quick scoop was allowed. When the bowl was finished, the pieces of fish would be examined and it would be determined if any girl had not had fish. "I did not get any fish," she would declare and demand an answer. The rest would chime in to declare their luck. This meant that one could never have an additional piece of fish too many times. Sooner or later it would be known who was dishonest. Sometimes I didn't have any fish, sometimes I couldn't stop chewing the second piece, and other times I spit out part of the second piece and shared with a girl who had not received her piece yet. One time, I bit into a piece that was too tough to be a vegetable, and too chewy to be fish. After grinding and feeling with my tongue, I decided to spit the piece out. I never told anyone about it, but I thought it must have been a piece of cooked overgrown jungle leech. Nothing else would make sense.

Every night after the meal, I scraped as much mud off my feet as I could with a stick before I went to sleep. After a while the stench from the cows below did not bother me. The cows also got used to us peeing on them. I learned to sleep with rain water dripping on me, but some nights there was no sleeping. The monsoon rains would persist through the day and into the night. The best nights were when I was able to sleep in a dry shirt. The only clothes I had were what I wore, so I always went to bed with wet pants from at least the knee down.

With each day, work kept taking us further and further into the jungle. We woke up before sunrise and worked to clear an area for about an hour before we lined up for a meal. Then we worked for another hour before it was time to return to the cattle shed.

After about two weeks, the Black Uniforms moved us closer to the jungle. This time the place had no name. It looked like a tiny island about one foot higher than the surrounding water. As before, we had to build our own shelter. I was told to gather wild grass to make thatched panels for the roof and wall. The grass cut like razors on my bare hands and lower legs, and the water stung my raw flesh with blood that tainted the area, inviting the jungle leeches to cling to me. My heart palpitated and I panted every time I felt the leeches puncture my skin, but it was useless to scream for help because there would be no response. I knew the leeches were on me, but I was too scared to look at them closely. I would rather tuck my tummy, hold my breath, squirm, and let them suck my blood than rub them off with the razor-sharp wild grass as some of the girls did. Like most of the girls, I wouldn't dare yank the blood-sucking creatures with my bare hand for they were too disgusting and creepy.

I helped make soft bamboo strips used for stitching the wild grass together for thatched panels that went on walls and rooftops. Before the huts were completed, my left thumbnail became thin from not knowing the proper way to weave the abrasive wild grass into thatched panels. It was sensitive to touch, as though the flesh under my nail was exposed.

Finally, we had a place that was away from the smelly cows. There were two shelters: the smaller one for eating and the other for sleeping. The shelters were surrounded by flood water, and we laid wild grass on the path between them. So when we walked up the island and between the shelters, our feet would be clean. Our feet had become so tough that the wild grass didn't cut through our skin as we walked. It was nice to be able to sleep with clean feet.

In this new place, the Black Uniforms left us all by ourselves. No men, no boys—just a few older women stayed in the eating shelter and about thirty girls in the sleeping shelter. It was the island of girls.

No one was a close friend to anyone, but since we had left the cattle shed there was a sense of pride, dignity, and peace, even though food was even more scarce. We seemed to do what we could to keep the Black Uniforms away. No one would stay homesick more than a day in a row. It seemed as though we pressured each other to dunk our feet into the cold flood water or stick our heads out into the rain before the sun came up, so that the Black Uniforms would leave us alone. When we were not able to work, we spent time weaving thatched panels for future needs.

After we had cleared the edge of the jungle as far as possible with our God-given limbs and pulling power from oxen, the Black Uniforms forced us to work deep inside the jungle. Every morning I walked to work through water above my waist, but it was peaceful. The Black Uniforms were not with us, and the leaders were slacking off and not rushing us. Even though I was exhausted, I enjoyed walking in the flooded ditch because there was less debris and bushes that could puncture or scrape my legs. The deep water eliminated the usual splashing sounds of every step, and it felt as though I just glided through the water with the other girls. Also, along this ditch there were big, tall, wild fruit trees: Anthocephalus cadamba (*tkouv*). The fruit was high up on the tall trees, but many had dropped and floated around me. After biting into a few bad ones, I became good at seeking out the good ones. There was plenty of tkouv for everybody. I thought about Em and wished I could share them with her.

Every day the boys' team would meet us in the jungle. We didn't know where their camp was, but every morning we saw their line in the distance, marching toward the jungle before entering the thickness of trees. We were to remove dead branches from the muddy bald spots and clear the area surrounding them. Usually these spots were flooded with knee-high water. The bald spots were surrounded by giant termite mounds covered with thick bushes and ancient *kakoss* trees. I had never seen a kakoss tree. They were huge and imposing, showing off their beauty and demanding attention.

Girls and boys would use these mounds whenever nature called. The boys would use the mounds on one side of the field and the girls would use those on the other side. I would use mounds from where I could still see the team working in the bald spot. Somehow seeing everybody made me feel safe—safe from being hunting down by a tiger. Like all the girls and boys who were there with me, I was afraid of tigers. However, no one dared to mention the word *tiger*, because of the superstition that if the name was mentioned in the jungle, the animal would be present.

I always asked for forgiveness from the occupants of the mound before I did my nature dump. And I always followed through by pleading for help to get me out of this misery. The thickness of the bushes by these mounds made it hard to find a bare spot to squat, but when one existed, the loose, black layer of the mulch made it difficult not to slide down the slope. During one of these ordeals, I found a marble. It revealed itself through the black mulch, beckoning for me to rescue it. A marble in the deep of the jungle reminded me of my little brother's happy face, but I felt sad. I picked the marble up as though it was tender and precious. I missed Kheang and prayed God would let me see my little brother again and would bless him with peace and happiness, wherever he was at.

One day threatening thunder rumbled nonstop during lunch break when a girl blurted her fear: "Does anybody here have a swirl on her calves?" The question must have been on most of the girls' minds as each one proudly replied: "Not me!" It reminded me of when I had confirmed another mark of bad luck on me. The bald woman in Water Mill sick-house said that if you have a swirl of hair on either one of your calves, you will likely be struck by lightning. It seemed to me that I fit the description every time I heard about a mark of bad luck, so I didn't answer the question. A few girls never heard of such marks, so they checked their calves as they asked questions about the swirly hair. After everybody was confirmed safe to be around, they looked at me, and I stared back at them with the expression that they were crazy to believe such a thing. When one of the girls reached to check my calf, I stared her down. I was able to evade the question, but I wasn't able to convince them that I was safe to be around when there was thunder. On that day, I became further detached from the world. No girl wanted to be near me. Deep inside, I feared the thunder more than the Black Uniforms on that day.

At the end of each day, everyone rushed to get out

of the jungle. As soon as the leaders yelled, "Time to head back," everyone seemed to gain a spurt of energy—not necessarily running, but everyone hustled just enough to be ahead of me. Even when I tried to anticipate the announcement and hustle just like the others, one by one, boys and girls splashed cloudy water toward me as they caught up and passed me by. Some older men turned their heads to stare at my soul through my desperate eyes. Instinctively, I looked back as though I wanted to be sure that they would always remember me in case I was living my last day. I didn't blame or shame them for leaving me behind, but I still felt bad. I wasn't afraid of dying as much as I was afraid of being knocked down and eaten by a tiger from out of nowhere. My father would say that when you are face-to-face with a tiger, you can't outrun it. You should look a tiger right in the eye. The spirit within each one of us shows though our eyes and can deter a tiger much better than our physical body can. I was sure that inside the jungle I would have no chance to look a tiger in the eye, but as soon as the thick trees and bushes were behind me, I slowed down. At least then I could see what might be coming toward me.

Rumor was spreading that not too long ago the Black Uniforms had killed a tiger at a nearby camp. A mixed feeling spread around the girls' camp. In the physical world, there was one less tiger to worry about, but in the spiritual world, we were intruding on their place and killing one of them. Their kind would surely come back on one of us.

Some days I would be so far behind the others that by the time I got to the camp some girls had already finished their meal. Meals on those days consisted of rice broth with bamboo shoots and salt. There was no meat whatsoever, not even a tiny sliver.

One day I woke up and was ready to go to the jungle when I noticed my spoon had been stolen from my sack while I was asleep. I knew I had not lost it because I carried that spoon everywhere I went. I put it into my sack every night and checked it every morning before I left the hut. What would I do without a spoon? How would I eat the watery rice soup off a plate? Em had warned me about this possibility. I should have been more careful.

I attacked the girl who slept next to me. "Did you take my spoon?"

She looked grumpy but didn't reply.

I knew she had done it. She was mildly retarded. "Show me your spoon!" I demanded.

"No!" she snapped back.

I grabbed her hand and flipped it up. There was the spoon that Em had branded by cutting the tip of the handle and uniquely marking the back of it.

"Give me back my spoon!" I pleaded and fought to get it back, knowing that it was useless to fight with a stubborn, senseless person. She showed no feeling, just a face determined to keep my spoon. I cried without a drop of tears, not for the loss of my spoon, but to protest to God and express my self-pity. The rest of the girls stared at me but did nothing. They were pathetic, and so was I.

That day I didn't report to work. A leader, a dark-skinned woman who was cooking for the girls, let me borrow her spoon while she was serving us. I heard a rumor that she kept her hair long but hidden under her krama and neatly wrapped around her head. I thought for sure her long hair must be left over from the old regime, for my hair never seemed to grow. It had stayed the same length since I left Poipet. Thus, I never had to surrender my hair to the devil.

Encouraged by the woman's kind gesture, I decided to push my luck by returning the spoon to her at night in hopes that she would be willing to help me more. My prayer was answered when she gave me a small bowl of solid rice. Grateful for some food with substance but scared that other leaders might see us, I grabbed the bowl from her. "It's okay," she said as gently as an angel. I wished to see her long hair. I imagined her hand patting my head, and I longed to feel her touch.

So someone did care about me and understood what I was going through every day. She must have been watching me come in last for the end-of-the-day meal. It seemed as though she knew me more than I knew about her.

I thought about Em that night. How was she doing without Pa? Did she have an angel like mine? Tears dropped onto my little sack, and I flipped it over because Em told me that whenever I missed her at night, I should flip over the pillow, and she would feel my love. I didn't believe in such things, and I didn't have a pillow, but I pretended to because that was our secret.

One day two older men came from Chark in a canoe to deliver rice and some fish for us. They looked like the old farmers from the past: big, strong, and jolly. With them was a young girl. As soon as they arrived, the girls hustled to receive them. It was the first time anyone from the river had visited our camp. One of the men was very loud and outgoing. He poked fun at every girl as he handed a small package to her. He made the girls laugh, giggle, and drool with every package he gave out. But not me—my focus was on the quiet man's face. At the other end of the boat, I quietly and politely asked the quiet man, "Uncle," to show respect, "do you know my mother? She just moved to Chark and her name is Chheng." My sinking heart and shattering voice stopped me from giving any more description of Em.

The quiet man called out to his loud friend, "Hey, this is Chheng's daughter." The happy thought quickly registered into my mind and stopped any sorrow that I felt for Em. I knew that whoever came to know Em would like her. She was a sincere and likable person.

The loud man turned his attention from the girls and scanned me from head to toe. Slowly and clearly, he declared: "Chheng is my wife."

It was known that the Black Uniforms forced marriage on ladies whose husbands escaped. I was instantly devastated.

The loud man's face turned from jolly to a satisfied devil laughing about his accomplishment. He laughed out loud and added: "I'm just kidding!" I found myself unwillingly laughing with him and everybody else.

I pleaded with the men to wait for me as I had something to send to Em. The men rushed me as if they were already late leaving. I hustled to get the little pouch of grayish and moist rock salt that I had been collecting and saving every day from my ration. On my way through the hut, I passed a girl who was writing a note to her parents. I pleaded with her to let me borrow her pencil and give me a piece of paper to write to Em.

"I don't have enough!" she replied.

"Just a small piece, please," I begged her.

She turned her back on me. I sat behind her silently begging and hoping that she had the heart to give me a small piece of paper. "Just a palm size, please."

Just then the loud man yelled that he was leaving. The girl was unable to concentrate on her writing. Frustrated, she sighed, turned around, and ripped off the corner of her letter and told me to shut up. I thanked her and quietly asked God to bless her and to be with her.

On the fragile piece of paper, smaller than the palm of my hand, I crammed my message to Em:

> My Dear Mother, I always miss and love
> you. Little Girl.

I folded the paper to protect the message and stuffed it into the salted pouch but wondered if it would ever get to Em.

After the men left, attention converged on the young girl who had just come with them. We sat around her, inquiring for the latest news from the river. The girl was happy to share the news: "Our Eastern Comrades treat our mothers and fathers in the village to one dessert per week."

"Dessert? What sort of dessert?" A few girls could not control themselves.

The young girl described all sorts of desserts and her memory of the way they tasted, smelled, and felt in her mouth. I couldn't help but drool like a dog. When she described the rice cake with mung bean inside, floating in palm syrup and coconut milk, I wanted to know and hear more and asked, "How big was each cake?"

She cupped her hands and replied, "As big as a small noodle bowl."

We all yelled at her in disgust, and she quickly lost her audience. "It's true!" She begged for us to come back.

"I've never heard such thing. As big as a bowl?" I asked, challenging her.

"You are lying!" chimed in everybody else.

The girl quickly replied: "You didn't let me finish. They were as big as a *small* bowl, the *bottom* of the small bowls."

Everybody responded with an outburst of laughter. It was the only time we laughed together in that hut.

I was happy for Em, even if what the girl said was only partially true. I wished Pa and Kheang could be around to see the changes. We also learned that along with the desserts, the Eastern Comrades allowed one day off per week.

Our work sites took us further and further into the jungle. Rumor was spreading that the work sites were getting too close to the Thai border. The quiet whisper was heard by all: "On the other side of the Malai mountain is Thailand." Sometimes we even heard the faint crow of a rooster, which I hoped was from a Thai village. Sometimes I imagined some secret Cambodian army was hiding and watching over us and looking for the opportunity to liberate us. Perhaps Ee and Hong were with this secret army. Maybe Pa, Ee, Hong, and Kheang were reunited and waiting for us.

Not long after we stayed on the isolated girl island, we were moved to a new place. Unlike the cattle shed and the girl island, this third place had large, newly built structures made of solid wooden slabs for the floor and large tree trunks for posts. It was an intrusive sight for such structures to be built at the edge of the jungle. The one that I was assigned to was shared with the Eastern Comrades.

Gradually over a couple of months, almost all of the Black Uniforms had been replaced by the Eastern Comrades, but no one knew why. Like the old Black Uniforms, the Eastern Comrades' sleeping area was next to the kitchen.

My sleeping area was away from the kitchen, next to a girl who peed her pants every night. Somehow, I always got wet from her urine.

I met a girl who had lighter skin and looked more

Chinese than I did, but spoke perfect Khmer. Her name was Savdy. We became good friends. She was goofy and fun to be with. On dry days, we would walk on a levee that was large enough to support a small car, if one existed. We were enjoying the height of the levee, the fresh and clean air, talking about anything, and laughing about everything. She taught me a new twist to the Khmer language that some girls in the camp had been using. It was a made-up language, where each word was broken into consonant and vowel sounds and adding a constant vocalic syllable to them. We had fun laughing and teaching each other this new language. Many of the girls couldn't comprehend it, and the boys weren't even interested. So we would talk in this new language in the open whenever we wanted our conversation to be secret. Some girls got frustrated because they didn't understand what we were talking about, which made it even more fun.

One of the Eastern Comrades was a tall, good-looking man. His light skin and Chinese eyes reminded me of my Uncle Khemm, whom my father had sent to study in Paris just before the Black Uniforms took over.

This man never left the comfort of the shelter. Just like my uncle, he spent most of his time flirting with ladies. They loved it. Every time I walked by him, he looked at me like I had something to hide. The first day

I was unable to report to work since arriving at this intrusive complex, I had to eat a meal with this man watching over me. He was lying in a hammock with one leg pushing on the wood floor. Every time I peeked to see if he was looking at me, I found his little, smiling eyes looking back at me.

Finally, he asked, "Comrade, what's your name?"

I pretended that he was not talking to me. A girl sitting next to me elbowed my ribcage. With a quick glance at his face, I replied, "Little."

In a firm yet calm voice, he asked, "Comrade Little, why are you not reporting to work today?"

I felt my stomach pushing the rice soup back up to my throat when I tried hard to calmly reply. "I had a headache." I felt the room turn silent. The spoons were softly and slowly dipping into the rice soup with hardly a sound. My breathing was slow and quiet as I tried to hide myself from the man's sight.

He went on. "Does your headache still bother you?"

"Better now," I replied softly.

The silence continued. I ate as fast as I could and walked back to my sleeping area without looking at anybody around me. I contemplated what had just happened and what could happen next, but I was not too afraid of him. I felt that he could see the history of my past through the color of my skin. While I was still thinking, the man called out my name again, "Comrade Little, come out here."

With my tail between my legs, I walked slowly to him and stood next to him and waited for the next command.

Using the same calm and firm voice, he said, "You need to help Nurse Seng carry her stuff to the river."

To the river? Oh, dear God, thank you! I will get to see Em again.

Chapter 15

Planting Season of 1978

Nurse Seng was a small-framed lady who limped to one side when she walked. Like the good-looking Black Uniform man, she also had light skin and spoke without a village accent. Her name was another give-away that she had Chinese blood.

On the way back to the river, I walked behind Nurse Seng and carried all her bags. Limping through the water and the mud, she lifted up her black sarong past her knees and hustled to beat the sunset. Feeling lucky and elated, I wanted to walk faster than her, but I had to control myself since I was supposed to be sick. She asked to make sure I was okay to continue walking without a break. That was the only conversation we had on the whole trip.

It was dark by the time we reached Nurse Seng's place, so she kept me there for the night. She had a large container full of water by the stairs for washing muddy feet and legs before going up to the house. It was a big house that could have accommodated thirty girls, but there was only one other black uniformed nurse staying there. The second nurse responded to Comrade Long. She had been waiting for us and served us a meal of steamed rice and salted fish as soon as we arrived. We ate next to a fish oil lamp that glowed like a soft candle. I tried to be civilized when I was eating, but I wasn't sure I would able to achieve it. I was grateful, but somehow I didn't thank the ladies for the food. I thought about Em and couldn't wait to tell her my luck. I knew I would see her again soon.

Nurse Long gave me a dry pair of pants to wear for the night. I slept next to two Black Uniforms that night and felt like I was their pet.

When the sun came up the next morning, I learned these ladies were not just any nurses. They must have been well respected among the Black Uniforms. Their place was high above the ground, with a red tile roof, wooden walls, and polished wood floors. It had three compartments: visiting, sleeping, and cooking. They had their own stove. There were no belongings in the place that might have indicated anyone other than the two ladies lived there.

I saw the river and other nice houses around it. They all looked new to me. I had no idea what village I was in.

Nurse Long had thick, curly hair and darker skin than Comrade Seng. Her Chinese name puzzled me. Her appearance reminded me of my Aunt Sareth, who was a dark-skinned lady with tight curly hair. She looked like an Australian Aborigine, but she spoke Chinese fluently, way better than Em's Chinese. Nurse Long was more talkative than her friend. When she saw I had already changed into my old pants, she looked up and down at me slowly with heavy eyelids, and she said softly, "Throw it away." Instantly, I became aware of my ragged appearance and felt embarrassed and sorry for myself. At the same time, I was grateful for her kind heart, but unable to bring myself to say thank-you to a Black Uniform who was so high up in rank.

The two nurses left me in their place that morning and every morning after that. During the day, I polished the wooden floor, filled the water container by the stairs, cooked, ate, and stayed away from the public eye as much as possible. At the end of the day, before the nurses came home, there would be a couple of cleaned fish delivered to the front stairs for me to cook. Most nights the ladies would entertain Black Uniform men with guns slung over their shoulders while I lay down quietly behind the wooden wall, listening to them flirting with the nurses. Some of the Black Uniforms saw me during the day, but they pretended they didn't.

Some of the mothers in the village checked me out whenever they saw me, but they were too afraid to ask the nurses about the situation. Some of the little kids in the village were afraid of me because I hung out with the Black Uniforms. It turned out that the place was in the upper river of Chark.

One night, Nurse Long woke me up and said, "It was just a dream."

I couldn't go back to sleep because my dream had been so vivid. I saw Kheang hiding behind the post of the house, whispering my name and saying, "It's me. Kheang." He was younger than when I last saw him. He was cold, hungry and asking for help.

I cried in panic and was scared for him. *What are you doing here? Why did you come back?* The next thing I knew, Nurse Long had awakened me.

The following morning, I determined that would be the day for me to look for Em. It had been more than two weeks since I came to the nurses' place. I thought it over and considered sneaking out, but if the nurses found out they might be really upset. They would be right to be upset, as they had been very kind to me, and still I had never opened up to them. I decided instead to ask permission from Nurse Seng, who was the leader of the two nurses.

"Would it be okay with you if I go to my mother

today?" Before she replied I assured her that I wouldn't go right away, meaning that I would wait until all mothers and fathers had left the village to go to the field.

The nurses looked at each other, ignored my request, and left for the day.

Before I left the place, I stared at the rice and salt that were at my disposal. I wanted to take some to Em, but I couldn't do that because these ladies trusted me. With empty hands, I walked down the river and behind the village, confident I would find the bin that Em and Stubby shared.

I became excited when I started to recognize familiar places that indicated I was closer to the bin, and I walked even faster when the bin was in sight. I was not so sure that Em was still at the bin, but the first thing I noticed was our old blanket as if Em intentionally kept it in the open to let Chenda and me know she was still there. I climbed into the bin and waited for Em. It didn't look as barren as when I had last seen it. The sleeping area now had small grass mats laid on the floor, and two or three more mats hung over a string for privacy.

I feared to find out how Em was doing without Pa, but at the same time I couldn't wait to show her I was all right and to tell her all the things I had gone through. As expected, Em came home for lunch. Perhaps she always hoped one of her kids would be waiting at home for her. My heart pounded with excitement when I heard footsteps next to the bin. Peeking through the grass mat, I saw it was her and I came out slowly so as not to startle her and called softly: "Em."

With a quick, short breath, she stepped back and felt her heart with her right hand. I smiled at her. She smiled back, but her lower lip was shaking uncontrollably. I stepped toward her and she toward me, and she grabbed onto my upper arms, shook them, stared into my eyes, and whimpered, "I thought I would never see you again. That man! The one you gave salt told me that you were so frail and pale."

I smiled and was glad he was wrong. Em looked happy and healthy. She showed no sign of weakness or sickness. She patted my forearms and chuckled. Then she pulled the fabric of my new black pants, which were oversized, making me look like a skinny Black Uniform.

Em rushed to show me what she had been saving for me. She unwrapped her sack and tossed two pieces of clothing on the grass mat and told me: "Your Aunt Sareth and little Cousin Pros came to see me. She traveled with her little boy across many villages, muddy roads, flooded fields, and a river, walking all day in the rain and into the night, all in the name of sister love."

I felt Em's love and pain at the same time.

"Your aunt could sense my pain. Her timing was

impeccable. She didn't even know about your father, but she came just when I needed help the most." Em looked into the distance, blinked her red eyes, and added: "Pros was crying and exhausted when he got here. He had to swim while his mom waded through some spots where the water was too deep for him to walk. He was wet and cold."

I thought that Pros probably had a little alligator twist from walking a long distance, the same alligator twists I had experienced after walking all day when the Black Uniforms evacuated us from Poipet. After all, his skinny nine-year-old legs had endured the journey from Phum Preah Ponlea to Chark, all the while sneaking past the Black Uniform radar.

Em gently shook her head in disbelief and added, "I felt so sorry for my little nephew." Then she broke a smile. "Your aunt and I were in this bin massaging his legs."

As I listened quietly, Em added solemnly, "Your aunt loved you just like her own daughter."

I wanted to reply, but my throat became tight and choked up by emotion. As I picked up the garments and unfolded them, I felt Aunt Sareth's love seeping into my body. She had made me and Chenda each a bra from one of my favorite old dresses that she had taken with her when the Black Uniforms evacuated her from our home in Battambang. The handmade bras had buttons, each carved from a piece of plastic into irregular circles, with two little holes in the middle for sewing them to the bras with thread. The cups were crisscrossed with stitches and a layer of fabric to support what she imagined were young girls' breasts, except I did not have any to fill the cups. I imagined my aunt missing me and thinking of me when she was making them. I wished I could see her.

It was a miracle for Aunt Sareth to survive the Black Uniforms with just her and her little son, for she was once a lady of high society who hardly had to lift a finger. I remembered being excited every time we got a chance to visit her beautiful apartment, which was situated between the royal palace and the waterfront of Tonle Sap in Phnom Penh. One of my favorite things to do at Aunt Sareth's apartment was to bathe under lotus water.[23] Some of Aunt Sareth's neighbors were European, and a Khmer movie star lived two floor above her. Chenda and I would giggle and whisper every time we saw Aunt Sareth's movie star neighbor.

I was happy for Aunt Sareth. That she could leave her village and travel across many villages to see Em meant she had an angel. Someone liked her and saw good things in her.

---

[23] *Lotus water* is a term we used to describe shower heads. Most Cambodians who lived in the city at the time had running water, but very few had a shower.

I hesitated but decided to share with Em my dream about Kheang. She listened and quietly asked me, "Did he talk to you?"

"Not exactly, but, I seemed to understand him without him actually saying the words." I was hoping Em would tell me what the dream meant, but she didn't offer and I didn't pursue it. Later in life I learned that Cambodians believe that when a person passes away, his or her spirit will communicate with you in a dream without actually talking out loud.

Em told me that the people in Chark had been very kind to her and Stubby. The village women visited them and provided them with a kettle for hot water and other essentials to get them back on their feet. The men dropped off fish occasionally, including the man who delivered salt to Em. I told Em the man teased me about being married to her, and she laughed and said his wife was also named Chheng and they had always been kind to her.

I told Em about my situation with the nurses and that I had all the food I needed, but I couldn't take any for Em because they trusted me. Em commended my actions and encouraged me to go soon so as to not get the nurses in trouble with their Black Uniform comrades.

On my way back to the nurses' place, I felt blessed to know the people in Chark were nice to Em and that she was making good friends.

One day, Nurse Seng wanted me to go to Banana Village with her to help carry fruit and coconuts back to her place. Banana Village was where I was in the sick-house when Pa and Kheang left. Fearing that I would be recognized by some of the nurses at the sick-house, I didn't want to go, but I didn't have a good excuse to share with Nurse Seng. I told her I didn't sleep well the previous night and I had a headache. The nurse told me she could wait until I felt better the next day. She was determined to take me with her. There was no way I would tell her about the men of my family and that I had run away from the sick-house. How could I tell this lady who was so kind to me that I was not good for her? And for the very same reason, how could I not tell her?

The next day, Nurse Seng limped in front of me all the way to Banana Village. All the while, I contemplated the idea of telling her about my father. What would she do if I told her? I was certain she would feel betrayed. All this time we were together, I knew more about her and Nurse Long than they knew about me. They never asked me about my family, and I made sure I didn't talk about them other than to say that Em lived in Chark.

At the sick-house in Banana Village, Nurse Seng was greeted with food and laughter from the local nurses as well as the Black Uniform soldiers. Nurse Seng was always kind, but rarely spoke to me. But with her Black

Uniform comrades, she was outgoing and soft-spoken and had many punch lines that brought laughter all around her. With my head wrapped in an old cotton krama, I was dismissed as being a shy young girl.

None of the nurses who had handed me my sick ration noticed me, but one soldier did. "Hey, you remember me?" He was fully dressed in his shiny black uniform with a gun hanging from his shoulder, and he was excited to see me.

I smiled in reply. He was the guy I met in the Chamnaom sick-house who came for his dead cousin. *Go away!* I wished in my head.

"How are your parents?" he asked. Apparently, he did not know about Pa. *Shut up*, I wished he could hear me thinking.

Nurse Seng chimed in with excitement that her favorite girl knew someone in the ranks. "You knew each other?"

The soldier did all the talking, and I slipped further away in the background, trying to appear more shy than scared. I pretended to be busy packing things for the return trip, trusting the soldier was smart and wouldn't say anything that would sound bad to the Black uniforms. Even more, I preferred that he not say anything at all.

Not knowing what Nurse Seng knew about my family

and how she would respond, I feared I would be moved again. The next opportunity I had, I snuck out to see Em and I told her what had happened at Banana Village. Em assured me I had nothing to worry about. "Nurse Seng will take care of you. Don't be lazy. Push yourself to do what you can to help her around the place, and she will help you." Em also told me that the soldier had stopped by the hut in Meeting Creek when Pa was around, and he brought food to Em and Pa several times.

I listened to her quietly but was still worried. Em studied my face and something else concerned her that she needed to tell me right away before she forgot. "Be sure to cover your face," she said. A mixed expression of pride and fear flashed on her face, and she warned me: "Your face is like a doll." I had heard Em give the same warning to Chenda before, but never to me until then. Em was always afraid that Chenda would be forced to marry.

Back at the nurses' place, I worked harder to keep the floor shiny and the place tidy. Nothing really seemed to change. Nurse Seng was always quiet while Nurse Long talked too much and laughed too loud. But one morning, after the ladies had chatted with a small group of soldiers the night before, Nurse Seng told me she had to let me go. "Your role here puzzles other comrades. I told them that you're my patient."

It was to be expected, I told myself. I was both relieved

and sad that our relationship was over. I was relieved they were free from me, for I had nothing but dirt that would smear them one day. I was sad to depart from my two angels, for they had looked past my appearance and had taken risks by having me under their wings.

Nurse Seng continued: "So I was told to take you to the sick-house."

The nurses waited for me to say something, and I wanted to tell them I understood, but I turned away and grabbed my sack instead. Nurse Long jumped to grab whatever she could find for me in the cooking area and tried to stuff it all in my small pack. The quietness made her nervous, and her hands shook uncontrollably. She pulled the sack from my hands and lowered herself to finish packing on the floor. She couldn't decide what to pack and what to keep. She kept putting items in and out of the sack by my feet. I lowered myself down next to her and held her hands. She stopped shaking. I felt her love. She hid her face. I waited for her to look back up, but she refused. I slowly pulled my sack from her hand, and felt her heart ripping. But I had to go. I got up slowly and left my friend, my unlikely friend, but my best friend.

Without a word between us, Nurse Seng marched me back to hell.

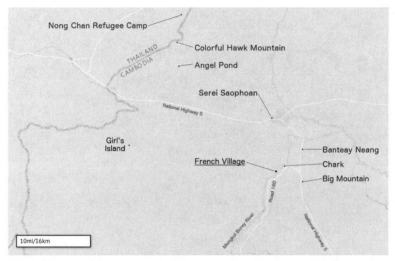

Flight to Freedom Map—After multiple escape attempts over a five-month period, Em, Chenda, and I arrived at Nong Chan Refugee Camp and were finally free. *(Adapted from National Geographic MapMaker Interactive by K. W. Laux, 2017.)*

Chapter 16

THE VIETNAMESE INVASION

Harvest Season of 1979

I was taken to a new sick-house in Water Mill Village. It had been moved across the river from the pagoda to an old elementary school. I should have been used to being a stranger to everyone around me, but I was not. I felt so lonely surrounded by unfamiliar faces. No one knew who I was, and no one wanted to know anything about me. No one trusted me, and I trusted no one. It was the price I paid to be close to Em, to let her know she was not alone and that at least one of her children was okay. Every day I was hungry, sad, and lonely, but I was confident that I did the right thing.

There was a beautiful, healthy young woman in the same sick-house. She was the most beautiful Cambodian woman I had ever seen, so beautiful that I couldn't help but think she could have been a movie star if the Black Uniforms hadn't taken over the country. Looking at her

made me feel relaxed. Even the Black Uniforms appreciated her beauty. They stopped by for friendly conversations, and extra food was always available for her. I wanted
to get to know her better, but she had no interest in me.
She looked at me over the tip of her nose while perching
her head to exaggerate her height. I missed my nurses.

At the new sick-house location, I had to cross the
river to visit Em. When I saw her again, she told me
the Eastern Comrades were in the village because they
were retreating from an invasion by some kind of army.
"Soon the new army will be here. Be prepared to escape from the sick-house. Don't be afraid. I will be here
waiting for you no matter what. I won't leave this place
without you." I was frightened by her concern and serious expression.

What if I can't be here? I thought. I didn't want Em
to get hurt by waiting for me. But if I couldn't make
it and we were both moved around, when would we
meet again?

At the sick-house, even the little critters seemed to
know it was a dangerous time since they all seemed to
stop making noise. Everything was so still. Everyone
quietly packed and organized their few belongings. The
Black Uniform nurses didn't stop by to chat with the
beautiful young woman. I thought about how I would
know when it would be time to escape to Em.

Waking up the following morning, I was disappointed to find things no different than any other morning. Everyone was still around me, mostly lying in bed, so still. As more and more people woke up and began roaming around, a girl rushed back into the building with wide eyes and short breaths. She grabbed her belongings while she answered all our questioning eyes that were on her: "They're all gone!"

My heart was pounding, and I was short of breath. I was ready just as Em had told me to be, so I grabbed my bag and saw all the other girls were hustling too, feeling lucky that I'd visited Em not too long ago and was prepared for this event. Surely not all the girls knew what to do. Outside the building and into the yard, many girls were running frantically in all directions. I decided I wouldn't go through the main building where the Black Uniform nurses stayed because I didn't trust the rumor that they were all gone. Instead, I snuck out the side of the building and stepped into the ditch with undisturbed mud coming up to my knees and grass slashing my skinny body like razors. I ran across Road 160 into the fields and across the river to Em, all the while fearing she might not be there.

When I got to the bin, I was overjoyed to see my sister there. It had been at least a year since I last saw Chenda in the girls' camp at Water Mill Village. She had to have been in contact with Em to know to come home with such impeccable timing. She looked so skinny and wore a persistent frown on her face as though she was in constant pain. It hurt me to see my sister so frail, but I thanked God for letting us be together again. Chenda was infested with lice, her scalp full of yellow pus and oozing blood. Em took a pair of scissors and snipped a few strands of hair at a time. Some were no longer rooted and came out on their own when Em lifted them to be trimmed. When it was all done, Chenda's whole scalp looked like one big ball of infection with lice sucking on it. Em picked off the lice as much as she could and rinsed her baby girl's infected head with water. Chenda moaned and squirmed as Em washed her. She wanted to put the old krama back on to rescue her dignity. But Em pleaded with her to let it be so that the fresh air would help dry and heal the infection. Em was right. A couple of days later, Chenda's head already showed signs of healing.

Soon after we were together, we heard explosions echoing from afar. I was excited and thought, *Liberation! Someone cares about us.* For safety, Em and Stubby spent the night sleeping under the bin next to an old chicken nest. Remembering the chicken mite problem at the Meeting Creek hut, I hesitated to sleep next to them, but Em didn't let me have my way. She said, "Come here, my children. We'll sleep next to each other." I was on one side of Em and my sister was on the other. "We live together and die together." Em added.

Stubby laughed out loud, "You're a vicious lady. Don't you at least consider extending the bloodline?"

Em was sure of herself and replied: "Too much torture to live without each other."

The next day a strange atmosphere pervaded the village from the sound of kids crying and people walking, talking, and packing instead of being in the fields working. Where they were planning to go, no one knew. The Black Uniforms were nowhere to be seen. Later that day, before night came, Em decided to take us across the river so that if anything happened we would be on the east side, closer to National Highway 5, opposite from the jungle. That night we stayed in a house of one of our former maids, Bong Onn.

The maid and her family lived in a lovely wooden house in the village. Since she had been a maid in the old regime, the Black Uniforms had selected her and her husband to be leaders. Em told me Bong Onn had sought her out and brought her fish and other foods. I did not remember her, but I had heard her name. Her main task had been to babysit me when I was an infant.

While growing up, I was told often that at night I would cry as soon as the hammock stopped swinging.

To ensure the swinging lasted longer, Bong Onn would push it hard. Once she swung the hammock so hard it launched me out of it, and I landed on the tile floor. I was told that was the only time Em ever struck a maid.

Bong Onn was happy to see me. She laughed with tenderness and told me the same hammock story. I was glad to finally meet the woman I had heard so much about, who had taken care of me and dealt with my baby tantrums.

Bong Onn was not a pretty woman, but her husband was a good-looking man. They had three little children. I heard as Em pleaded with Bong Onn and her husband for help. "Please help us. Have mercy on my girls. I don't know what to do or where to go." Her plea morphed into a sad story and a plea to a higher being. "I have no destination. I have lost everything I owned. They emptied me. What do I do now? Dear Lord, hear me; help me. Show me a way to a better life for my girls."

On that very same night, like thunder, the bombs dropped nearby and all around us. People screamed, kids cried, mothers called to their babies. Em rushed us out of the house with the words: "Run, run, hurry, hurry!" We were with many people, all of them running *toward* the bombs, seeking a chance at freedom, a chance to be free from the Black Uniforms.

Like a calf in the middle of a buffalo stampede, no

matter how much I tried, people passed me by. I could no longer see Em, but I heard her voice constantly calling out our names: "Thom!²⁴ Tuch! Stay together, my dear children."

"Jah,²⁵ Jah." We replied. I stepped in a dry fish hole,²⁶ and my right knee sank into the earth. I was unable to get up, and at first feared I couldn't keep the promise that I made to Kheang. Worse yet, I might be the one who slowed Chenda and Em down.

"Em, Em, Em! I'm stuck!" I cried. In a few seconds, Em and Chenda pulled me out of the hole.

"Let's go! Hurry, hurry!" Em urged me as though the Black Uniforms were right behind us. To my surprise, I was able to move forward. But I'll never forget those moments of fear and agony.

After a while, the bombs stopped, people stopped running, and we were walking on a dirt road under the moonlight without Bong Onn. By then most people were resting or sleeping, but a few of us kept going. We

²⁴ *Thom* is Chenda's nickname, referring to her status as the older of the two daughters in our family.

²⁵ *Jah* is a Khmer word that means "yes."

²⁶ A *fish hole* is about 1.5 feet deep and 8 inches in diameter, dug near flooded fields, with a smooth pathway between the water and the hole to encourage little critters such as small fish, crabs, and snails to crawl in. The hole is then covered with twigs and branches. Once in the hole, the little critters, including frogs, are not be able to escape.

were marching, adding more distance between us and the river. I saw Em and Chenda's profiles as we walked on the dirt road, each with a load on her head that was too heavy to keep their bodies straight. In my head, I recited the promise that I gave Kheang: *Don't worry, I will take care of Em. Dear God, please give me strength and show me a way to keep my promise to my brother.*

I decided then that I would be the one to make shelter and find food for Em and Chenda. I was not sure how, but I would do whatever I could to make sure Em and my sister were taken care of. For now, we truly had nothing left, not even the Black Uniforms to give us rations.

A second round of bombing started. Like thunder, the bombs exploded, burning bushes and trees nearby. This time the bombs were so close that they changed my perception from being liberated to being eliminated. Chenda bent her knees to lower her height and cried out for Em when the bombs whistled through the night sky and rattled as they lost speed, preparing to explode on impact. Em yelled and commanded us to charge forward, behind her.

Each of us carried a load wrapped in cloth on our heads. We took turns carrying the heaviest load, which Em had packed with the kettle and some food. After a while the load was so heavy that all I could think about was the load itself. Still I bit my lips and counted every step to get my mind off the weight, pushing myself to carry it as long as I could, giving Chenda and Em a longer break. I would refuse the first few offers to trade loads.

The next morning, we found ourselves among many people from other villages gathering near the crossroad between Road 160 and the National Highway 5. It had been over three years since I had last been on an asphalt road. I felt as though I was walking on foam. *Is this real, or am I in a dream? Am I really free? Are the Black Uniforms really gone?*

At this crossroad, we had the option to turn left toward Thailand or right, which would lead us back to our old home in Battambang. I knew Em would never go back to Battambang. There was no one there waiting for her. I pleaded with Em to stay one day at the crossroad to give me enough time to build a push wagon so we wouldn't have to carry our loads on our heads any more. In my mind, I could do this. I didn't have tools, but I could ask for help and borrow tools from men who had hearts. Many did. Em was either not convinced that I could build a push wagon or she didn't care about the weight of our belongings. She made up her mind to get us out of there as soon as possible. We turned left and walked to Banteay Neang, a town along National Highway 5.

At Banteay Neang we slept on the veranda of an old general store along the highway. I was awakened by adults who couldn't wait for the sun to come up. Em decided to take us back to the crossroad. We followed her without asking any questions. I sensed it would be dangerous for two young teenage girls and a lady to live on the street in a country that had no law and order now that the Black Uniforms had left. On the way back, Em constantly apologized for pushing us to come to Banteay Neang only to take us back to the crossroad the next day. As we walked back, she pleaded with us to keep pushing and not give up on her. She motivated us with her love. "Try a little harder for me, my dears. Have faith in me."

I thought, *There was nothing to forgive. Of course, Em, I would do anything for you.* I was sure that if we'd had enough resources to live on for more than a couple of days, we would have proceeded forward toward the Thai border.

As we marched back to the crossroad, I saw more and more people on the highway. It was nerve-racking to march in the direction opposite to everybody else. I started to doubt Em. *Where are we going, Em? What is the plan?* As if she could read my mind, she told us we were going to see if we could reunite with Ouv and Mair. It made sense. At least with Ouv and Mair, we could help them find food, and we would not be all by ourselves. Besides, we needed a man to exist in this man's world, and Ouv was a man both strong and kind.

Back at the crossroad, streams of people continued to come from the villages along the river. We got off the highway and turned onto Road 160, which led us back to the river. I really didn't want to leave the highway, but I didn't protest Em's decision. We were the only ones heading down the road to the river. Oncoming flocks of people looked at us as though we were crazy. Once we got closer to the river, but before the road turned, we stopped so Em could recover from her asthma, which seemed to get worse as the sun was getting hotter. We anxiously waited and hoped Linda's family would show up, but they were nowhere to be found.

Finally, Em let us proceed forward toward the river while she watched the road for Mair and Ouv. My job was to get some food from the Chark eating shack. Chenda was to go further up the river to convince Linda's family to leave the French Village, assuming they were still there. Em thought that Ouv would not leave French Village, since he would be more comfortable foraging food in a village and open fields than having to deal with people in old towns and cities. However, Em feared that if she was right about Ouv, there was a good chance that his family would be recaptured by the

Black Uniforms. Her thought was first we need to get some distance from the Black Uniforms, then we can worry about other problems, in which case we would be better situated to deal with a problem together.

I felt proud that Em counted on me to get food for us. I hustled back to Chark Village in a hurry and was not afraid. By the time I got there, most of the people were gone. I went to our bin and grabbed two small buckets and a carrying stick, then headed to the eating shack.

Even before I got to the eating shack, I heard men yelling and fighting for food. From the distance, I could tell there was little chance that I could fight my way in to get some of whatever was in the big basket the men were fighting for. But I had to. I charged at the crowd of about fifty men and elbowed my way to get in. I was pushed in and out as my face and head were banged by strong arms and elbows. Determined to get some for Em, I pressed myself between the men to get a look at what was in the basket. It was obvious that there was no way I could reach in to scoop what was left at the bottom. I looked around in desperation for a longer arm to help me. A man grabbed and yanked a bucket out of my hand. "Get out!" he yelled, and indicated with a quick facial gesture that he was going to help me. I recognized him—the man who was teasing me about being married to Em—so I slid down and slipped out of the crowd between someone's legs. From my knees I still saw the man with my bucket. He handed it to me full of rock salt. "One more bucket, please!" I screamed for more. He hesitated a little, but he did help me.

I stepped away from the crowd, hurriedly hooked the first bucket onto one end of the carrying stick, and waited for the man. As soon as the man handed me the second bucket, I hooked it onto the other end of the carrying stick. With the carrying stick on my shoulder and the buckets of salt suspended on each of its ends, I ran out of there as fast as I could.

More and more people were leaving the villages along the river, heading toward the crossroads—many more people than when I left Em less than an hour ago. The road was so packed that it was nearly impossible to move forward. People were moving with oxcarts and belongings they had taken back from the Black Uniforms. Trying to make the crowd move faster, someone in the group yelled: "They're coming! They're coming!" The crowd hustled and ran as far as they could before slowing down again.

Approaching the turn in the road, I saw Em stretching her head and neck, searching frantically for her babies. In bare shoulders, she was giving herself coin rub therapy on her chest, marching back and forth on the road and whimpering: "Dear Lord, help me. Help my baby. My baby. My baby."

"Em!" I shouted.

She continued to whimper, "Oh, dear God, I am so grateful. Thank you for giving me back my baby. Help me, child. Help me look out for your sister. I should have never let my babies go."

I felt sad and frightened, not only for Chenda but for Em as well, because I had never seen Em crying frantically. Fearing for Em's mental state, I couldn't stop worrying for her while I was on the lookout for Chenda and Linda's family. Em spent the next thirty minutes or so sitting down, getting up, marching back and forth on the road, and crying out for her baby girl, but no one seemed to noticed her.

Finally, Chenda emerged from the crowd with Ouv right behind her on a fully loaded ox cart and the rest of the family behind him! Em's distraught behavior immediately disappeared, and I gave thanks to God.

Reunited with Chenda and Linda's family, we learned that Ouv had an old friend who lived in Big Mountain (*Phnom Thom*), which was not too far away, south of the crossroads, along National Highway 5. We stayed with them for the next few days. On the other side of the highway were hills covered with green shrubs, trees, and overgrown vines. It must have been the big mountain that the town was named after. Linda and I went there to pick wild greens for cooking. The area behind the house was full of banana bushes and a line of bamboo bushes that served as a fence for the property.

Just like Ouv, his friend used to be a Buddhist monk. Hoping for spiritual support and advice, Em shared with Ouv and his friend the dream I'd had the night before Pa left. Both men looked disappointed. With hesitation they interpreted the dream to mean that Pa and Kheang had moved on beyond this world. To them, this is what the enlightenment on the last portrait along the wall of the worship house in the dream indicated. At that moment, I witnessed Em's pain again and was angry at the men for making such harsh statements when they didn't know for sure. Until then, Em's interpretation of the dream had been that Pa and Kheang had reached happiness and were suffering no more.

The day after we arrived at Big Mountain, I saw a truckload of our liberators on the highway. Instantly I felt sad. The Vietnamese were the last group of people we expected to liberate us. Historically, our two countries had endured bitter wars. Growing up, I had heard horrors stories of how Vietnamese soldiers tortured Cambodian children. Nevertheless, I was happy that we were at least free from the Black Uniforms.

Every day, the Vietnamese soldiers would be on the

highway, driving to and from Serei Saophoan, where they were stationed. More and more people were marching, biking, and even riding on buses heading to Poipet, hoping to find refuge in Thailand. Some were marching to Battambang, hoping to claim properties or to be reunited with loved ones.

Em met many of her old friends from Battambang and learned that Uncle Song, my father's oldest brother, and his family were in Serei Saophoan. The next day we left Linda's family and walked to Banteay Neang, the same town where we slept on the veranda. Not knowing where we would be staying or if we could find our uncle, Em managed to get us on a small, old, beat-up bus from Banteay Neang to Serei Saophoan to buy some time. I was excited and nervous to be in a bus. During the four years under the Black Uniforms, I had never even seen a bus, much less ridden in one.

In the bus, men were cheering and talking about what was going to happen and what kind of government was going to lead the country. Some said it didn't matter as long as the Black Uniforms didn't come back. They cheered for their freedom. An outspoken Chinese man (who reminded me of Pa) warned everybody: "Don't celebrate too soon. The Vietnamese are also communists. It's like we are in the same bus going to the same destination—just a different driver, that's all."

At Serei Saophoan we were reunited with our cousins and learned that Uncle Tre's oldest son had been tortured by the Black Uniforms after his family escaped to Thailand with Ee and Hong. He was a skinny twenty-two-year-old walking with a cane. Physically and mentally he had been damaged for life.

Uncle Song's family made fun of Chenda and me because we now spoke with village words and thick accents, which was not socially desirable. I thought they were lucky the Black Uniforms didn't change *them* that much.

Seeing my uncle and his children made me wish Kheang and Pa were with us. It had been only a few months since Pa and Kheang left. If Pa could have endured the Black Uniforms just a little bit longer, we would be together now. There were many possible reasons that forced Pa to decide to leave: It could be because the Black Uniforms moved Pa and Em from their friends at the edge of Meeting Creek Village to the longhouse. It could be because Pa's group leader reported on him. It could be because Kheang was growing fast and soon would be taken further away from Pa and Em. It could be because of Stubby's husband, the one that claimed to know the way to the Thai border. Or it could be because of me.

Chapter 17

Harvest Season of 1979

The large number of Vietnamese troops stationed in Serei Saophoan made the town a relatively safe zone from the Black Uniforms. However, those who ventured beyond the Vietnamese post toward Thailand were often raided by the Black Uniforms during the night. Many families were killed after their short taste of freedom. We heard terrifying stories of how they were slaughtered, including beheading and emptying out guts. Many people who survived these latest atrocities returned to Serei Saophoan to stay close to the Vietnamese Troops.

After staying with Uncle Song and his family for about a week in Serei Saophoan, it was clear that we needed to move on. We were unable to pitch in and help with food. The rice fields near town were already emptied, and there were stories of the Black Uniforms still capturing and killing people who set out seeking rice in remote fields. People had tried selling and exchanging things, but we didn't have any valuables left and we had no men in the family to help us wheel and deal in this man's world. We walked back to Linda's family in Big Mountain.

At Big Mountain, we went out every day to gather as much rice as we could. Our stomachs were always full those days. We competed with others to gather the rice, but we worked for ourselves, not for the Black Uniforms. We would get up and head to the fields as soon as we could see the trail in front of us, and left the fields as late as we could. I thought that if we worked hard enough, we would have extra rice to exchange for other goods—as long as Ouv's friend was not like Mr. Sovan's family, who welcomed our hard labor but didn't share the fruit.

When the nearby fields became empty, we stayed home waiting for Ouv and his friends to scout a new field for us to work in. One day while resting with my cousins under the house, I heard a man yell in anger: "This man is a Black Uniform guy. You killed my children! You devil!" The yelling man swung and punched the suspect, who was tied with his arms behind his back. Soon other men joined in. They were swearing and reminding the suspect of the loved ones that he had killed, all the while taking turns kicking and punching him like bulldogs attacking a bull. The suspect was larger, stronger, and taller than any of them. He didn't deny any of the accusations. With his hands tied, he couldn't fight back, and finally they were able to take him down. Blood was all over his face as he lay on the ground taking more kicks, but not a scream nor plea for mercy ever came out of his mouth.

Em asked God, "Dear Lord, why so much suffering?" I thought about my plan to get revenge on the Black Uniform girl leader who kicked me and dragged me on the ground by my hair in front of Em, but after I saw what happened to this Black Uniform, I was certain that revenge was not for me.

People should have been happy. With the Black Uniforms gone, there should have been no more killing, but still there were killings. Not long before, a man was killed in a fight over ownership of a pig. His body was thrown in a ditch, partially cremated. His bottom half stuck out in the air and swelled up in the heat of the sun. I saw this accidentally, not knowing where they had attempted to cremate him.

Ouv took us to Phum Preah Ponlea where Aunt Nay Hak, Aunt Sareth, and their families were staying. We hoped to find more unharvested rice there, but as we approached the village, it was clear the rice had already been harvested. We were disappointed, but we still hoped to see our aunts, not knowing whether they were still there.

The village people told us where Aunt Sareth and her son lived. Aunt Sareth was happy to see us. She constantly smiled, showing her white teeth. I was happy to see her as well, but for some reason I was reserved and didn't show much affection or curiosity. My little cousin had not grown much since I last saw him. He stood a little higher than my belly button and looked dark and skinny.

As we were getting reacquainted, Aunt Sareth learned about what happened to the men in my family, and I learned that Aunt Nay Hak's husband had died, and she had gone to Serei Saophoan with one of her sons, Ou. I also learned that my best friend from Battambang and her siblings had been axed by her chauffeur before taking his own life. The chauffeur had spent many months taking care of my friend and her siblings, who had been separated from their parents when they left Battambang. One day he'd had enough and decided to finish the suffering by his own hand.

We brought Aunt Sareth and Cousin Pros with us to Big Mountain. Since Aunt Sareth was with us, Ouv's friend offered us an empty rice bin to stay in. Ouv built an extension of the rice bin with a bamboo floor, a grass roof, and walls for us. We used the extension as a cooking area, and all the girls slept in the bin.

One afternoon, Om Leung's brother-in-law from Meeting Creek stopped by. He was happy he had found us and couldn't wait to share the news. With a smiling face, he told us, "Your husband and your son didn't make it."

"How do you know?" Em replied, fearfully demanding to learn more.

His reply shocked all of us. "Stubby's husband and Pad's son came back."

The man tried to explain the details, but it didn't matter. Em and Chenda just started to cry. Em knotted her face in agony and cried out loud. She howled her plaint like a baby throwing a tantrum: "I won't ever get to see my son again!" She and Chenda leaned on each other, sobbing. Em whimpered, "I won't get to see my baby again. Lord, please help me. I begged him again and again to endure a little longer, but he didn't listen to me. If he could have waited just a little longer, we would all be together."

Catching her breath, she screamed with the most painful feeling she had ever experienced. "He took my baby boy away from me!" For four years Em had suppressed emotional and physical tortures. This was the first time she was free to cry out loud.

I felt the lump in my throat, but I couldn't cry. All I

could do was wonder why this guy was smiling while telling us such horrible news. I was mad at him for bringing the bad news and making Em suffer again. It seemed to me that the man was so excited to have first-hand knowledge that he forgot about the impact of this terrible news.

I watched Chenda weep and imagined the pain that I would have felt if I lost Em. Chenda was close to Pa as much as I was close to Em.

I wondered why I couldn't cry like Em and Chenda did. Perhaps I latched on to the man's smiling face and anticipated good news. Perhaps I didn't believe the news. Before the man came, I had been daydreaming that our father and brothers would come to rescue us soon, now that we were free from the Black Uniforms. Perhaps my heart was with Em and Chenda since the news had struck their hearts in the most vicious way. Or perhaps I was ready to move on and didn't want to feel the pain. Whatever it may have been at the time, today I wish that I had been able to cry and allow myself to feel the pain instead of spending years hoping for something that would never come true.

The following days I relived my last conversation with Kheang over and over. How I wished I hadn't encouraged him to go. How I wished I'd said something different in those few seconds. How could I tell Em that I had a chance to change the outcome, but I chose the wrong path?

Chapter 18

THE SECOND EVACUATION

Harvest Season of 1979

The Vietnamese troops stationed in Serei Saophoan would drive by Big Mountain in their vehicle once or twice a day, but they never stayed around. Just like the Vietnamese troops, many people would come from Serei Saophoan to trade rice with us, and they would be in a hurry to go back so they wouldn't get stuck here after the sun went down. After dark, Big Mountain was like a ghost town, and we were left to fend for ourselves. Every sunset my heart was heavy for fear of being captured by the Black Uniforms. I felt abandoned with despair. Many times I wished Em trusted me enough to find food for us so we could be safe in Serei Saophoan.

One day while we were eating lunch, we were interrupted by bombing. We were unprepared and never thought the Black Uniforms would attack in the middle of the day. We ran into the banana patch behind the house where I stepped into a pile of human excrement that was still warm to my foot. We all squatted there and said prayers. We couldn't sit because we were in the middle of a place that we had been using as our bathroom. We were supposed to dig a hole before we did our jobs, but not all of us did, and sometimes there wasn't enough time. Still, we were supposed to dig a hole afterward and bury it, but some of us must have forgotten.

We couldn't stay in the shitting place any longer, so we sought shelter by a bamboo bush. Then Em decided to move us to a dried-up pond so we could be below ground level and away from any flying bomb fragments. The dried pond was behind a neighbor's house, across from a rice cleaning field. Between the bombings, we all dashed to the dried pond. Bending as low as I could while running across the rice cleaning field, I saw people crowded by the pond. When we got there, the pond was already full of people, and it was impossible to get in. I squatted by the rim of the pond, protesting to Em that it wasn't possible to enter it. Before Em had a chance to reply, another bomb dropped and pushed me flying into the pond, landing me on top of people. Women screamed and prayed, and kids were crying. All the men were outside the pond, and some of them exclaimed their amazement at the powerful impact of the bombs. Smoke, flame, and the crackling and popping sounds of burning were all around us.

An old woman next to me was shaking like a wet rat and said her prayer in a shaky voice. Someone else was yelling, "You peed on me!"

With a shaky voice, the old woman replied, "I didn't even know." Then she crawled back to the rim of the pond and tried to empty her bladder in front of everybody. While she was squatting, her husband kicked her—not hard, but enough to humiliate her—and followed it with disgusting comments. I felt blessed to know that my father would never have done this to Em. In fact, I never heard Em and Pa fight. Pa would yell at Em, and Em would be upset, but I never heard them yelling at each other.

When the bombing stopped, we learned that the bamboo bush we had left to go to the dry pond had been burnt to the ground, and with it a family of five.

I had never seen any dead Black Uniforms or Vietnamese soldiers, only the villagers were wounded and killed. Looking back, I wondered whether the Black Uniforms were actually fighting the Vietnamese. Or if the Vietnamese were trying to scare the Black Uniforms off with the bombings, why would the Vietnamese soldiers sacrifice their lives for Cambodians? And why would the Black Uniforms confront the Vietnamese soldiers when all they had were their own two feet and whatever ammunition they could carry with their bodies? They didn't even have horses. They had been so comfortable being bosses, patrolling the rice fields, and controlling their own people that they had forgotten to defend the country.

A few days after the bombing, Bong Tav (Uncle Song's son-in-law) came to Big Mountain asking for directions to an orchard along the way to Meeting Creek to pick mangoes. Since he came all the way from Serei Saophoan and my uncle had helped care for us, Em felt obligated to let me take Bong Tav to the mango orchard. To get to the orchard, we had to get off National Highway 5 onto a small dirt road toward the river. Sitting on the back of the bike with Bong Tav peddling as fast as he could, I wished Em had not let me venture into Black Uniform territory. The faster Bong Tav peddled, the more nervous I became. When we arrived at the orchard, we got to work quickly as though we were stealing from the Black Uniforms all over again. When Bong Tav climbed the mango trees and shook the branches, the mangoes and giant red ants fell on me and on the ground. I picked up the falling mangoes and packed them in a cotton sack. We rushed back on the dirt road to the highway with a sack full of mangoes on my laps. On the return trip, Bong Tav seemed to peddle harder and harder while I encouraged him to go even faster, knowing we were both scared of the same thing: the Black Uniforms. I had to endure this trip multiple times, and every time it got scarier and scarier.

One night we woke up to a combination of gunfire, the Black Uniforms yelling, and the sounds of terror from mothers and children. We ran to the fields behind the house and kept going to get away from the terror and to make sure that the Black Uniforms would never recapture us. That night we slept in a field full of hard and pointy little mounds six to eight inches in diameter at the base and about six inches in height that had been home to many giant earthworms. I had never seen such mounds before. It was impossible to lie down without getting prodded by these hard and pointy mounds. We had no mats to lie on and no blankets to cover us as we slept under the open sky and on top the dried giant earthworm mounds. I thought about how worried Ouv's friend must be, for he and his wife left town early that day, and their kids were stuck here with us. They had a girl named Tiny (*Pech*), who was a little older than me. Tiny's little brother was about three years old and was always tickled about everything. He had white teeth, a chubby face, and a brown body that was naked all day long.

The next morning, the sounds of gunfire were gone, but we remained in the field until the little ones could no longer bear the sun without water. The adults led us back to town, assuming that the Black Uniforms left the town and the Vietnamese troops would be back patrolling the highway.

But as we approached the town, I sensed something was not right. It was too quiet, but we went in anyway. As we walked past the burned-down bamboo fence, I wanted to go back to the field, but the adults were hustling and tiptoeing quietly to the house. Bending down as I hurried on light feet behind the adults, my heart was pounding, and I longed to be somewhere else.

At the house, we crawled under the rice bin that stood about one foot off the ground. We were lined up and packed against each other like sardines in a can. I was at the edge of the pack, hidden by a stack of firewood and next to Em. The little ones seemed to understand the situation as they became very quiet even though they were thirsty and hungry—except for Tiny's little brother. He was the youngest of the kids, and he started to make noise and plead with his sister for food. Tiny took him from the hiding place to feed him in the cooking area.

We waited quietly for the Vietnamese soldiers to rescue us, sure that they would come. It was just a matter of time since they needed to have access to the highway. Time ticked by slowly. I heard the Black Uniforms yelling for people to get out of the houses and threatening to shoot them. I closed my eyes, and in my head I chanted the Buddhist song over and over to protect myself, to occupy my mind, and to fill my senses with nothing but Buddha's wisdom.

The Black Uniform devils brought me back to reality when they shouted at the family two houses away from us. Through an opening in the firewood, I saw them hovering by the house. I squeezed Em's hand, and she squeezed back in reply. Where were the Vietnamese? I closed my eyes and tried to go back to chanting, but I kept getting interrupted by my own fear, the fear of getting my head chopped off. I had heard many stories of the Black Uniforms coming back to the Vietnamese side, chopping off people's heads, and mutilating their bodies.

I looked again. This time they were at the house next to us, shouting nonstop. Some of them stabbed the thatch walls with their bayonets. One of them looked right back into my eyes and grinned. I froze and felt exposed. I was sure they were coming for us. Heavy-hearted, sad, guilty feelings replaced my fear: I had exposed my family to them.

If I'd been squeezed in closer to Em, he wouldn't

have seen me. There was no need to tell Em what had happened. What good would it do? As they marched closer and closer toward our place, I hoped the Black Uniform who saw me was not true to their cause and that he would let us go since he hadn't tipped off his comrades. Besides, he had smiled at me. I saw their feet as they walked next to us, but there was no sign that they saw us, no shouting or demanding. Just then they looped around. It was just a game they liked to play: giving us hope and taking it away.

"Out! Out—before I kill you!" they shouted in their devilish voices.

There was no pleading, no confession, nor even a cry from the little ones. One at a time we quietly crawled out through the tiny opening.

"Why are you hiding from us? Are you supporting the Vietnamese? I ought to kill you right now!" one of them screamed at us.

I could only imagine what they would do to Ouv, the only man in the group of eleven people.

I was the last one to get out, right behind Em. As I stuck my head out through the tiny opening, I thought of nothing but my neck and the swinging motion of a machete. I imagined my neck without a head and the blood shooting out. I repeated in my own head: *Any time now they are going to chop off my head.* As I came completely out and stood up straight, I was still thinking that they would like to chop it off while I was standing. When they yelled at us to move, I was greatly relieved.

We walked slowly to the edge of the town, still hoping that the Vietnamese would catch up with us. "Hurry up!" they yelled as they pushed us with the tips of their guns. There were more people held up at the edge of town. When we got there, they moved everybody across the highway onto a dirt road. I thought of how lucky Tiny and her baby brother were. Since the Black Uniforms had seen us under the bin, they didn't bother to check in the eating area, which was separated only by a slab of thatched wall. Not long after we stepped off the highway, we heard explosions. Walking even slower, we hoped that the Vietnamese would drive down the dirt road to rescue us.

One of the Black Uniforms calmly commented on how slowly we walked: "You don't walk like you are trying to get away from the enemy. Do you understand that the Vietnamese have been our enemies for centuries? You don't know it, but we are giving our lives to rescue you." I wasn't sure how to take this. Nevertheless, we hurried a little more to pretend that we were listening to him.

We walked past the mango orchard that Bong Tav and I had come to a couple of weeks earlier. As we got closer to Meeting Creek, my heart was heavy. I was nervous and not sure if I should even take a glimpse at our old hut. I forgot all about my current situation. Finally, when we walked past our empty hut and through the empty Meeting Creek Village, all I could think about was Pa and Kheang, hoping the news from Um Leung's brother-in-law was incorrect.

We crossed the river and walked past villages that had been abandoned, grabbing up belongings that had been left behind. There were many overripe tomatoes along the way. Whenever we were allowed to break for cooking, we would take the chance to prepare the tomatoes and make tomato paste out of them.

We walked past Syhsamon, which was not recognizable without flood water. I thought about Pa and Kheang again and hoped the news we received a couple of days ago was incorrect.

After a couple of days of walking, we were resettled not too far away from the thick jungle, near the Thai border. I thought about how unlucky we were: We'd had a chance at freedom, and then it was taken away from us.

Everybody that was recaptured pitched in to build longhouses where we were staying, and we gathered rice from the surrounding fields. We had one of the best spots in the longhouse, which was at one end so we didn't have to be sandwiched between two neighbors. This was because Ouv had farming skills, including knowing how to build longhouses quickly. After his hard work helping everyone put up the longhouse, no one challenged him when he claimed the prime spot.

Living under the Black Uniforms this time around, there was no common kitchen. Everybody made their own meals. Em stayed at the longhouse to take care of my little cousins and find creative ways to fill our stomachs with wild water spinach, some small fish, and other small critters, while everyone else went out to gather rice from the same fields I had helped plant when I left Em at Chark after Pa and Kheang had gone.

There were no leaders among us except the few Black Uniforms themselves, so most of the time the Black Uniforms left us alone. With this lack of control and the fact that I was a skinny girl, I would pretend to be sick. I would lie down under a blanket when people lined up to go to the fields, but as soon they left, Pros and I would head out to a creek that was nearly dried up. There we sank our feet into the sticky clay mud that came up to my knees to try and catch little fish and critters that were sheltered underneath water hyacinth in shallow water.

Pros was very good at finding and catching fish. He would lead me to where he thought would be a good spot, and many times I thought as I walked behind him, *You are such a good boy, and so cute.* I imagined he had done this for his mom all of these times since his father had been separated from them and there were no other big brothers or uncles to help out. Many times he helped me and was cutely frustrated with his pouting and tired face when I screamed for help to remove leeches from my body. Even a few steps away, it was an effort to plow through the deep, sucking mud with each step. Sometimes he would be the only one going into the mud, and I would wait for him to throw little critters for me to collect so he didn't have to waste his energy coming to help me with the leeches.

The creek was far enough from the longhouse that by the time we got back, the mud on my legs, arms, and face would dry up and pull my skin apart. For Pros, it was all over his body. To save water, we would pull the dried mud off of us instead of rinsing it off. We never came back to Em empty-handed. It was always with a handful of small fish and snails, and sometimes we even got a fish as big as Pros's big toe. With eleven people in the family and not much vegetation available, these catches were not enough, so we filled our stomachs mostly with rice and tomato paste.

One day my right foot was punctured near the big toe and blood oozed out even though the foot was coated with mud. The next few days, my whole foot was swollen and throbbing. I was bored, hungry, and waiting for my family to come back from the field when I heard thunder. Suddenly, I realized it was the sound of a bomb. Again and again I heard faint explosions far in the distance—more like at the end of the horizon. The women at the longhouse looked at each other with a tinge of excitement that only those who shared the same feeling would notice.

The next day people hesitated to leave their families to line up to go to the field, but the Black Uniforms came on horseback and led them to the field. That was the only time I saw Black Uniforms on horses.

That day the explosions were louder than the day before. Em was prepared to leave any time, but as she looked at my foot she was sad and worried. I can only imagine what she was thinking. Truly bad luck. At that moment I made up my mind that I would not let Em worry about me. I did not know how, but I was sure that I would do the best I could to not slow my family down.

The following morning, we woke up to the sound of horses prancing and their riders yelling for us to move. Everybody was busy packing, but I couldn't do anything to help. I sat up and watched everybody around me hustle when the horse came around again.

"Hurry! Hurry! Go! Go! Now! Come back later to

collect what is left behind," shouted a Black Uniform rider.

Bombs exploded, and this time I felt the ground rumbling. Em, Mair, and Aunt Sareth were directing us. Due to Ouv's good nature, his farming skills, strong and hardworking attitude, he was the caretaker for two oxen and a wagon from the Black Uniforms. With these oxen and the wagon, all of our belongings were loaded, and everybody was ready to move when Em turned around and said to me, "What are you doing?"

Sitting at edge of the of the longhouse by myself, I told Em, "I can wait here."

"Are you crazy?" Em yelled in disbelief. "No wonder families get separated," she added as she came over to put my right arm around her neck and help me limp to the wagon.

We moved further away from the river and closer to the jungle. We had no idea where we were taken to. We just followed those in front of us. We marched without any water for quite some time and with no Black Uniforms in sight. When we came across a water hole, my excitement was trumped by the warmth, thickness, and brownish color of the water. I couldn't bring myself to drink thick, clayey water, but Em stirred some kind of crystal rock into the water to allow the cloudiness to drop to the bottom of the bucket. The water tasted sour, but at least we weren't drinking mud.

At the water hole, everybody was helping to get rice cooking, unpacking, fetching water, and finding firewood. Sitting in the wagon and watching all of the action around me, I felt bad that I was not able to help. However, I also felt lucky that Ouv had access to the oxen and the wagon. Otherwise Em, Chenda, and I would have been left behind at the longhouse.

Looking at the surroundings, I realized I was next to girl island. Without the flood water, the place was hardly recognizable, even though it was only about five months ago that I had been there planting rice and clearing jungle patches.

Although only part of the hut was there, what was left was the spot where I sat for many days in the planting season, making grass panels for thatch walls and roofs until my right thumb started bleeding. Somehow, I was excited, and I wanted to tell Em that I had been here before. When I finally told her, she gave me a quick smile and said, "Live like a wild animal. You are blessed to survive. Angels are looking over you. Pray to them and the keeper of the jungle to show us a way out." Those words sent me back to the reality that I might have to spend the rest of my life in a jungle and never again experience civilization.

Even before I got a chance to finish pleading to the angels and the keeper of the jungle for help, someone in the group was hustling and moving away from the water hole. The next thing I knew, more people had turned around and were running away from the jungle. We threw everything back into the wagon and joined the stampede, taking the chance of getting shot at by the Black Uniforms if they came back, but also the chance to be free again.

The sound of pots and pans banging and the stampeding footsteps were so loud that if the Black Uniforms were within a few miles of us they would definitely hear. But no Black Uniforms ever came to corral us, so the people kept running across the shrubs, through the fields, and toward the river until they could no longer run.

After a while, the walking became more like crawling. At that point some men tried to motivate the crowd to move faster. "They're coming! They're coming! Faster! Faster!" they would say to scare us. The stampede started again then eventually slowed down again. All the while, I was the only one in the family who was allowed to ride in the wagon because it was loaded with rice and other belongings, and Ouv did not want to risk breaking the wagon or pushing the oxen too hard. Even the little ones had to walk. Mair seemed to be mad about my situation, which was understandable. Even her youngest baby, Red, who was about two years old at the time, was not allowed to be in the wagon, but she was carried by everybody except the younger ones. I felt blessed and guilty at the same time.

We cycled through these stampedes and crawled many times until finally, just before the sun went down and soft breezes blew by, people began to walk and talk with excitement and laughter as we approached the river. More people were coming back to villages along the river. Their greetings and curiosity were the best we could hope for. Someone in the group was yelling, "They're coming! They're coming! Hurry! Hurry!" and this time we all laughed in response, leaving the village people puzzled. We crossed the Chamnoam bridge, and retraced our way back to Big Mountain. Less than one month later, we were back to civilization.

Chapter 19

THE FLIGHTS FOR FREEDOM

April 1979

When we arrived at Big Mountain, we learned that fragments from bombs that exploded not too long after the Black Uniforms captured us had hit Tiny's little brother while they were hiding in the cooking area. Tiny had been cradling him on her lap before he was hit and killed instantly. Tiny's inner thighs had been damaged and deformed. The grownups speculated that she would never have a baby of her own.

Not long after we got back to Big Mountain, Bong Tav came to take us with him to live in Serei Saophoan again. The goal was to wait in Serei Saophoan for any opportunity to escape the country. Em wanted to take Linda with us, but it was Aunt Nay Hak's gold that would allow us to stay in Serei Saophoan. Asking to take Linda along would have been too much for Aunt Nay Hak. If Linda had stuck with us through thick and thin, I was pretty sure that Em would not have left her with Ouv and Mair. Instead, Em asked for Aunt Sareth to go with us because she had enough gold to take care of herself and her boy. However, Aunt Sareth hesitated. She wanted to stay in the hope that she would be reunited with her husband. Aunt Sareth encouraged Em to leave without her, but Em pleaded for Aunt Sareth to go with us. The two sisters tried hard to convince each other while all of us quietly watched and listened to them. Mair and Ouv probably felt left behind because there was no chance that they could even think of going.

Aunt Sareth opened her small jewelry pouch, trying to choose a gift for us to remember her by. She reached in and with a gentle smile handed me a gold ring that had once belonged to my grandma, whom I never had the chance to know. I knew then that my aunt had made up her mind to stay behind. Aunt Sareth, Mair, and Ouv took turns blessing our journey. That was the last time I ever saw them.

Chenda and I walked while Em sat on the bike that Bong Tav was peddling. Every few steps I looked back, and there everyone stood together, looking back at me. When I could no longer see them, my tears fell and everything stood still except my beating heart. Suddenly I became conscious of my own existence—the sensation of being so small compared to everything around me. I took one small forward step at a time, away from people who loved me, but I would be with Em. Bong Tav was hustling and going back and forth with his bike to give us a ride and keep us together, but most of all to make sure we would be in Serei Saophoan before nightfall. Traveling on the highway at night during this time carried with it the risk of being captured or shot at by the Black Uniforms.

When we got to Serei Saophoan, we stayed with Aunt Nay Hak and Cousin Ou in a house that was occupied by at least eight other families. Some families stayed under the house with a mat that had been laid on the dirt floor. We were the lucky ones who occupied the wooden veranda of the house where we ate and slept. Uncle Song and his family were nearby. I spent most of the day goofing around with my cousins, cooking and carrying water from the river for the grownups. All of our food was paid for by Aunt Nay Hak, since Em didn't have any valuable jewelry left.

Prior to the Black Uniforms era, Em had kept American currency with her for emergency in addition to jewelry. She was able to hide a thousand dollars from the Black Uniforms until Pa left. She told me that when Pa left, he took with him five hundred American dollars and left five hundred dollars for Em. Anticipating that the Black Uniforms would come for her, Em asked a friend to keep the money for her. When things settled down, Em went back for the money. Her friend told her that Em was delirious and that she had never ever received any money from Em.

"It's okay," Em said. "What goes around comes around. It is part of fate."

She also said, "It's better to lose that money than to lose something worse." Cambodians believe that your destiny was determined before you were born. If something was going to happen to you, you couldn't get away from it. How bad it would be was not certain. Thus, if a minor bad thing happened, the curse was lifted.

One day after a few weeks of staying in Serei Saophoan, the atmosphere was restless. I felt something was not normal about the day, but I couldn't put my finger on it. The grownups were talking too softly. Em's face was relaxed but sad as she stared into the distance, far away from any physical world. Finally, in the late afternoon, she told us we would be escaping that night. I was neither scared nor excited. I got into a mode of telling myself that I would not let Em worry about me. I would be strong and take care of Em and Chenda. That night I put on my favorite undergarment knitted by one of Em's friends whom I adored. It was the very first time

I wore this special undergarment, that I brought with me from our house in Battambang.

We pretended to sleep until we were sure everyone else was truly asleep. Then we quietly slipped away from the veranda.

We gathered by Uncle Song's place and picked up three of my cousins and the Saram family of six. Uncle Song had six children with him at that time. How he had decided to let his oldest son, one of his daughters (Cousin Kiny), and Uncle Tre's son go on this journey we did not know.

There were fourteen of us in total, and we tiptoed and hustled along the bushes out of Serei Saophoan and into a nearby village. Two men with guns slung over their shoulders received us, and there we waited for other people to show up. My heart pounded as I kept thinking, *What a waste of precious nighttime! Can't we just go?*

Finally, another group of people showed up. Together we were around thirty people. The guides led us as we rushed quietly out of the village and along the bushes as much as we could. Sometimes there were no bushes to protect us, so we would hurry through the open field.

A baby cried—yes, an infant baby. Someone in the second group had snuck a baby in, and he wouldn't stop crying until his mom stopped walking to nurse him.

My heart sank. Every time that baby cried, we all had to stop and wait.

I thought, Someone please make a decision to leave the baby and his mom. Please!

There was anxious and furious but quiet discussion among the adults. "Unbelievable," Em said under her breath.

Still, there was no change of plans, and the guides made us stop every time the baby cried. Every time we stopped, it would take at least five minutes that seemed to last forever. We stopped several times before we arrived at a good side road. In the open field closer to the road, we lowered ourselves as close to the ground as possible while moving along to reach the road. One of the guides took the first crossing, and his friend waited for the signal and nudged us to go in small groups, two or three at a time.

"Stay together," Em told Chenda and me. When it was our time to go, I almost hesitated, but I didn't want to slow Em down. As I climbed up the slope toward the edge of the road, my blood pumped stronger and my heart rushed to get out of my body. I could not think of anything else but moving fast and staying low. As I crossed over the road, I felt as though I was a target, and I fearfully imagined bullets flying toward me.

We walked all through that night, and I didn't feel

tired at all. Just before the sun started to come up, we were deep in the woods and feeling protected by the trees. There was a calmness in the atmosphere.

The guides stopped and turned around to face us. "The border is not too far away from here," they explained. "We can't go any further. We need to get back to our post before the Vietnamese look for us."

Someone in the group pleaded for the guides to take us further until we could see Thailand. The guides replied, "The border is on the other side of the mountain. You will be there in less than half an hour." When it was clear that they would not take us any further, all the men approached the guides and asked for specific directions.

An old lady with her grandson, who was about six years old, stood next to us. She said quietly to Em, "They have guns. They could easily shoot all of us and take our belongings." Em looked concerned but didn't say anything back to the old lady. We stood and solemnly watched the guides turn back and leave us.

After several hours of walking, there was no sign of any village. The sun was getting hotter and hotter. The little boy started to tell his grandma that he was thirsty. The grandma lied: "We are almost there, my dear grandchild."

People started to walk slower and slower. Someone

in the group said, "We've been scammed. They took our gold and left us to die."

Another one replied, "If they were bad men, they would have shot us and taken all of our precious gold and jewelry. So I think the border is not too far, just as they were saying."

Feeling exhausted and thirsty, I wanted to stop. "Please, can we rest for a while?" I asked Em.

"Try harder, my child. We have to keep going. Stay close to your cousin. If we stay behind, no one is going to come back for us." I remembered the commitment I made to myself before we left Serei Saophoan: I would be strong and take care of Em and Chenda. So I pushed myself.

We continued walking up the slope of the mountain. I stopped and waited for people to pass me by, and Em pleaded with me to continue. I told her I needed to urinate.

"Wait," she responded quickly. "Don't waste it," she added as she hurried and pulled out a plate from the cloth wrap.

As she handed the plate to me, I remembered hearing stories of people drinking their own urine to survive when there was no water. I thought, *Is this really happening to me? What is coming next?*

After I was done, I looked hesitantly at the plate of

yellowish liquid with its strong aroma as Em encouraged me to drink it. My stomach was already tight and ready to eject anything going in, but still I made myself lift the plate to my nose as Em told me, "Hold your breath, my child."

I did exactly what Em said. A gulp of my own concentrated and warm urine went in, and Em hurriedly grabbed the plate from me as every muscle within me worked to eject the urine along with any liquid that was left in my stomach. I was still hunched over when Em wanted me to try again. "No," I pleaded with her. She studied me for a while and decided that she would not push me. Instead she lifted up the plate and drank it herself.

Everyone seemed to head out their own way, searching for water out of desperation. We lost track of my three cousins and found ourselves in a small group of thirteen people: the Saram family, the old lady and her little grandson, and the five of us. Cousin Ou led us, hoping to get to the other side of the mountain and the Thailand border. On top of that mountain and under the full sun with hardly any shade, I felt the dryness of my throat and mouth, and all I could think of was water. I pleaded quietly to no one: *I'll do anything for just a drip of water to wet my parched mouth and throat.*

Finally, we could no longer inch forward and were

all lying down, scattered randomly on the gentle slope of the mountain with a few tall trees and hardly any shrubs. Cousin Ou took off to find water. He took with him an aluminum tea kettle and an old gasoline canister. I wanted to plead with him to stay because he was the strongest in the group and our last hope to lead and guide us, but if he stayed, he couldn't help us. I thought, *Will I see him again? Will he be able to find his way back to us, even if he does find water?*

Meanwhile, the little boy was screaming non-stop for water, while his grandma tried gently to calm him down on her lap. His desperate cry echoed through the mountains, and he could no longer obey his grandma.

He took off from her lap and deliriously screamed for water: "Need water! Need water! Need water! ..."

The grandma cried back: "Come back. Come back. Come back, my dear child ..."

As the boy's cries got softer, the old lady's cries became louder. When he finally stopped, she let loose an agonized scream and softly cried, shaming God for his harsh punishment on her sweet little boy, the only family she had left.

As I waited for Cousin Ou to come back, every second seemed like an hour. I wasn't thinking of death, nor did I fear it. My only need was to subdue my anguishing thirst. I found myself taking comfort in calling

out my cousin's name every time I exhaled, "Ou …
Ou … Ou …"

I was awakened by the sound of people begging
Ou for water, and the old lady howling softly for her
baby grandson to come for water. When she received
no reply, she cried again, and under her breath she
summoned: "My dear grandson. My precious child.
My only grandson." Her cry turned into a tantrum at
God. "Why do you take him this way? Take me instead.
Please, Lord, take me instead."

I opened my dried-up eyes to the afternoon sun,
crawled to Ou, and wondered how long I had been
sleeping. Or was I unconscious? Had it been days, or
just a couple of hours?

Days later, Ou told us how he found water:

> While searching for water and a village
> that was supposed to be nearby, I climbed
> the tallest tree I could find to get a sense
> of direction. Looking in all directions, I
> could see no sign of a village nor any body
> of water. Sensing our grim future, I lost
> hope. I wanted to scream, but then I no-
> ticed a tiny green frog (*kunchagn chayk*)
> jump out of a black hole of the burnt tree
> trunk. With excitement I reached into

the small dark hole and felt moisture on my fingertips. Adjusting myself so I could reach deeper, I still didn't feel any water. The next thing I did was to unravel the krama from my neck and dipped it into the hole. There I felt the water seeping into the krama fabric. Every drop of the water that I brought back for you was squeezed from the tip of my old, sweaty krama.[27]

Ou handed me about three sips of water, and I pleaded with him for some more, thinking that since I was his little cousin he would give me more. However, I got no special treatment. "I know it is very little, but we have to make it last," he told me in a calm and gentle voice that sounded like a monk's blessing. I imagined my own desperation as I drank and crawled away for others to take turns. A part of me was asking why Cousin Ou had to give water to everybody and not just our family.

As I lay still on the mountain, I tried to figure out how long I had been sleeping. It was possible that I

---

[27] During the writing of this book, Cousin Ou and I talked and recounted additional details of this blessed event.

had only a couple of hours of sleep before Cousin Ou brought us the water, but there was no way to know for sure. On the other hand, if I had slept there more than a day, then I must have been unconscious. I had lost all reference of time.

Ou and the rest of the grownups except the old lady were discussing the next option. Cousin Ou explained: "We don't know how far we have to go. Thus, we may not be able to make it. There is no water left at the last place I went to. If we go back down, we know how far we have to go, and we know there will be water."

Several of the grownups spoke at the same time: "We have to go back down." I felt despair at the thought of not continuing the journey even though I was not able to walk too far. I imagined how people would receive us, how shameful it would be, and how the Vietnamese soldiers would treat us.

Cousin Ou continued with his plan. "We will rest until nightfall. Then we will walk down."

The old lady spoke out: "I cannot leave my grandson." She stopped abruptly, waiting for some response.

All the grownups and Cousin Ou pleaded with her to go with us. "You cannot help him, even if he comes back to you."

The old lady whimpered as she replied without hesitation. "I have no need to live without my sweet grandson. He is my only hope. If God has no mercy and chooses to take my dear grandson this way, he will have to take me too."

She had made up her mind to stay near her grandson. Feeling sad and empathizing with her, I forgot all about my thirst. She pleaded with Cousin Ou to look for her grandson. Ou walked to a patch of shrubbery where I had last seen the boy. He circled it and called out the boy's name, but there was no reply. We begged the old lady again and again to go down with us, but she was sure that she would not leave the mountain without her baby grandson, and she encouraged us to leave without her. She reached into her sack and handed Ou a smaller sack that was still larger than her two hands.

She said, "Take it with you." She wanted to make sure that at least her precious jewelry was not wasted in the jungle. She had foreseen her grim future.

Ou was not sure what to do, and he didn't respond right away. Finally he said, "Keep them with you. They are for someone who can help you and your grandson. Have faith and don't give up hope. Someone might be able to help you."

That was the last conversation I heard before I fell unconscious again from the heat, but I was brought back to life by the coolness of the night. As I moved around, I felt my body burning against the rocky terrain. I saw

Cousin Ou sitting up on a small boulder, looking over us like a watchdog, and I wondered if he ever slept.

"Up. Up. Up. It is time to go while it still cool," Cousin Ou said, waking everybody up. Slowly, everyone got moving. Em encouraged Chenda to get up. Chenda was rolling around but not yet up, and I was waiting until everybody was up so I didn't waste my energy.

Finally, Cousin Ou stood up and encouraged us, "Let's go. Let's go." As he reached over to help his mother, the old lady sat up, but she didn't get up.

Em crawled to her and said, "Please come with us, aunty." The old lady did not reply.

Cousin Ou knelt down and gently comforted the old lady as much as he could, saying, "Keep those precious belongings with you. If I make it, I will send someone to find you." There was still no reply from the old lady.

When Cousin Ou stood up, we all followed him. Our faces down, we slowly and quietly walked away from the old lady. We left her all by herself in the middle of the jungle in the dark night.

Cousin Ou led us by following the stars in the dark sky for direction. We continued walking slowly without saying any words. All I could hear were footsteps on dried leaves. Every step was an effort, every muscle that I had was dead weight, every bone was too heavy. Even my eyelids were too heavy.

Along the way Cousin Ou kept encouraging us: "Let's try harder before the sun comes up." Every time he said so, I felt a tiny spark of energy to march further. As we marched down the hill, without a pleading word to stop and rest, someone decided to lie down on the ground, unable to continue. Cousin Ou would yell, "Let's take a break," and he would give all of us another round of water to wet our throats, then we would all collapse on the ground. Soon afterward, He would command us to start again, and Em would plead with me to get up. I wanted to beg Em to let me rest a little longer, but that would take too much energy, so I got up and stayed close to Em.

We were all getting weaker, advancing at most a hundred yards before someone crashed. I would feel relief when that happened, because it meant I would get a break. We took many breaks throughout the night. By the time the sky started to lighten, the water was completely gone. After that it took more time to get us started again after each break. Still, Ou continued his regiment of lying to us that we were almost there and encouraging us to get up and continue.

After sunrise, we wandered across a patch of wildflowers that looked like water hyacinth. I had never seen or heard of this kind of flower before, but someone in the group said, "These are agar flowers (*phak chrawhoy*). They're edible." We were like a pack of sick bunnies picking and chewing on these flowers. The moisture in the flowers helped to coat my dry throat and allowed us to continue further.

Not too far after the flower patch, we came across a cool, moist spot of earth. In hopes that we would find a spot with some muddy water left, we scattered, anxiously hunting for it.

"Stay together. Don't go too far," Em commanded softly. Chenda and I found a tiny muddy spot. A strange sound of excitement without any words came from within us. I scooped some mud onto the end of my cotton krama. Tilting my head backward, I tried to squeeze the water through the krama and into my mouth. Only a couple of drops hit my tongue, and I wanted to cry, but instead I put the mud into my mouth and sucked on it. Not much came out of it, but I felt the cold, grainy moisture. I gave up on trying to extract water from the mud, and instead I scooped it up and spread it on my neck, torso and arms.

Once again, the sun was at its peak. I could no longer see too far ahead, nor did I care to know what was there. All I needed was the awareness that Em and my sister were next to me. Even with that, I was unable to hold on. I also had diarrhea, likely from the wild flowers and the muddy drops of water. I was aware enough to squat down, but too weak to care about my favorite underwear, so I just got up and left the underwear on the ground. Not much further along, I couldn't walk any more, and I couldn't try any harder. I dropped down on the forest floor and told Em, "I can't go any further."

"Please try harder," Em quickly replied.

"Please, let me be. I can't go any more," I pleaded, crying without teardrops.

"You need to try harder so we can stay close to your cousin."

Too tired to reply to Em, I thought: I know, Em. I know, but I can't walk.

Em could read me, but she refused to accept my response. She gave me the ultimate plea: "Do it for me, my child."

I started crying, knowing that I couldn't physically do it. "Please go without me," I said.

"My dear child, don't you know I have been living just for you? I'd never leave you. Without you, life has no meaning. We will make it together, or we will die together." Em's response was determined and calm, but agonized as well.

Although I was unable to say it, I was thinking: You have to go and you have to let me be. Please don't stay, I beg you.

Then Em on my right and my sister on my left lifted

me, carried me, and bore my weight so we could catch up with the group.

We were by the foot of the mountain when Cousin Ou left us again to search for water. We stayed under the only tree in the area that offered some lush shade. Mrs. Saram's family was in a sparsely shaded area about ten yards away from us. In between consciousness and unconsciousness, I dreamt that we were all lying under the protection of a seven-headed dragon.[28] When I opened my eyes and looked at the shade tree above us, I noticed that the tree had two trunks. One was broken and burnt with charcoal marks on its tip. The second trunk was taller and alive with branches and healthy leaves hanging over to protect the burned trunk. In the two trunks, I saw the powerful seven-headed dragon that protected Angkor Wat. I feared the consequences of our intrusion on what I believed to be a sacred place, and at the same time I felt blessed that the guardian angel of the forest brought us here.

"Em, I dreamt that we are staying under the seven-headed dragon," I said with a glimmer of excitement in my weak voice.

Em looked up at the tree and said, "Pray, my dear,

---

[28] In Khmer culture, a seven-headed dragon symbolizes a powerful spiritual protector of a sacred place.

pray to the angel who came to your dream, and to the guardian of the jungle to guide Ou to water."

I was awakened by a loud roaring sound echoing through our surroundings. I looked over for Em's strength and protection. Instead, it was the first time I ever saw Em lying unconscious on the ground. Aunt Nay Hak never said a word during this time, for she was also unconscious. I saw Mrs. Saram sitting and fanning her family. Chenda was thrashing, but she sat up to the roaring sound and started to cry for help, "Help us! Help us! Please."

"Stop it!" Mrs. Saram warned Chenda.

What is Mrs. Saram afraid of? I wondered. Was it from runaway Black Uniforms? The sound may have come from some kind of machinery, but it wasn't continuous. Elephants? But I knew what elephants sound like, and this was not an elephant sound. Was it some other wild animal that I didn't know?

Many years later I had a flashback of this suffering when I heard the same sound during the feeding of the lions and tigers at the San Francisco Zoo.

I had probably become unconscious again but was awakened by Chenda, who cried in fear, "Em, what's wrong? What's wrong, Em?"

Em had regained consciousness and replied to Chenda with a strong voice, full of energy. "Make music. I want to dance!"

Chenda sat next to Em, trying to shake her out of it as she cried and pleaded, "Em, what's wrong? Em, wake up."

I sat up next to Chenda and watched Em hallucinating.

"I said make music for me. I want to dance," Em insisted, and this time she raised her hands above her chest and started to make traditional Cambodian dancing movements with them. Since I knew Em had never danced in her whole life, I was fearful of the spirit that was possessing her.[29] It wasn't just a hallucination.

Again Chenda pleaded with Em. This time Em replied immediately and with irritation but playfully: "You're not listening to me. You talk too much."

Mrs. Saram crawled over to help us out. "Yes, of course. Let's make music for our guardian." Mrs. Saram no longer referred to Em as she normally did. She led us to make music for the guardian, singing "Ting-Ting-Tingtac-Ting-Ting ..."—the same sound that Cambodians make for their babies to get them excited and dancing. Like a baby, Em was dancing and smiling. Mrs. Saram pleaded with the guardian: "Please help us."

---

[29] Cambodians believe a spirit sometimes possess a person in order to communicate with us. The possession most often happens in rural areas, especially in the jungle or places that are undisturbed by technologies. Perhaps in rural areas people are more open-minded to such possibilities.

The guardian interrupted her. "I *am* helping. That is why you are here."

Chenda asked Em, "Who are you?"

"I am the guardian of this forest (*Lok Ta Prey Phnom*)!"

Chenda asked the guardian: "Is my cousin finding water?"

"Yes. Yes. He is on his way back. Don't worry."

When there was no more music for the guardian, Em became carefree and started humming her own music, dancing to it as though she wasn't suffering from thirst.

Chenda interrupted the dancing. "Dear guardian, please help us with some water."

"Coming soon. I told you he is coming soon." The guardian didn't have much patience.

"Why is it taking so long?" I challenged him.

"Do you think he is coming in an airplane?" the guardian snapped back. I chuckled and felt my abdomen tighten up for a moment but was unable to laugh out loud.

Chenda mourned, "Grant me water, please."

"You are complicated to deal with—saying the same thing over and over. All you want to know is water. I told you it is coming!" the guardian said through Em, sounding annoyed.

"Do you know if my two brothers are okay?" Chenda was referring to Ee and Hong.

Em's arms waved above her chest with excitement and she said, "They are so far away, and they are so happy. Don't worry about them," and she laughed cheerfully.

"What about my father and my little brother?" Chenda added.

The guardian started to cry. Em's hands collapsed and slapped her chest as the guardian moaned. "Please don't ask me anymore. It's a sad story of suffering." He paused to cry. "It makes me sad to think about them. Neither the father nor the son ever did anything bad. They were loving people." For a short moment, I forgot all about my suffering, feeling very sad. I'd lost hope that I would see my father and younger brother again.

I must have become unconscious again, but when I woke up, I wandered around desperately by myself until I saw a young lady in her mid-twenties who smiled and looked at me as though I was the cutest little thing she had ever seen. Exhausted and annoyed by her expression, I looked away and kept on with my search for water.

"What are you looking for?" she asked.

I was disgusted by her question, sensing that she had to know I needed water.

Still smiling and filled with adoration and energy, she gave me two options: "Do you want water or these?" She bent down to show me a basketful of precious jewelry.

Frustrated, I unhesitatingly summoned up one word: "Water!"

The beautiful young lady straightened herself, still smiling, and pointed with her finger, saying, "Follow the trail." She laughed with happiness while I wobbled off in search of the trail. It was a short trail with a thick wall of tall green grass at the end. I stuck my hands into the grass wall and pushed it apart, revealing a tiny, perfect square pond no longer than my arms outstretched. It was full of cold, clear water and surrounded by the thick, tall, green grass. I drank and drank—until I woke up to the heat and the dryness. I sensed that if I had told the beautiful young lady that I wanted the jewelry, I never would have woken up. Cambodians believe that everyone gets a second chance in life depending on how greedy one is.

I think I'm going to die. I think I'm going to die ... That refrain kept repeating in my head. The air was too hot and still, and there was no sound of any life. My mouth and throat were dried up and getting drier with every breath. I heard footsteps walking toward us thru the vegetation and thought, *I hope it's Cousin Ou. Please let it be him.* The sound got closer and closer.

Finally my tall, strong, energetic cousin emerged from the thickness, loaded with water in a kettle and an old gasoline canister on his carrying stick. I was not able to speak, but in my mind and my heart I was saying thanks, not only to my Cousin Ou, but to the guardian as well. I was grateful to be safe and protected by the guardian, but at the same time I was fearful of the guardian's power.

After everyone received a sip of water, Cousin Ou stood up to assess the surrounding area and try figure out which way to lead the group.

With some hesitation, I shared the vision that had come to me: "An angel told me in my dream there is a trail near the foot of the mountain."

Ou turned around and stared at me, then walked toward the nearby hill about ten feet from where I sat.

"It's true!" he exclaimed, looking back at me. We stared at each other feeling blessed and fearful.

"And there will be water at the end of the trail."

"Little Girl's dreams come true. The angel will guide us to safety," Ou said to the group.

The trail was close to us, disguised by brown grass so it was recognizable only when you stood on top of it and saw the profile of the shorter brown grass that formed a path. We followed Cousin Ou single file along the trail with the mountain behind us. At the end of the trail was a large body of water. I said thanks to my angel and the guardian. We had to walk around the body of water to cross to the other side. Along the way we found a swollen, dead body floating in the water, its bare butt stuck up into the sun. My mind told my stomach to throw up, but the tainted water was already being absorbed by my body.

On the other side of this angel pond, I saw green trees that outlined a village and wondered: *Can we hide at the edge of the village, restock on water, and try again?* But I didn't say anything.

When we reached the village, we walked to a wooden house and pleaded for mercy. The owner of the place made us rinse ourselves before she let us go up into her house. Squatting on two slats of wood raised above the ground by two logs, Chenda and I took turns scooping cold water from a large urn to rinse ourselves. The cool water and the afternoon wind made me shiver; my teeth rattled in my stiff jaw. Red, bloody water flowed down my body when I rinsed myself. That was my very first period. After I changed, I was going to clean the dirty pants, but Aunt Nay Hak pleaded with Cousin Ou to help us girls, not knowing that my pants were bloody.

"Ou, could you help your cousins so they can rest?" she asked. Normally, I would not let *anybody* wash my bloody pants, let alone a man, but during that time I was so exhausted and cold. I couldn't wait to crawl into the house and lie down. Cousin Ou, who was only about three or four years older than me, washed my bloody pants.

The next day we were shipped via truck to be questioned by the Vietnamese soldiers in Serei Saophoan. As they unloaded us, Em reminded us to cover our dolly faces. Squatting on the dirty floor, hugging my legs, and facing the dirt floor, I listened to the grown-ups convincing the Vietnamese Leader that we were not the Black Uniforms.

"Why do you want to leave your country?" The Vietnamese leader asked in a calm and respectable tone through a translator.

"Starvation, sir. After four years of starvation we just want to go where there is food, sir." Em replied.

"My brother's family is here in town. If you suspect that we are Khmer Rouge, he will be able to speak for us," my aunt added.

Hoping that he would be paid in the form of gold, the Vietnamese leader put us into their jail. We were separated. My aunt and the three of us girls were placed in a thatched jail pen that was built with bamboo and dried grass panels. It had no openings except the door that shut behind us after a Vietnamese soldier shuffled us in. It was not the worst place I had been, but knowing I was in jail, the feeling was devastating. In the same pen was a woman seated in the corner and by herself. *A lone Black Uniform*, I thought. While we were still standing and studying things around us, Em dropped her sack on the dirt floor and squatted next to it, letting go a strange chuckle that expressed relief, disbelief, and carefreeness.

"Huh," she said. I noticed a little smile in the corner of Em's lips.

"I think your mother is going crazy," my aunt commented, observing Em's behavior in disbelief.

I was sad and scared—scared that my aunt was right. I had heard stories of people going crazy in confinement. I waited for Em to dismiss my aunt's comment, but she didn't. There was nothing I could do but hope that Em would be okay. I had no clue what would happen to us, but I always trusted that Em was able to make things better. I hoped my aunt was wrong.

I heard a woman speaking loudly and anxiously just outside the cell. She sounded familiar, but I couldn't make sense of who she was or what she was saying. It was all in Vietnamese.

Meanwhile, Aunt Nay Hak and Em were so excited that they both exclaimed at the same time, "It's your aunt!"

It was Aunt Neang, Uncle Song's wife. She must have

pleaded and bargained with the Vietnamese leader, but most of what I heard was her talking, yelling, and crying, and very few words from the Vietnamese leader. Before then I'd never known that Aunt Neang spoke Vietnamese. The guard let us out, and Aunt Neang hugged us and cried louder when she realized that her children were not with us.

We went back to the same veranda that we left three days ago. I learned that the place where we got lost was called Colorful Hawk Mountain (*Phnom Klairg Poir*). The nearby villagers believed in the mystical power of the mountain, hence its name.

A couple of days later, my three cousins also found their way back to town, and again Aunt Neang paid the Vietnamese leader to get her babies back. Cousin Kiny thanked me for her survival. "I was trying to find my way and was ready to give up, but I found your underwear in the woods and I knew then that you had left me a trail marker." I thought of the angel and the guardian. Nothing had been left to chance.

Cousin Ou saved ten people's lives with water, and my dirty underwear saved the lives of five—my three cousins and two more people that had been with Cousin Kiny at the time. Out of about thirty people that had attempted to escape, sixteen of us returned to Serei Saophoan. The rest most likely died on the mountain.

It didn't take long for the news of our botched escape attempt to reach Big Mountain. Cousin Linda came over to visit, and I couldn't wait to show her the proof of my story. My whole body was marked with scrapes and cuts from the failed journey. Yellow pus on my skin was forming into small beads, and red flesh around each one was warm to the touch. When Linda ran her fingers over them, she let go a sound of sympathy, and all my pain and soreness went away.

My infected body was not quite healed when I heard adults talking about escaping again. That night, Em quietly prayed to God, our ancestors, and to the guardian of Colorful Hawk Mountain to guide her.

"Dear God, ancestors, and guardian of Colorful Hawk Mountain, who has protected my girls this far, I plead with you one more time to show me the way in my dream. What is the best thing to do?" she prayed.

Right then, I knew Em was not fully committed to the escape plan. The next morning, she was excited as she explained her dream to Aunt Nay Hak. "I saw an old man who aggravated me. He couldn't even walk straight, but for some reason he kept pushing me with the edge of a dulled axe blade. The man said: '*Go! Go, I say. Hurry up!*'"

Encouraged by her dream, Em decided to try to escape again. Just as before, Aunt Nay Hak paid our way with gold. This time, however, Uncle Song and his whole family were with us as well. There were nineteen of us in all. Just as we did on our first attempt, we left Serei Saophoan at night, but this time there were so many people. I couldn't see well in the night, but I perceived the crowd by the sound of the footsteps, the whispering echoed through the woods, and the stirring of the surrounding air. There was no single-file line to follow. I sensed people all around us, thus I had little confidence that we were following the guides. I was frustrated and feared we wouldn't make it. The sloppiness of things happening around me was a hundred times worse than a crying baby. Despite this, I was not as scared as in our first attempt.

We took hardly anything with us but water. Two at a time, the young men in our small group (Cousin Lim, Bong Tav, Cousin Chhun, Cousin Ou) took turns carrying water in a large steel gasoline container suspended from a bamboo bar resting on their shoulders.

As the morning sun started to shine, I began to feel safer, especially when I noticed that there were *many* people, far more than I had imagined during the night. The number of people was in the hundreds, maybe even closer to a thousand. Each one of us had to pay the guides in twenty-four-karat gold.

Kids were crying, and mothers were calming them

down in normal voices. There was nothing discrete about the whole thing. It felt as if we were in a marketplace. Most of the people had no water with them. I feared for them, but at the same time thought that we needed to move faster so we would not be attacked for our water.

As the sun began getting hotter, more people pleaded with us for water. Babies were crying, and their mothers pleaded with us for mercy toward their little ones, "Please. Just for the baby, please." The more they pleaded, the faster we walked. We closed our eyes and ears and walked away, for we didn't know how far we still had to go, or how long the water would last.

We stayed as close as we could to the guides. They looked just like us, except that they had guns and had no family members with them. One of the guides stopped abruptly in his tracks and held up the rest of the people following him. "I can't go any further," he told us quietly.

I've heard this before, I thought. The man pointed, and I saw two other men with guns camouflaged in the trees and looking back at us.

Our guides walked backward and at the same time encouraged us to move forward, saying, "Go, go. Those are Thai people. We cannot go any further."

What if they shoot at us? I asked quietly in my own

mind. I saw the sad look on the guides' faces that said they didn't want us to leave them, and I worried about what was going to happen to us. The Thai men yelled back with hurrying, demanding, vicious voices that sounded more like the Black Uniforms. A few Cambodian families started to move forward toward the Thai men and lowered themselves as close to the ground as possible, their feet still moving, putting their hands up while holding on to their belongings. I walked away from our guides toward the Thai men while hoping the guides would stay around to make sure we weren't executed by the Thai people who had no fear of retaliation by us.

One of the Thai men spoke Khmer Surin,[30] and he translated his friend's vicious demand for a fee to take us past the rest of the jungle and into a Thai village. The men made us sit in a circle as they collected their fee. I was right behind Em as we began forming the next circle for the Thai thieves. Em quickly yanked me toward the Surin man and away from the mean thief. Unlike his friend, the Surin man held a bucket in front of us to collect whatever we could give him as if it was a donation. His friend, however, demanded the fee by

---

[30] A group of Khmer natives who lived in Thailand for generations. Most of them live in Surin province of Thailand. They speak Khmer with a strong accent. They call themselves Khmer Surin.

yelling and pointing his gun at the Cambodian refugees. When the bucket came in front of us, Em truly didn't have much left, so she reached into her wrap and grabbed a sterling belt for her sarong and handed it to the Surin man with two hands and said, "This is all I have left. I lost everything."

I watched Em give away her precious belt that was so special to her. It was the belt she bought for herself to remember a special day, the day that she delivered her first baby, my brother Ee. All of us had been told the same story many times and understood its sentimental value to Em. Em reluctantly let go of the only memento of her firstborn into the bucket, knowing it was not worth much to anybody else. The Surin man continued to park his bucket in front of Em, hoping she would give him more, but after a long second, the man decided to let us go.

Chapter 20

THE REFUGEE CAMPS

May 1979 to June 17, 1979

After paying the Thai thieves, we walked about a mile to what we believed was Thailand. There were no signs to indicate that it was except the thieves themselves. We arrived in an open space where we were stopped by a Thai patrol in uniform. At that moment, I knew for certain that we had reached the Thai border. But the Thai patrol prevented us from venturing any further into Thailand. Later in the day, trucks with Red Cross markings delivered water, rice, salty dried fish, and basic supplies. I was overwhelmed and touched, not only for the food, but for the caring that reached out to help us and give us hope that things would get better. I felt the urge to express my feelings regarding what we had been through, but the language got in the way. The thought of being reunited with my father and brothers was becoming real, despite the bad news of Pa and Kheang that I heard at Big Mountain. The hope for real freedom occupied my thoughts. *Em was right: someday I might be able to wear a miniskirt again. And I'll grow my hair as long as I want.*

That night, all the women and girls in our group slept under the open sky, surrounded by our men to protect us from Thai patrollers. The place was called Nong Chan. We were among the first group of refugees to stay in Nong Chan. The next day we received more food and donations from other organizations. One of these organizations was the Chinese Thai Community Association, and leading this group was my father's business partner, the same man who Em had entrusted with her precious jewelry before the Black Uniforms pushed us to the countryside. The man confirmed what the guardian told us: my brothers Ee and Hong had made it to safety and they were already in America. And just like the guardian told us, there was no news about my father and my baby brother Kheang.

The mixed news struck my heart with a feeling of heaviness. I should have been happy for the good news of Ee and Hong, but the pain and misery from news about Pa and Kheang seemed to overshadow that happiness.

No matter how many times I heard that my father and Kheang may not have made it, my instinctive response was heartbreak followed by a silent demand for the messenger to *prove* it to me. "There is still hope," I said to myself. "I may not see them again, but it doesn't mean that they are no longer living."

The Thai Chinese man told us that he had given all our jewelry to Ee and Hong. We also learned from other people who had entrusted their life savings with the man that he did not give them back what was theirs. Em realized what had happened and gave up. "What goes around comes around." If Aunt Nay Hak had hoped we would pay her back when we made it to Thailand, she lost all hope right then and there.

Some of Pa's old friends helped us by providing clothes and additional food besides just dried fish and rice. Because we were living in a man's world, they provided their assistance via Uncle Song instead of directly to Em. One day Uncle Song came into the tent with donations, right away my cousins fought for what they wanted while I watched on the sideline. I felt that I was given the left over. When we received fresh fruit, one of my cousins placed it on her sarong, and I sat among everybody to receive my ration. Instead of being happy, I felt hurt and a sense of self-pity, wishing my father was with us. I wished that Uncle Song had given our share to Em so I didn't have to feel what I felt and Em wouldn't have to witness it. Em certainly must have seen that I was feeling self-pity.

Not long after we arrived in Nong Chan, a makeshift fence was built with barbwire to segregate us from the Thai villagers. Some refugees were exchanging gold and fine jewelry for Thai currency. The refugees then used Thai currency to buy fresh fruit and produce from nearby Thai villagers. Thai currency was also used for exchange among the refugees within the camp.

To help Aunt Nay Hak pay our way, Em would buy fresh pineapples every day from the Thai villagers. We cleaned and sliced each one of them into eight wedges. The thought of standing in public and begging for money in exchange for pineapples filled me with shame, but if I didn't do it, then Em would have to, since it was not likely that Chenda would. I didn't like it, nor was I proud of the way I felt, but regardless, it was a feeling that I could not deny. We were the poorest of the poor, but what we had to do was part of what we wanted: the freedom to make our own living and control our own destiny. I compared myself to my cousin, who was the same age as I was but never had to do anything. Her situation allowed her to still be a kid, pampered by her parents, laughing and giggling under the protection of a makeshift hut. Even though I wasn't proud of how I felt I couldn't overcome the feeling of jealousy. I wondered whether I would have had to do this if my father had been with me. Most likely not. I didn't understand why, but I felt more ashamed when I was with my cousins than I did when I was with strangers. Em seemed to understand the way I felt, and she decided to go with me to sell the pineapple wedges at the main pathway that ran through the camp.

While we were walking to the main pathway, she encouraged me: "Don't be shy or ashamed, my dear child. Think of yourself as being able to help us to survive. When people look at you, they will see what a good daughter you are. I am so proud to be your mother. You are my inspiration." There was no sound of self-pity or sadness in her voice. Her energy inspired me, and her encouragement made me feel that I could move the world. I had nothing to fear, for in her eyes I was a special daughter.

Standing in the hot sun on the main pathway with other sellers, I no longer felt ashamed nor shy. Instead, I felt sorry for Em when I compared what she was doing to what my aunts were doing. However, I didn't have time to think deeply about it since we were busy selling. People who had the means to spend seemed to want to buy to help us out. There was no bargaining. We had only a small plate to put the pineapple on, so Em went back to the makeshift hut to clean some more pineapples for refills. My goal was to empty the plate and go to Em for refills instead of forcing Em to come to the main pathway, which I proudly did a couple of times. We were making four hundred percent profit on each pineapple. I sold so many pineapples every day that I couldn't wait for the next day to sell more. I had great fun until the skin of my palms was eaten away by the natural acidity from the pineapple.

Water was hard to come by, and there were no gloves or plastic to protect my hands. My whole body shook each time I had to clean pineapples, but I bit my lip and did it anyway, telling myself I would never eat pineapple again.

Every day more refugees arrived at the camp. It quickly became extremely filthy. Miserable living conditions, offensive foul matter, and chaos rapidly filled the air. But still people were happy. Old friends greeted each other who recognized each other by their voices, not by their deteriorating physical appearances.

Em met many of her old friends. One of them was our next-door neighbor from Battambang. It was miraculous that every one of their families had survived the atrocities of the Black Uniforms. Em was also reunited with E Lang, her best friend, whom she had known long before they both got married. E Lang had five children, and all of them were with her, as well as her husband and her sister. The ladies cried when Em told them about Pa and Kheang.

About two weeks after we got to Nong Chan, we were interviewed by some kind of official, and during this interview, we told them that Ee and Hong were in America. Early the next morning, they called out our names along with a small group of other people. Bus drivers were yelling and hurrying us to get on board. We were being separated from the people that we knew, unsure of what was going to happen next. Em frantically looked for E Lang and our next-door neighbor to say goodbye. As they hugged and cried, they said prayers for each other. In the bus, we didn't know anyone. It was just Em, Chenda, and me again.

A few on the bus were excited until someone reminded them that we didn't know where the driver was taking us. Along the way, Em asked us to look out and try to take mental pictures of the places that we passed, just in case we needed to know. However, as we traveled through bigger towns along the way, the fear subsided.

Finally, we were in the middle of city lights. I remember thinking how many lights were needed to brighten the night sky! How could this be possible? What a waste. Why were so many cars driving around at night? Don't people go to bed?

The bus stopped. We had to cross the widest road I had ever seen. Cars were charging and roaring by us. They were moving so fast I couldn't tell what they looked like. All I could see were the bright lights beaming in front of them. I thought it was going to take a long time to cross this road. Em grabbed my hand, and with Chenda on the other side of her, she stopped us from stepping into the road.

"Wait!" A man's voice warned us. "Be careful! Hold on to your kids. You don't want to be known as a survivor of the Khmer Rouge only to be killed by a car in Thailand." A small group of people dashed across the road, and cars honked them out of the way. I was scared. Only two weeks earlier, I was more comfortable in the jungle.

"Can someone please stop these cars before we cross?" I pleaded quietly to myself.

"Stay close to me and follow. When I say go, you go," Em instructed us.

I thought but never had the chance to ask: But what if I fall? Cars are also coming from the opposite direction on the other side of the road.

Em tugged my arm and commanded: "Go!"

My heart flew faster than my feet. I saw no cars and heard no horn; I just followed Em. After the longest seconds, we were on the other side of the road. How did we do that?

We sat outside a complex with a guard post and

a bright light overhead. Inside the guard post was a stern-looking rifleman in uniform. A couple of men at the gate called out each family's name, counting their members and admitting them into the complex. While the rest of us waited for our names to be called, we cheered the families onto the other side of the gate. Commentators in the crowd always seemed to have something to say to make fun of each family when they stood up to their name and proudly presented their family to the crowd and the officials.

"Ly Chheng," the official called out.

We stood up proudly as the crowd cheered us on. The cheers burst into laughter when a commentator voiced his disappointment. "That's it? I thought I would get to see a movie star." Em softened her walk and chuckled with a big smile on her face. We all laughed together. There was a famous Chinese movie star who had the same name as Em.

The place was called Lumpini Transit Center, and it was located in Bangkok. Once inside, we were thrilled to find out that the Saram family made it as well. They came in a different bus. We didn't even know that they had been in Nong Chan camp. We staked out a spot next to the Saram family against the wall and next to a window, which provided us some privacy and fresh air. We learned from Mrs. Saram that the lady and her crying baby that were escaping with us during our first attempt had made it across the border as well. The news brought me back to the suffering on Colorful Hawk mountain about a month earlier. I thought of the old lady that we left on the mountain. It made me sad.

One of the Saram daughters was about the same age as Chenda. I called her Bong Prom. Every day Bong Prom, Chenda, and I tried to remember old songs and wrote the lyrics down in a notebook. We sang, laughed, and corrected each other on the lyrics that had been prohibited during the Black Uniforms era.

There were many other refugees besides Cambodians in Lumpini. Some were from Vietnam and some from Laos. It was the first time since we left Poipet four years earlier that I was able to bathe in running water and use a toilet with plumbing. It was so unreal, like a dream. When I woke up the next morning, the first thing that came to my mind was: I am blessed! I am so lucky; I hope it lasts.

A few days later, more refugees began streaming in. We were reunited with Uncle Song and his family, also Aunt Nay Hak and Cousin Ou again. Not long after that, we were told that the remaining refugees in Nong Chan were bussed and forced to go back to Cambodia. Many were shot at by Thai soldiers and forced to go off the cliff of Phnom Preah Vihear of Cambodia. Those who survived the cliff had to walk across minefields that killed many more.[31]

Em waited by the gate for E Lang and her family, but they never showed up. Neither did our next-door neighbor. Em cried for her friends. She told me that the neighbor snuck a hundred-dollar bill to Em when they said goodbye in Nong Chan, right before we got on the bus. There was nothing more touching than a donation that had no strings attached and came when we really needed it most, just to help out and make life easier for a little while. Em was heartbroken, not knowing when she would see her best friend again or how she would be able to pay back the kindness that her neighbor had shown. Em made sure that we never forgot the kindness that we received from others.

When I heard that the Cambodian refugees were pushed back to Cambodia, I had a flashback to Em's dream about the old man rushing her to move fast. Had we hesitated and left a few days later, we would have been forced to walk back to Cambodia, off the cliff, and

---

[31] The Thai government leader strategy was "to demonstrate to the international community that his government would not bear alone the burden of hundreds of thousands of Cambodian refugees." Some 42,000 Cambodian refugees were sent back. Wikipedia: "Preah Vihear Temple: Expulsion of Cambodian refugees" https://en.wikipedia.org/wiki/Preah_Vihear_Temple#Expulsion_of_Cambodian_refugees.

through the minefields. I felt blessed and thought of the different ways our angels had helped and guided us.

With so many refugees coming in, there was not enough room in the building. Many refugees were sleeping outside on the concrete with a tarp hanging over them for protection. Outside our window was an old Chinese man with his little boy. The boy was not old enough to talk yet, but he could stand up. Every morning the man would complain about the boy peeing on him. "What did I do in my past life to be stuck with you now?" The words were harsh, but his tone and actions were gentle, and his expression was loving. Every morning I watched the man clean up the bedding as the boy stood there with a bare bottom, watching his unlikely mother. Whenever the boy cried, the man would comfort him like a silverback gorilla babysitter, so lovingly awkward.

Many times the man would ask, "What do you want?" or "Tell me what to do?" and all the nearby mothers would help him care for the baby. It appeared that the boy was adopted. He was a cute little dark-skinned baby, but the Chinese man was very pale-looking. It appeared that the boy had given the man a new purpose in life, and the man had given the boy the love that all babies need. I saw that Em was taken by the love that the man gave to the boy, and I thought several times that I wouldn't mind if the man and Em got together.

News of our arrival at Lumpini traveled to one of Pa's closest business partners and his family, who had escaped the Black Uniforms and were now living in Bangkok. His wife came to visit us. She and Em cried and hugged each other through space between the bars of the fence. She had lost her husband as well. He had been dealing with the Vietnamese government after the Communists took over Vietnam, and he never returned from a business trip to Vietnam. Through her we got Ee and Hong's address in Lincoln, Nebraska. Right away, Chenda wrote a letter to them.

We stayed in Lumpini about one month waiting for news of our next destination. During this time we had nothing to do but chat, sing old love songs, and wait for the next meal. Without much to do, the days went by slowly.

When it was mealtime, we stood in line to be served by Laotian refugees who got there before us. A young Laotian girl about my age was always standing on the other side of counter to serve us food. She acted as though the food belonged to her and would slam the food on my plate with her unpleasant expression. She went the extra mile to avoid scooping meat for my portion, and made sure the portion was as small as possible. With her own group of Laotian refugees, she would be smiling and chatting, especially if she happened to be talking to a boy. My cousins and I often talked about how unfair and disgusting she was. One time while I was in line for food, the girl scooped a little bit of soup onto my bowl of rice. Without speaking her language, I could not ask for more soup, so I stood pushing the bowl closer to her to let her know that I wanted some more. She yelled at me, and with her hand gesture, she ordered me to move on. I was furious, and the next thing I knew I dumped all of the food on my plate into a pot full of soup. My actions caught her off guard, and the soup splattered all over her. As the girl screamed, I walked away without food, but I felt great. I never had to deal with her unsteady and unsure hand again. All of my Cambodians friends continued to tease me about the incident. "Don't mess with Little Girl. She won't put up with crap. I feel sorry for her future husband."

We also had to deal with the Vietnamese women and their different bathing habits. The bathing area was shared, and because there were no showerheads, we had to scoop the water from a big tub that was about waist high. There was no door nor were there partitions for privacy, so anybody could walk by the bathing area and see us. All we Cambodian girls and women would bathe with sarongs wrapped up to our chests, and we would lower ourselves behind the tub for added privacy, but the Vietnamese mothers would bathe naked.

It was the first time I had ever seen a naked woman, and it made me feel uncomfortable and frustrated. I tried hard not to bathe near the Vietnamese women.

There was a stocky American lady whose strong demeanor was more like a man than a lady. Her name was Judy, and everybody made room for her whenever she walked into the camp. One day she rushed through the crowd to get to the office. As soon as she got there, a translator spoke into the microphone and called out our names.

There was a chair behind a small desk in the center of a small room. When Em, Chenda, and I walked in, the translator stood by the desk while Judy sat on the chair. Judy was smiling ear-to-ear while she was talking to the translator. When she could no longer contain herself, she stood up and walked around the desk to take a closer look at us while we squatted on the floor listening to the translator.

"Judy talked to your son," the translator told us.

Em placed her shaky hands together and raised them above her head as she said thanks to God and Judy in a shaky voice of excitement and relief. "Thank you, God. I am so grateful for the chance to see my sons again," Em said, and tears softly flowed down her cheek.

I thought, So it is true that my brothers are safe and living in America.

"Ms. Judy is going to try her best to get you and your

sons reunited as soon as possible," the translator added as Judy took in the satisfaction of her efforts.

While they were talking about the logistics of what needed to be done—how and when—I couldn't help but study Judy more closely. I had never been so close to a Caucasian person before, let alone an American lady. She had short hair, almost like a man's, and carried a briefcase instead of a purse. She leaned on the desk, and when she sat on it, she lifted one leg and rested it on the desk as she grabbed onto her knee with two hands. I was about to die—this was a mannerism that a Cambodian lady would never do. When we left the office, I kept remembering Judy's excitement for finding Ee and Hong and her commitment to ensuring that we would be reunited. With Judy's passion to save us, I felt more and more confident that we would never have to go back to the Black Uniforms.

While we were still in Lumpini, we received a letter from Hong in reply to Chenda's letter. Em read it over and over. One of the many things that he told us was to lower our ages so that Chenda could attend high school when we arrived in America. Along with the letter was some money and instructions to buy some clothes because in the US clothing costs too much. I was proud and felt special that I had brothers who already lived in America and that they were sending us money.

But not Em. She was sad every time she read the letter. She would say, "My boys are struggling."

I wondered why she said that because in the letter there was nothing to indicate that they were struggling. I reread the letter, and again I didn't see what Em saw. Aunt Nay Hak lightheartedly said to Chenda and me in front of Em, "Your mother always has something to worry about."

Em explained her logic. "They gave us an odd amount of money. Not $100, $200, nor $300, but $250. That means that they had to scrape to get as much as they could." She added, "Yes they are safe, but how can they be happy without having their mother next to them? I can't imagine what they had to go through to be in a new country without a mother."

While we were at Lumpini, I felt inadequate when I saw my cousins wearing jewelry. My craving to be like my cousins was so great that it must have touched Em. She bought me a thin, short gold necklace. I was happy and felt special and beautiful every time I saw myself with that pretty necklace on. But the feeling was short-lived. Two days later, the pretty necklace must have broken and fallen off my neck while I was bathing, and I didn't realize it until afterward.

"Such bad luck!" Em exclaimed when she learned about the loss. My first thought was about how much bad luck I brought to the family. All my life I had been labeled with bad luck in so many things that happened. I felt guilty and wished that I had been more careful, but I started to feel better when Em said, "Now we can move forward. All the bad things we would have had to endure are done."

A formal documentation of our identities had started, and to simplify the process, we were given numbers that uniquely identified each family, one that started with the letter *T*; thus we called it the *T-number*. In this formal documentation, Chenda's age was decreased from eighteen to seventeen and I decreased mine from seventeen to sixteen. Everybody was doing it, and Em increased her age by two years because her friends had told her to do so in order to qualify for retirement sooner. The concept of retirement was new to us, and we didn't understand how it worked, but Em did it anyway per her friends' recommendation. I remember thinking, *How can a person retire without working?*

Every family had to choose the country for their final destination. Many Cambodian refugees were picking France because most Cambodians knew more about France than America. Uncle Song picked America instead and tried to convince his sister, Aunt Nay Hak, to do the same. His logic was: "I would rather be a slave for a rich guy than a slave to a poor guy." Aunt Nay Hak picked France because she wanted to be near her sister and three brothers, who were already living there. For us, it was not a question. Of course, we wanted to be with Ee and Hong again.

A few days before our trip to America, we were allowed to go shopping outside the camp. We were picked up and dropped off at a shopping area. We spent all day shopping for clothes and luggage from many small shops along the streets. Em spoke enough Thai to carry a conversation and to bargain for better prices. Many of the shop owners told us how lucky we were to be getting a chance to live in America.

When we left a shop, I showed Em a cute small red coin purse with a zipper that I had just shoplifted. When Em realized what I had done, she was shocked, very disappointed, and scared for me. "You are killing me," she said as her shock turned to anger. "Do you realize that you could be put into a Thai jail?"

I had no response for Em, and I felt scared and ashamed. Em added, "We survived the Khmer Rouge, crossed the border, and came all the way here, to come so close to being put in jail for a little coin purse."

On the way back to the camp, I couldn't forget about the possibility of coming close to being put in a Thai jail. Em added one last exhortation to set her child straight: "You must promise me that you will stop stealing from now on. You don't need to steal for food any more. You need to stop this bad habit."

Em, Chenda, and I were among the first few refugees to leave Lumpini. The day before our flight, while Em was packing, she picked up her patched-up pants that she wore every day working for the Black Uniforms. I had an instant flashback of all the things that we had experienced together with Pa and Kheang, and of the time when she was walking on the levee by the Banana Village sick-house the day after Pa and Kheang left, which was almost exactly a year ago. Uncle Song saw Em studying the pants and asked, "Why are you packing those pants?"

"For a souvenir, so we won't ever forget what we have been through," Em replied.

"Don't bring those bad luck items with you," Uncle Song added.

Em agreed with that viewpoint, so she left the old rags behind. However, she kept her old bra from Battambang that had the secret pouch for storing her jewelry, and the blanket that Pa, Em, Kheang, and I had shared many nights while we slept over the low-burning coal like smoked fish. I packed my pants that Em bought for me when we visited Thailand days before the Black Uniforms took over and the bras that my Aunt Sareth made for us. The rest were clothes that we had bought just a couple of days ago. The only jewelry I packed was Aunt Sareth's ring that she gave me when we said goodbye in the Big Mountain and Em's emerald pendant that had no value in the black market during the Black Uniform era.

After one month of staying in Lumpini, we said goodbye to Uncle Song and his family, my Aunt Nay Hak, and Cousin Ou. As we stepped onto the bus to the Bangkok airport, I thought of Aunt Nay Hak and Cousin Ou. Without them we would still be in Cambodia. Aunt Nay Hak paid our way to escape twice, and Cousin Ou saved us from dying on the Colorful Hawk Mountain.

Chapter 21

"COKE, PLEASE"

June 18–20, 1979

The bus unloaded us in front of a large building with big automatic doors. I kept thinking about how amazing it was that we were on our way to America and that we would see Ee and Hong again. I remember every step of this journey as if it were yesterday.

It felt wonderful to be in a place that was so clean and as big as the Bangkok airport. You could definitely feel the excitement and happiness among the refugees without understanding the different languages that were being spoken. Kids were having fun jumping in front of the automatic doors and laughing when they opened.

The airplane was full of happy Cambodian, Vietnamese, and Laotian refugees. As the plane took off, everybody cheered and shouted in their respective languages. While we were flying across the Pacific

Ocean, I daydreamed about what my new life would be like. Without any schooling for the last four years and not knowing any English, I was sure I would have to be somebody's maid. I imagined the three of us working for a family, just like the Chinese maid and her two daughters that worked for my old neighbor before the Black Uniforms era. The thought of working for someone as a maid didn't bother me. What bothered me was thinking that Em would also have to be someone's maid. So I began to formulate a roadmap for success: First I would save my money from working as a maid. Then, when I could speak better English, I would do whatever was necessary to be a hairdresser and would save enough money to open my own beauty shop so Em would never have to work again. I was happy with this idea because it sounded doable.

I also prepared myself for a hard time living in a place that was so cold that ice formed and fell from the sky. There was no Cambodian word for snow, so any form of frozen water was called ice. When Judy told us that the place we were going was cold enough in the winter that snow fell, my brain automatically envisioned blocks of ice falling from the sky, and people having to be protected in ice shelters that would be similar to bomb shelters. Before the Black Uniforms, I had heard a story that in France some people had died from falling ice.

Chenda was our translator during this trip because she had taken a couple of years of English class prior to the Black Uniforms era. Even though she had not had the opportunity to use her English skill, it was better than no communication at all. The flight was so long that the stewardess came around and offered us food, and there were options for drinks. I wanted Coca-Cola, of course, which I had not had in a long time. As the stewardess handed us the drink she said, "Coke", and Chenda repeated after her: "Coke." The stewardess was pleased that had she taught us a new word.

It was dark when we arrived at a military base on Guam Island. It was the first time I saw American servicemen in full uniform, and they scared me. We were served instant noodles before being loaded up for our next destination.

We were in the airplane for many more hours, and the sun seemed to set quicker than I expected. This was confusing to many of us. A man who looked more Chinese than Cambodian marched up and down the aisle translating for people. He was trying to explain to us why the day seemed short, which made it even more confusing for me.

During this long flight, Em was thirsty for water, and she told Chenda to ask for water. Chenda hesitated to bother the stewardess, so she convinced Em to wait until mealtime. When the stewardess came by to serve our meal, for some reason Chenda asked for Coke again. So I drank Coke again, even though my teeth felt sore from the sweetness.

We arrived at an airport in Hawaii in the afternoon and were quarantined into an area. The Chinese man told us with laughter that Hawaii was a special vacation place with heavy tourist traffic and that we were separated from the crowd so we wouldn't scare them. We all had a good laugh.

While waiting for our next flight, we really needed to use a bathroom, but when Chenda and I got there, the door was locked. I could hear girls talking and water splashing on the bathroom floor, so I knocked and knocked, but there was no response. More and more people started to show up and waited to use the bathroom. Finally, two Laotian girls emerged with wet hair wrapped in towels. The girls were yelled at in all different languages, and they yelled back feistily.

When night came, we were escorted to the terminal area and told to wait for our next flight. The whole place was empty as though it had been reserved just for us. We were all amazed at how beautiful the wall-to-wall carpet was, and we hesitated to walk on it with our shoes. Our feelings were expressed by the little children, who didn't know how to contain their emotions.

They kicked off their shoes and chased each other in bare feet, screaming with joy. I remember wondering how they clean such a beautiful rug.

When we got to our terminal, we all sat and lay on the carpet that felt so good to our bodies and was much better than the chained-up chairs. It was one of the best beds I'd had in years.

Em was relieved when we were given orange juice, but as soon as she tasted the juice, she almost gagged. The juice's taste and smell were much different than what we expected. It tasted more like medicine: sour and bitter, and didn't smell fresh. But still it was much better than Coke.

On the flight from Hawaii to San Francisco, Chenda requested of the stewardess, "Coke, please," and again Em complained as she sucked on the ice cubes.

After the plane landed, we were received by two Laotian ladies who guided us to board a bus. The bus took us across a bridge to a motel. In the bus, the Chinese man was so excited that he talked nonstop. He explained the significant landmark of a golden bridge. Upon hearing his explanation, I imagined a bridge made of gold, and I thought how rich America is!

Later the man spoke fast and loud, gasping for air as though his spoken words impeded his ability to communicate faster. He rushed people to view through a window a glimpse of what was supposed to be the golden bridge. I never got out of my seat to see it, for I was supposed to be a lady now per Em's description.

After the golden bridge excitement, the man began to speak in a calm and subdued tone of voice. "Well, this is the last time most of you will hear from me. Tomorrow I will be reporting to work. My master is a salt farmer." He chuckled and added, "I am going from farming rice for the Khmer Rouge to farming salt for an American." I listened skeptically as he spoke, for I trusted no master nor government, understanding how unpredictable they can be. I also felt deep inside me that whatever happened would not be as bad as what I just came out of.

He finished his volunteer speech by saying, "I wish you all the luck with your new masters."

I found myself thanking him quietly and wishing him the same. It was not the hard work that worried me, nor was it the food. Instead, it was the uncertainty of the kind of treatment that I would receive. How much freedom would I really have? How much respect would I ever get? How well would I fit in with people in this country? Would I be welcome? Would I be a burden to this new country?

We were dropped off at a motel to spend the night until our next flight to our final destination. The Laotian ladies told us to meet at the office the next morning. The lodge was a beautiful place on a hilly landscape with green grass and a flower garden near the office. We were given a room to ourselves with a real bed and mattress. I found myself sniffing the bedding and confirming its cleanliness. And there was a television! We were able to turn on the television and watch an old black-and-white cowboy show. Without understanding what they were saying in the show, it got confusing very quickly, especially when all I could see was the same lady and the same guy in the show.

Someone knocked at the door and brought food for us in a bag with more Coke. I remember Em biting into the sandwich with hesitation as though it was a medicine patty. Her tongue was not sure what to do with the new flavor and texture of sandwich. She needed rice. Just rice and dirty rock salt would have been much better than the pretty sandwich. Again we dumped the Coke and sucked on the ice cubes.

It was nighttime, but we couldn't sleep, and we didn't know why. We kept opening up the curtain to check for people gathering at the office, fearing that we would be left behind. I wished we were with everybody and not in our own private room. Maybe the Laotian ladies told us a specific time, but we had never had to worry about time for the last few years, so the significance of time didn't cross our minds. We decided to be at the office as soon as the sun came up. To us back then, morning didn't start until sunrise. After briefly dozing off, we woke up to a bright sky. We looked out the window, but no one was by the office. We hurried to get out of the room and walked to the office. No one that we recognized was there. Not a single Asian person was around. Our biggest fear had been realized: We had been left behind. Not understanding how the system worked, I thought for sure that we were lost in a vast place called America and might never get to see Ee and Hong again.

We squatted by the street next to the office, shaking uncontrollably from the cold of the morning and hoping that the Laotian ladies would come back for us. A taxi stopped by, and a big-bellied black man came out and talked to Chenda. Between Em, Chenda, and the taxi driver, they reached an understanding, and the driver took us to the San Francisco Airport.

When we got to the airport, the driver helped us unload the only luggage we had. Then he demanded his fee by putting out his white palm. That was strange. All throughout the trip we never had to pay for anything. Why did this guy want us to pay? Through Chenda's broken English, Em asked for the Laotian ladies. The driver chuckled, showing his white teeth while trying to explain the situation to us. Fortunately, Chenda was able to understand his explanation. He had nothing to do with the Laotian ladies. Frightened and not believing what had just happened, Em flashed her hundred-dollar bill and demanded that the driver take us back to the lodge. The driver quickly helped us load the luggage back into the trunk and drove us of out of the airport. On the way back to the lodge, I was frightened and felt vulnerable now that the driver knew we were lost. He could easily take advantage of us, but he did not. He unloaded our luggage at the exact same place he picked us up. We sat there with a sigh of relief, and this time we waited calmly for the Laotian ladies.

A couple of hours later, the Laotian ladies showed up, and we went back to the same airport. At the airport were many people going in different directions, and all seemed to be in a hurry, going to places or being late for something. We walked all over the airport with our belongings. Chenda had two carry-on bags, Em had a handbag and a big plastic UNICEF bag that contained all of our documents, and I struggled with both hands to carry the big, heavy luggage.

The Laotian ladies walked briskly ahead of us without looking back. When I noticed they were taking us down on an escalator, my heart beat fast in fear that I would fall or be stuck for I had never seen or been on an escalator before. Before I could say anything, Em and Chenda were already on the escalator, so I had no choice but to follow them.

As I got closer to the escalator and noticed other people were looking at me strangely. I took it as a warning that I should not do that. I felt self-conscious, but what could I do? When there was no one between me and the escalator, I became mesmerized by the constant movement of the slotted staircase and I couldn't move any further. The pressure of people backing up behind me pushed me forward without any strategy of how best to get onto this automatic staircase. The luggage was wider than the escalator, and it blocked my legs from moving further, but the moving rail pulled me through and automatically adjusted the position of the luggage, allowing me to regain my balance and prepare for how to get off the escalator.

The escalator moved faster than I could come up with a strategy to get off. Then the luggage became frozen at the bottom of the escalator in front of me. The moving escalator pushed me over the green luggage and I found myself faced planted with my butt protruding in the air. Embarrassed and frustrated for being left behind to fend for myself, I felt the heat on my face.

We said goodbye to the Laotian ladies after they delivered us to the gate of our final flight to our destination. As I sat and watched people walk by, I saw many old ladies in skirts with swollen calves and feet that bulged out of their high heels, and a few young ladies, too, but they all looked alike and walked too fast to be called ladies. The men were too big and obnoxiously clumsy. They were all in a hurry and too busy to notice that we might need help. I felt dizzy looking at them and was feeling sad that the new world was too different for me.

We were hungry, so Em gave me some money to grab food from a nearby shop. I went in and paid for something that looked like bread. When Em bit into it, she exclaimed, "Too sweet!"

I bit a piece and it tasted like soft palm sugar with some kind of nut, and I wondered why in the world anybody would buy a block of candy.

The next thing I knew, Em asked for water again. This time she demanded that Chenda go and speak slowly and ask people for some water. Chenda didn't want to stand out in public asking for water in broken English, so Em asked me to go. "I don't speak any English!" I protested.

"Don't worry, Chenda will teach you," Em said to encourage me.

I sighed, but learned and repeated the words, "I want one water." I asked Chenda why the same word was used twice in the sentence.

"What?" was Chenda's puzzled and frustrated response.

"There are two *wons* in the sentence. 'I won won water.'"

"They are two different words!" Chenda was annoyed by me.

"They sound the same to me." I was not giving up.

"Just do it!" she demanded.

I don't want to sound stupid! I was frustrated, but I wanted to get water for Em, so I repeated the stupid phrase over and over again until Chenda approved of my accent. She encouraged me by walking with me to a restaurant where we thought we could ask for water.

Before approaching the restaurant, I watched waiters and waitresses serving the tables. I selected my favorite waitress by the way she carried herself. I believed she had a heart, but I was not quite ready, so I asked my sister to evaluate my English again.

"I won won water." As soon as my sister approved, I took a deep breath, held it, and marched into the restaurant and stood by my waitress while she was serving. When she straightened up and looked into my eyes, I repeated the phrase that I had been practicing: "I won won water."

Another thought came into my mind after the phrase came out of my mouth, but I could not put it in English. *It is for my mother.*

Just as I imagined, my waitress spoke softly and calmly, but I could not understand her words. So I stood there, determined to get water for Em. With her serving tray in one hand, she gently tugged my arm with her other hand and led me outside of the restaurant and left me in a waiting line at the shop next door.

I watched people come out with trays of food and cups of drinks. I was excited when I saw that the young man behind the counter taking orders was Asian. I was very hopeful. While I was waiting, I repeated quietly in my head, "I won won water." The closer I got to order my water, the more I was afraid that the phrase would not come out right. I was not scared, but I felt my heart beating faster and faster. So when the young man spoke a set of English words so fast, I froze and said, "Coke please!"

We came back to the seat where Em was waiting. Em was very disappointed and tired. All she could think about was a refreshing gulp of plain water. I dumped the Coke into the bathroom sink and brought back the inadequate ice cubes for Em.

While we sat and waited for our flight, we noticed on the opposite wall from us that there was a stainless-steel object attached to the wall with a water spout that people were drinking from. I watched and wondered how people got the water out. Em encouraged me to get the water for her, since she was so sure that she had seen people drinking from it.

"What if they just use it to rise their mouths, Em?" I asked.

"If they can put it in their mouths, I can drink it," Em replied, confident that the water was good enough to drink.

When the crowd lightened up, I decided to give it a try. Trying to be as inconspicuous as I could, I walked over and stood next to the object with a cup full of ice cubes and tried to catch the water. No water came out. I realized that I was doing something wrong, but didn't know what that was. I couldn't find the obvious knob to turn it on. Feeling embarrassed and exposed, I walked back to our seats, where Chenda and Em were giggling at my actions. I didn't appreciate that Em and Chenda were laughing at me, but Em's plea convinced me to try again. After a few more observations, I was ready to try again. This time, not only I was standing next to the thing, but I even bent over it and waited, but still there was no water. After a few tries I gave up and walked back to Em.

"Get me the water from the bathroom sink. I don't care," Em demanded.

"How do we know the bathroom sink water is not from the same water in the toilet?" I reminded Em of why we had not done this earlier, but she didn't care.

As soon as we boarded the plane to our final destination, all I could think of was imagining what it would be like to see my brothers again. I could not believe that it was real. During the flight, I had flashbacks to all the horrible things that happened during the last four years—the four years of suffering that seemed like forty years—the four years that still lingered with me in my core, my now dark skin and village accent. I thought about my last conversation with Pa and Kheang right before they left. What would Ee and Hong like to know? What would *anybody* like to know? Would I be able to tell them without reliving the pain? Why would I want to relive the misery?

When the plane landed, my heart beat with excitement, and I wondered what my brothers must be feeling right then and what they looked like after all these years. I thought of Pa and Kheang, and wished with sadness that they were with us.

As we walked through the Jetway, I wanted to make sure I captured Em's reaction when she saw her boys again. Finally—before I was ready—I heard a cry burst out from Em, Ee, Hong, and Chenda. Em was propped up by Ee and Hong on both sides and walked to a seat. Chenda was crying and holding on to Hong. But when I looked at Ee closely, I was confused and my emotions were frozen by his head: He had a puffed-up Afro hairdo. And then I met my new masters for the very first time, Mr. and Mrs. Howe, my American angels.

Mr. and Mrs. Howe drove us to our new fancy hut in Lincoln, Nebraska, on June 20, 1979.

Afterword

Inever saw my father and my little brother again. Many times, over the years, I daydreamed of news that they survived and that we would be reunited.

In 2005, my mother told me that she had called and spoken with Stubby. It was true that Stubby's husband and Om Pad's son made it to Thailand. They had gone back to Cambodia during the Vietnamese invasion. Stubby and her husband were reunited, but he passed away a couple of years prior to her conversation with Em.

Through Stubby, we learned the details of what happened to my father and my little brother. They got lost in the jungle. After many days in the jungle, my father was suffering knee pain and fever. The group stayed with my father, but eventually they conceded to his last wish: to leave him behind and save Kheang. Soon afterward, they were spotted and shot at by the Black Uniforms. Om Pad was hit and died instantly. Everybody else dispersed and hid. After everything settled, Stubby's husband, Om Pad's son, and another man who was escaping with them regrouped, but they were unable to find Kheang.

Part of me still hoped Kheang had been found and spared by a Black Uniform since he was just a boy. The pain is too great every time I imagine what my father must have had to endure, words he must have had to use to convince Kheang to walk away, and the blessing he must have given to his baby boy before their last goodbye. I imagined the agony my father must have felt to watch his boy sob as he walked away. I imagined Kheang must have pleaded to stay with Pa, but in the end, he could not do anything but honor Pa's last wish, which was for Kheang to walk away and continue without him. I imagined Pa suffering alone. Every time I allow myself to imagine what Pa and Kheang had to go through, my heart aches with painful and agonizing tears. I hate what the Black Uniforms did to us.

I imagined Pa situating himself to ensure that when he was no longer conscious, his head would be in the eastward direction, so that his death would bring good luck to his children and to ensure that his spirit would be able to continue care for them.

I have wished many, many times that I had done something different during my last conversation with Kheang. Had I done so in those fleeting moments, perhaps my baby brother and my father would be with us today.

My mother thought my father could not bear the suffering any more after he learned I was raped. At other times, she thought it was because he could not bear to watch the Black Uniforms take his last baby, for he feared Kheang would be brainwashed and become one of them.

The date was April 13, 1976, when Ee and Hong left Seur and spent five days walking through the jungle of Roneam Daun Sam to reach Thailand. Once in Thailand, they were robbed at the border and moved to Aranyaprathet to be detained for one week before being released to the Aranyaprathet refugee camp, where they stayed for the next three months. They were sponsored by the First Lutheran Church in Lincoln, Nebraska. Mr. and Mrs. Howe were their sponsor family and eventually their American parents. They arrived in Omaha, Nebraska, on August 2, 1976.

Ee and Hong never even stopped by the girls' camp to try to get Chenda and me to escape with them. Ee told me that the only reason he and Hong were included in the escape plan was because Uncle Tre needed help carrying my little cousins. For this reason alone, Ee and Uncle Tre were not on good terms until many years later.

We learned that the Chinese friend who had kept Em's jewelry gave Ee and Hong the two gold Omega watches that he kept for Em, and nothing else. However, the watches were both stolen from their apartment in Lincoln, Nebraska. Em's emerald pendant was also stolen when I was a senior in high school. It was almost a laughing matter to have everything stripped from us even after we arrived in the US.

I have never gone back to Cambodia, but during the last few months of finishing my story, I have virtually ventured out to the towns and villages where my story took place. Many things have changed, including redistricting and name changes, but most of all, each town and village itself has transformed. My old neighborhood in Battambang is not as pretty as I remember, with dirt and trash everywhere. Places that used to be a jungle are now villages (such as Malai Mountain), remote villages that were not accessible by motorcycle now have roads that are accessible by cars, and some villages have disappeared from the map entirely. It is possible that some of the villages are still there, but being of no importance to anybody, are thus yet to be discovered.

Some places have been untouched and are now even more beautiful than what I remember (such as Water Mill pagoda).

I have countless nightmares of being recaptured

and back among the Black Uniforms. It has been over forty-two years since they took over the country. Things have changed for the better. New blossoms have filled the landscape. New goals and challenges that I face each and every day have eased me from my pains and guilt. I have not forgotten, but I have learned to forgive. I forgive those who have done evil to me and my family, and most of all I have forgiven myself for things I was guilty of.

Through this story I have been freed, not only from the Black Uniforms but from the label of unlucky child.

I attended Lincoln High School a couple of months after we arrived in Lincoln, Nebraska, and went to earn a bachelor of science degree with double majors in computer science and mathematics from University of Nebraska—Lincoln (UNL) and a master of science in applied mathematics from Santa Clara University. I worked in Silicon Valley as an engineer in the aerospace and biotech industries for thirty years. I am also the proud owner of Apsara Foods, manufacturing Cambodian food products here in the USA.

I am married to my college sweetheart, Kent Laux. We have two wonderful children, Natasha and Richard. At the writing of this book, Natasha is working on her PhD at USC Pharmacy School, and Richard is working as an actuary in Irvine, California.

My bother Ee is the owner of a successful small business, where he and his wife Cathy serve bagels in Santa Clara, California. They are the proud parents of Rita, Ryan, and Jessica Chhi, and grandparents of Malakai Chhi. They are blessed with a beautiful and kind daughter-in-law Jolyne Talosig.

My brother Hong was the first Cambodian to graduate from UNL with bachelor of science and master of science degrees in electrical engineering. He also worked in Silicon Valley as an engineer in the aerospace and biotech industries. He is married to Kandy, and they have three children: Andy, Rachel, and Alan Chhi.

My sister Chenda earned her bachelor of science degree with double majors in computer science and mathematics from UNL. She is the founder of Coral Tree Education Foundation, where she helps rebuild Cambodia through education. Through this effort she built a school that she dedicated to our brother Kheang. Chenda has three sons: Joseph, Zachary, and Eric Smead.

My mother, Chheng Ly (Em) had a wonderful life in America. Soon after arriving in Lincoln, Nebraska, she attended English classes daily, and once per week she went to a nighttime English class provided by a local church. As soon as she was able to read and write some simple English, she went to work at a local cafeteria. She went on to work as a housekeeper at Lincoln General Hospital. To earn some extra money, my mother and I cleaned homes for people, and small offices at night and on weekends. We were able to become independent from welfare programs within a year after we arrived in Lincoln.

Em was very happy and proud to be able to donate her extra money to UNICEF. "We need to help those who helped us, so they can help others." In the early 2000s, she became a US citizen by passing the verbal and written exams in English without a translator. She learned to love hamburgers and french fries, but not Coke.

She was most proud to be part of the Nebraskan culture, including hosting and cooking for Cornhusker football fans. She treasured every second she had with all of her eleven grandchildren. She had taught and touched every one of them in their own unique ways. She passed away in 2010. We all love and miss her so much. She is our angel and our inspiration. We are so proud of Em and love her so much.